Shakespeare
and The Lost Myth

A Revised Version

Ariadne
Books

Shakespeare
and The Lost Myth

Alan Hardill

©Alan Hardill 2002, 2004
Shakespeare and the Lost Myth

2nd (Revised) Edition 2004
ISBN 0 9543537 1 4
(1st Edition 0 9543537 0 6)

Published by Ariadne Books
26 Bromley Road
Shipley
West Yorkshire BD18 4DS
United Kingdom

Printed by
The Amadeus Press, Cleckheaton

Page Layout by
Highlight Type Bureau Ltd, Bradford

Cover designed by Robert Charlesworth
Printed in England.

In Gratitude

Soon after the publication of his book on Shakespeare's work as myth, the late Ted Hughes, our former Poet Laureate, agreed to read a neglected manuscript on the same subject, offered by the author. His enthusiasm and encouragement then, and at various times thereafter, helped a good deal towards the writing of this present book. Very few of his position and commitments would have shown such generosity of spirit and have bothered so with a complete stranger.

– – – –

I am grateful also to my two daughters, Katherine and Celia, who over the years have given much time, care and expertise to the tasks of re-typing and re-setting the manuscript at different stages.

I wish also to thank the following for kindly agreeing to read the text and for their comments and suggestions for its improvement:–

My brother Frank, former scholar of St Catherine's College, Oxford

Friends and former colleagues, Mr John Greensmith of Huddersfield and Mr Kenneth Harwood, sometime Head of English, Bradford Grammar School

And Rev Dr. David Jasper of Glasgow University.

– – – –

Acknowledgement

CONTENTS

INTRODUCTION

This book takes up the subject of a recurring myth in some of the most significant works of older English literature. It is a myth that originated in even earlier times and was passed on, as by an inheritance, to the writers of those works. Though it shows itself there in different forms, and with different degrees of wholeness and clarity, it is recognisably the same in all, and recognisably of the same voice, speaking for past ages and their understanding of life as a strange cyclical process imbued with a spirit of purpose or destiny.

What seems to have been a fundamental change of mental outlook, beginning to affect the age of Shakespeare but setting in strongly thereafter, caused interest in this myth to wane, along with an older mystical sense of life that had been the foundation of the religious and poetic spirit in earlier ages.

Interest in the myth revived, though marginally and briefly, in the Romantic period, and is found strikingly in the *Prophetic Works* of William Blake, who, like Shakespeare and Milton before him, was committed to combine many of its aspects and variants into single form, showing thereby their essential kinship. But attempts at mythical revival, as he well knew, and as some other poets of that period knew, were against the strengthening main stream of the modern age, whose allegiance to rationalism and realism was likely to erode the kind of mind, or imagination, in which mythic understanding could survive.

Before going into a first description of the myth in question, which this study will shortly undertake, perhaps it would be useful here to look further at this idea of an altered mental outlook or mode of thought that some, including Blake and others of the Romantic period, have believed to separate us from older literature, and its mythical elements in particular, though we might limit ourselves to two points for the sake of brevity.

The first is that in the literature of earlier ages part of the mythical quality or texture to their stories reveals itself in the way the sexes are sometimes portrayed in them – that is, not simply as actual men and women but, as often survives in fairy tales, in a way more open to a symbolic interpretation as 'sexual' forces, elements or spirits operating in all aspects of life. Accordingly, the feminine personages might connote, for example, the genius of the bodily and emotional, with all the attendant determination, deep powers and wisdom; and the masculine personages the energetic and creative (or destructive) character in life, with the attendant spirit of desire and imagination. Despite the well-known theories of such as Carl Jung, we tend nowadays to be more literal-minded in our reading of literature (as in our reading of life around us?) and so might benefit from reminders of this mystical tendency in older texts.

The second point of separation is the prevailing assumption in a good deal of older literature about our present 'fallen' condition. That is to say, it takes as understood the view that our earthly existence is but a lower and interim drama to which we are plunged by a disastrous disorder in the soul of life, and in which, despite all joys, higher moments and merits that randomly embellish, we must expect the common lot to be of pain and ordeal, though hopefully with the possibility that our endurance and struggle will be rewarded at last with a transformation – salvation, in whatever sense and by whatever agency – by which we shall return to what we rightly and rightfully are. The loss of this 'fallen' perspective, along with the loss of the myth that was used to express it, is perhaps the most definite factor in the separation, for better or worse, between the modern outlook and that of earlier ages, and might indeed serve to distance us from such as the Medieval and Elizabethan worlds as widely as they in turn were distanced from the earliest civilizations of Anatolia and Crete.

★   ★   ★

Chapter 1
Basic Story-Pattern and Characterisation

English literature before the modern age contains many cyclical stories of a similar pattern. This pattern shows (or implies) an opening loss of some higher, happier state of life, followed by a time of ordeal or quest in a lower, harsher existence, and an ending in which what was first lost is regained. As this story-line might in itself suggest, there is often a sense of fate or destiny behind the action. Another feature is that the first state of life is usually lost through violence, wrath, or upheaval of some kind; and its final regaining in turn follows some kind of violence to the lower interim existence. Broadly generalised, then, the pattern of the story falls as follows:- Higher happiness - Calamity - Lower ordeal or quest - Final climax - Restored higher happiness.

Once aware of it, we realise, perhaps with some surprise, just how often this cyclical story-pattern - or 'myth' pattern, as we might more accurately call it - actually occurs in our older literature. From Chaucer's work and the Arthurian stories right through to Milton's 'biblical' epics, it turns up with quite uncanny frequency. And not least in Shakespeare's plays, where it seems to occur wherever his sources allowed him any scope for symbolic or mythic treatment. Moreover, in some cases of his work, this cyclical myth-pattern is not only present in the main storyline, it is often added to, as if in reinforcement, by reminders of stories with the same pattern. In *The Tempest,* for example, readers will readily recognise in the shadows of the main action traces of the Troy cycle and the Persephone myth. In *King Lear,* likewise, the main cyclical story is shadowed by Arthurian myth and the Grail accounts, and also by folktales that in their humble way bear witness to the same destinal cycle.

At the same time, it has to be admitted that in some cases the pattern is not immediately apparent. It is not always a case like Chaucer's *Knight's Tale,* for instance, which shows it fully and clearly - the violence at Thebes, the prison-ordeal, the deciding tournament of arms, and the final happy marriage. Sometimes the pattern is obscured by the absence of the first calamity by which the higher happiness was lost, which is then only retrospectively hinted at in the story taking place. In *The Faerie Queen,* for example, as in some of the Grail romances and in *Hamlet,* events start with only a shadow of the past calamity to explain the tortuous search or ordeal going on. In the case of *The Faerie Queen,* this 'shadow' or retrospective glance appears in Book 1 as the violent tragedy of Una's royal parents. This adds to other past events recalled in the Book, one of which (Fradubio's tragedy in Canto 2) actually influenced, as we shall see later, Shakespeare's account of what *really* happened to Hamlet's father.

In other respects, *The Faerie Queen* shows the expected pattern clearly. That is to say, each of the six quests or adventures, tending towards a final restoration of the lost golden realm of Arthur (or the Court of the Fairy Queen herself), reaches the usual decisive climax by which the interim state of ordeal is ended. Four of these climaxes are shown as physical combats, against a monster or an enchanter; one is shown as a final victory over an enchantress (the wrecking of Acrasia's Bower of Bliss); and one - in the story of Scudamore and Amoret - is shown in the truly medieval style of a mysterious quasi-sexual test in the House of Venus.

So much for the idea of a recurring myth-pattern - at least for the time being. The next stage is to try to give some explanation for its odd recurrence, before we go on to the more complicated matter of the 'meaning' to this myth.

In explaining its recurrence, we could simply shrug and say: 'That's the way they thought of life in those days - a matter of cycles - whereas we nowadays tend to think linearly or in terms of continuous progression'. Well, it's a fair comment, but it obviously does not get us very far. It doesn't, for instance, explain the two points of crisis found so often in the old story-pattern, nor does it explain why the middle part has to be one of ordeal or relative unhappiness.

Another possibility is to say that the mentality of that age was steeped in a religious understanding mainly formed by the Bible, in which the cyclical idea of Fall/Ordeal/Salvation was a key point in life's estimation. According to this view, the story-pattern was due to the strength of a religious indoctrination. Looking at the Bible with this in mind, we see indeed that it contains many stories of a cyclical destiny, complete with two points of crisis and an intervening ordeal – Samson, Ruth, Job, Joseph, and the Egypt-to-Canaan cycle. Moreover, the Bible as a whole embodies the cycle in its overall scope: the shattered higher happiness of Eden, the lower ordeal of Adam's generations, and then after a final wrath the restoration. This final restoration appears in the Old Testament as the reconciliation of Jehovah and his people and in the New Testament as the final victory over the world of sin and death, with the promise of a restored Paradise like a resurrection.

It is obviously true that a bible-based religious outlook would deeply affect the way stories were written, and perhaps reinforce their cyclical pattern. But a moment's reflection discounts this as a full explanation. Other cultures little affected by the Bible, or even independently of it, had themselves long been writing stories of this pattern, as we can see well enough in the Osiris myth, the Persephone myth and the *Odyssey*. We should also note that even in our own culture there are many traditional stories of this cyclical type - folk and fairy tales, for instance - that likely had little or no biblical influence in their shaping. So we need to look further.

I think at this point I can hear some of my readers offering advice. It goes roughly like this. For at least a century and a half, scholars in mythology have held fairly consistently to the view that 'Nature myths' had some influence on the development of later myths and traditional stories, both religious and secular.[1] It follows, then, that the basic seasonal pattern of Fall, Winter, Spring, as would be found in some of these myths, may well have passed down into the later cyclical pattern of Loss/Ordeal/Restoration in secular myth, and of Fall/Penance/Salvation in religious myth. Moreover the seasonal pattern may in fact have given these later stories both the idea of a central ordeal - corresponding with Winter - and the feature of a first and last crisis or violence, because the onset and end of winter are often marked by stormy weather.

According to this view, the recurring cyclical pattern in the

---

1   See Longer Notes at the end of the chapter.

work of our older poets is partly due to an inheritance from Nature myth: something passed down in traditional material, which authors well-known for their loyalty to tradition would pick up in their source material.

There is probably a good deal of truth in this. We cannot read far into medieval literature without finding traces of Nature myth, for instance, or even Nature ritual, and so the possibility of an inherited 'Nature' pattern is real. A danger in accepting this too readily, however, is that it might allow us to run off with the idea that people like Chaucer and Shakespeare, in their 'unoriginal' use of plots, simply picked up willy-nilly an older cyclical form, and that it survives in their work merely casually or by accident. The truth is likely to be more complex, and I believe it begins to emerge when we ask why they were so ready, as by tradition, to adopt stories of this pattern. We then begin to suspect that perhaps some profound wisdom was perceived to be locked within them, something so important to the understanding of our situation in this life, and of our journey through it, that they almost demanded to be taken up and re-worked for this wisdom to be brought out. In following this up, I hope the reader will allow a spell of personal reflection.

I believe there is in all of us a story - a dream-story, if you like. It centres on a sense that there is, or was, a much better place and time, and that one day we shall win back to it. Despite all the rationalist propaganda, the seductions and numbings of entertainment, social pressures and formal education, our minds are still to some extent 'religious', and have this dream. And as we look upon a scene in mid-winter, we realise that Nature also follows this dream and story, for even in its sorrowful deadness it seems to hold a memory of a summer, which like a potential in it will one day allow the summer to return. And, just as we see that we were first conceived and brought into this 'wintry' life by a 'wrath' upon our mothers, and that we shall end by a last 'wrath' (of death) upon our lower existence, so Nature, brought into a darkness by the first wrath of winter, dreams of its coming last wrath which through a violence will restore it to what it was.

In this way, Nature reflects our 'dream' story, representing in non-human terms our own sense of being fallen from a long-ago summer and our hope that at some final crisis to our state there will be a return to it. And I believe that poets of our earlier ages were even more aware of that reflection between their 'dream' story, the cyclical pattern of their lives, and the story of Nature annually about them, as if all arose from some common source or nether 'mind' that impels the same destiny. It is this, I think, that made those writers seize upon the story-pattern in the narrative material they inherited in those versions of the 'dream' passed down from earlier ages. It matched with the pattern of their own perception of life, as a cyclical drama in which all are involved in a single destiny. It is also, I think, why those poets and artists not least in the Middle Ages so often brought Nature into the total story, as a rightful partner in the destiny, with its own drama part of the all-story - as perhaps it had always been, even in early times, and never simply 'Nature' myth as some believe.

A good example of this poetic and mystical recognition of life's all-in-one destiny appears relatively late in the period under examination - Shakespeare's *The Tempest*. In this play, we find at the centre of the dramatic tapestry the cyclical story of one man - Prospero - to which is attached the destiny of a whole group, who seemingly represent the human race in general, 'shipwrecked' upon this terrestrial island of ours amid the seas of space and time. Into and around this central figuring and their action are woven many reminders of other stories that throughout the ages have pictured and attested a cyclical destiny, comprising both biblical and pagan myths.[2] Then, surrounding the whole, as if to reinforce the idea of a circle of time, we find suggestions of the seasonal cycle. So, for example, the first wrath and tempest still reminds of the onset of winter, and the last wrath - Prospero's storm towards the end - reminds of the most ancient imagery of the end of winter. Indeed, the siting here of the Masque of Ceres (Demeter) adds to the 'seasonal' idea, for her rites at Eleusis were in symbolism much tied to the seasonal cycle. But, more than this, we next see how the whole picture - its figures, its myths, its wheeling natural backdrop

---

2   The mythical composition of the play will be looked at in the late chapters of this study.

– is suggested to arise all from one source, like a "dream" from a single sleeping intelligence, the lost 'mind' figured in the "drowned father". It is the 'dream' – this life – that emanates in all its aspects from the dark Unconscious, in Jungian terms, and mythically as from a sleeping Arthur, Osiris, Albion,[3] or a Cronos.

★   ★   ★

Having now taken up a sense of the myth as an overall life-story, we find in our hands something powerfully significant, which this study will explore. And yet the subject still lacks definition. We need to find something more specific, even something like a basic 'model' of the story, providing an idea of its structure, its working, its characterisation. The way I propose to do this follows from the foregoing argument. Wherever else the story is to be found, it is written most simply 'out there' – in the seasons. If this assisted the primitive mind in first shaping the myth, it will certainly assist us. We shall go back, then, to a primitive situation, and use a "dramatic conception of Nature", as Wensinck phrased it.[4]

Imagine then our distant forebears, in the fall of the year towards winter, wondering what it is that takes away the summer happiness. Some weakening in the assuring king of light and life, as in the sun, seems to alter his fair queen of Nature. She tires and sours away from her former beauty of response and fruitfulness, and hardens against her partner of vigorous and generous strength, seeking to deny or restrain his love. Does this not cause him then, as by a 'frustration', to darken from the power of life into something glowering and angry, eventually a winter demon of life-wrecking?

Thus, in that decline into winter, away from the happy summer balance of creative Masculine and kindly Feminine, may have been glimpsed a derangement in a sexual harmony, giving rise to the kind of myth whose opening phase shows a link between natural decline and a sexual alteration, or even a marital collapse, resulting in

---

3   Blake's figure of the original unified humanity that passed into a sleep of death

4   A phrase quoted in the opening chapter of *Before Philosophy* (H. & H.A. Frankfort, J.A. Wilson & T. Jacobsen) – a useful book for any who are interested in the development of myth.

destructiveness. Hence the common story-sequence in some stories that possibly had their roots in Nature-myth:-

A weakening in the King causes some dark alteration in his Queen, which leads to his turning into (or being replaced by) a destructive 'double' of himself, the ravisher or murderer of all that remains of the first happy 'summer'. It is a pattern discernible in later stories as far different as *Snow White* and *Macbeth*.

By the same play of imagination, the reverse process could also be 'dramatised'. So, for the return of Spring after Winter, our same forebears may have seen how the Queen, the wintry Nature, in bearing the scathes and blastings of her now fearsome lord, begins slowly to soften and repent her state of barren power, forming in her heart a longing for what she had once been. And he meanwhile finds that his anger has begun to change also, to transmute even in its fury from life-wrecking to life-desiring, from violence to virility, like his former power returning, ready to shed or break his present monstrousness. Because of these changes in them, it comes about that in a final climax, as in a last storm of fierce grappling, this demonic couple die from their wintry selves, and afterwards rise again, but fully changed, like two beings amazedly resurrected or reborn from the dark earth, the barren bark: the restored true marriage of the Spring.

Now, with signs of a 'coital' analogy in this - "final climax", "fierce grappling", and the idea of dying into a new birth - and with at least a dim recognition that the same analogy lingered like a quasi-sexual dynamic in some of the finest cyclical stories of our older poets, I am tempted to leap at once into later stages of my investigation. Instead, I will stick to the rudiments of the 'model' of the story I have just constructed, assessing it as follows:-

The story comes down to a cycle, involving essentially two characters, the masculine and feminine powers or aspects of life. In balance and harmony, these appear as the summer king and queen, whose harmony is then soured, throwing them and all their state awry (in some versions violently) and causing them to be changed into the winter king and queen. Their destiny thereafter, during the time of ordeal or 'winter', is to work out mutually the errors and distortions that have befallen their characters, and by a final 'violence' shed these dark deformities, and so find themselves again. Adam and Eve? Hud and Merry Ann? Oberon and Titania? We shall see.

This simple 'sexual' dualism in fact survived as the basis of many of the myth's later versions, when the 'Natural' connection had been partly or wholly forgotten. Its survival was partly due to chance no doubt – an inherited pattern that stuck with the story as it passed down to later writers – but also partly, I suspect, because this 'Nature' pattern agreed with the later poets' own perception of our life and destiny as something bound up with a basic contention of sexual opposites, reaching back to the oldest mystical concepts. However, whatever the explanation, the pattern remained. Beneath the psychological and religious subtleties and the diversification of character that the story later took on, the pattern is often visible. Sometimes distinctly.

One example is the biblical story of Samson (*Judges*). Perhaps not so surprising, since Samson's name – linked with *Shemesh* (the 'sun') – suggests the story's origin in Nature myth. In this biblical version, the first 'wintry' change in the feminine is remembered in the behaviour of the bride of Timnath and Delilah: the change from compliance to something resistant or binding upon life's masculine energies. The result, too, is the same: the hero turns to ravaging fury. The sequel also tallies, as the hero undergoes the painful ordeal of his anger, until a true strength returns for a final breaking wrath upon the feminine character (by that time imaged as the Temple of a false earthly power, as in the Christ-myth's shattering of the Temple during the final 'wrath' of the Crucifixion). Milton's own version of the story (*Samson Agonistes*), though different in some ways, is, if anything, even more centred on the 'sexual' contest. The poem's whole dramatic energy seems to be generated by the conflict of Samson and Dalila.

Another example shows in Chaucer's *Wife of Bath's Tale* – again a story that, through the many *Ragnel* variants, probably has links with Nature myth. In this, from start to finish, there are virtually only two personages – male and female – acting out what is recognisably the older story-pattern. As the free-flowing happiness of Arthur's fairy realm is blocked,[5] the male life-energies again turn

---

5   For later examination in Chapter 4.

to destructive outrage – the rape. There then follows the expected ordeal by which the darkness of the masculine and the 'wintriness' of the feminine (now linked with the power of pride upon him) are mutually broken in a final sexually-imaged climax, restoring the 'Spring' harmony of the sexes – the true marriage.

In Shakespeare's work, the main plot of *King Lear* is one of the best examples of the old myth-pattern's survival. Here we find the first weakening of the King, setting off a 'wintry' change in the feminine character (imaged as Cordelia's replacement by Goneril and Regan), and then a whole Act (Act 2) in which Shakespeare pointedly describes the resulting frustration of the masculine mind and energies as a major cause of Lear's derangement into wrecking anger. The ordeal that follows is unmistakably dark and wintry, with Lear himself as the winter-king of blasting wraths, finally worked to a climax in which both his own monstrousness and the resistance of the winter-queen (now partly imaged as the proud Law) are purged away. Then – as befits the pattern – the play's 'Persephone' (Cordelia) returns in simple kindness, bearing flowers of health and youth restored. It is a brief return to 'Spring' that is then roughly shattered by the play's tragic ending, the reasons for which we shall later ponder.

Once we take the standpoint given by the 'Nature myth' idea, we realise how often indeed these older writers were inclined, whatever number of personages they used in their stories, to concentrate on a central sexual duality, or even on two main characters, male and female, round which the other personages act in duplicate or as aspects of the main contention. Is not Shakespeare's *Winter's Tale,* for example, really the story of 'Leontes and Hermione', or *As You Like It* really 'Orlando and Rosalind', and so on? Rather like some fairy tales, in which the main focus is on a sexual duo – *Beauty and the Beast,* for example, or *The Frog Prince.*

It is as if the writers of these stories, wittingly or not, were staying true to the primitive story-pattern of 'sexual' contention. And staying true especially to one point in the pattern – the climax by which that contention is resolved. If we look again at the 'model', we see that in its climax, the 'last storm', two ideas are combined: (a) a final death or sacrifice by which the sexual factors, hitherto distorted and opposed, are freed again into their true characters and harmony, and (b) a final sexual act, by which the same factors are likewise freed into a new 'birth' of their joint being. And the same thing is found in many later versions of the cyclical myth. The final climax often still contains one of the two ideas – the death or the consummation – and sometimes both, as did many religious rites of 'death-and-renewal'.[6] The meaning of the characters involved had changed, and the significance of the climax had changed also – from one of 'fertility restored' to one of spiritual rebirth or renewal – but the climax itself remained, and still used the old sexual/sacrificial symbolism.

In Arthurian romance, for example – and not least in those connected with the Grail – the climax is found often to involve both a kind of death to the hero's interim character and some symbolic suggestion of the sexual act. Gawain's final test in both *Parzival* and the *Green Knight* story, for instance, centers on the idea of violent death in a setting tinged with sexual suggestion. The same is true of Guinglain's final test in *Le Bel Inconnu*[7] – in the darkness of the lady's chamber and the receiving of the fearsome serpent's kiss. In Chaucer, likewise, we find the climaxes of *The Wife of Bath's Tale* and *The Franklin's Tale* yoke together the notions of a final sacrifice and the sexual consummation.

In Shakespeare's plays the same quite frequently occurs, and, if anything, with an even stronger sense of connection between the two symbolic ideas: the final 'sexual death'. It is sometimes unmistakable. Few can have failed to notice, for instance, that Cleopatra embraces death as if in sexual surrender of her body and mortal powers: the old winter-queen of spells in her passing through the last, sweet wrath. Similarly in *Measure for Measure,* in the prelude to the restoration at the end, there is a fairly obvious coincidence of an execution and a sexual act. Perhaps, though, most telling of all is the example of Shakespeare's last play, *The Tempest.* As he sums up his life's work and the cyclical myth he has so often dealt with, he remembers most accurately this climactic event. During Prospero's 'last storm', with imaged reminders of both biblical and pagan

---

6   A link between ancient ritual and medieval myth has long been recognised.

7   Renaud de Beaujeu's fascinating medieval romance.

versions, there is still pictured the last grappling of the winter-king (or his agent) and the dark queen of this life, now shown in the lovers' entering into their nuptial union as into a rocky cave of death, a sepulchre of renewal.

Readers will have their own views on how the ideas of coitus and sacrifice metaphorically connect, pondering perhaps how both connote an annihilation of the old for the vital realisation of the new. However, a closer inspection of that matter will be given later. What counts for now, at this preliminary stage, is that we have begun to see in later forms of a myth not only a strange survival of an underlying 'sexual' contention but – and perhaps more obvious in many cases – the survival of the old climax by which that contention was resolved as by a dying consummation.

It is a strange matter, and one that will grow stranger as we proceed through later chapters. In anticipation of these, a few questions of wonder. What was the 'sexual death' enacted in the cave of Demeter, or Isis, or Cerridwen, that Shakespeare seems to remember in writing *The Tempest?*[8] And why is the event in that play given a reminder of the Crucifixion, as "king" Stephano and his gang like Caesar's men take away the old clothing? And why, too, is Lear, at the climax of his restored vigour, like the pagan champion of the last battle, and yet the crucifixional "bridegroom" – Christ at Calvary – meeting the same 'sexual death', and visualising "the pit" that he must enter as a woman's nether parts?

It will be shown why the last climax had to be remembered, and the circling myth itself of which it was the next-to-final stage. The myth was an artistic mirror of our situation in this dark life, and the climactic death a mystery of our means out of it to the 'summer' that once was ours. Shakespeare was one of the last of the primitive ritualists who knew the story and that it had always been the same. As he wrote his versions, he therefore gave reminders of its many forms, from ancient to Christian, both pagan and biblical, that had ever embodied the wheel of our mortal or 'wintry' destiny and its strange climax.

Perhaps he wrote partly in sadness or anger, knowing that the

---

8   To be dealt with in Chapters 9 and 10.

coming age would break the mirror and scatter its wisdom for a supposed liberation into clever barbarism. The Greeks were about to pull down his Troy of medieval Britain. Many now do not even notice the seasons as they move outside the window, let alone those seasons in the mystical mirror, and the giant forces moving there. And for the artists who used it long ago, including Shakespeare, we probably have little more understanding, without a special effort, than of the runes.

★   ★   ★

To sum up on the chapter. I have argued that the frequency of a cyclical myth-pattern in the work of our older poets was due to their recognition of a profound secret hidden within the cyclical form of inherited material, which corresponded with a pattern they apprehended in the seasonal round, in human existence, and in an inner dream-story. All these cycles mirrored for them the *same* story, the *same* destiny behind our lives, beginning with some higher state of happiness disastrously lost, and followed by a fallen or wintry state of ordeal in which we toil and yearn to be loosed into the finer life we once possessed. Central to this cyclical story is the idea that the woe was caused by some dislocation in the first harmony of the masculine and feminine factors or characters in life, whose journey then is through contention to some last climax by which the lost 'summer' might be regained. This story-pattern stayed visible in many versions of the myth across a wide range of time, as also did the mixed sacrificial/coital symbolism of the final climax.

I have in this first chapter mainly avoided the many variants in which this basically simple story-pattern appeared, particularly where the sexual factors or characters divided into a number of complementary roles. The avoidance was deliberate, for my chief purpose was for the reader to see, or perhaps strengthen him in already seeing, the main idea of a recurring story of sexual destiny, by which he might for himself discern a lurking singleness of meaning behind a variety of forms, whether that be of Samson or Llew Llaw Gyffes, of a wandering Odin or a Gawain in the wilderness of this world, or of a Psyche or Cinderella in a task of sorrows. I hope the aim for clarity about the main idea has justified the avoidance of complex investigation at this stage.

★   ★   ★

Chapter 1 Longer Notes

p. 3 The subject of Nature myth in the development of later myths and stories is wide and well-researched. It is hard to pick out particular scholars with justice. However, for the general reader a few works might be cited. Sir James Frazer's *The Golden Bough* is a standard work, though some judge its theories outmoded. It is also very long, even in the abridged version. A useful summing-up of the subject, along with other things, can be found in Edward Carpenter's *Pagan and Christian Creeds: Their Origin and Meaning,* now available in a cheap and easily obtainable reprint (Senate - Random House) under the title *The Origin of Pagan and Christian Beliefs.* For the pagan-mythical background to medieval literature, the reader will find useful J.L. Weston's *From Ritual to Romance* and R.S. Loomis's *Celtic Myth and Arthurian Romance.* But also valuable is John Speir's *Medieval English Poetry* and his opening chapter in the Pelican guide to English Literature (ed. Boris Ford): Book 1 - 'The Age of Chaucer'.

In addition to the above is the relatively recent *The Myth of the Goddess* (Ann Baring and Jules Cashford), which traces in a thorough and highly readable way the history of ritual and myth centred on the figure of the goddess, from ancient times to the Middle Ages. Though not aimed as background to the literature of the Middle Ages, it provides a fascinating insight into attitudes and ideas that influenced that literature.

Chapter 2
The Development of the Myth

The main idea of Chapter 1 was that some of the finest works of the medieval and Elizabethan period had inherited from a primitive myth their underlying story-pattern: a cyclical destiny in which the Feminine and Masculine factors in life's composition, having fallen into a 'wintry' distortion of character, pass through an unhappy ordeal of contention towards the restoration of their true selves and harmony together.

This chapter will give some more carefully examined examples of the primitive survival. By these it will be further seen that, whatever division of character-role arose in the story, and whatever the later psychological and religious development of its meaning – sometimes considerable – the original story-pattern and its main idea remained. It is as if the same mysterious mind that had informed the early understanding of the story continued to work through poets in their use of traditional material for their own versions of the destinal cycle.

One major change we need to recognise, however, in the myth's evolutionary journey towards the medieval world was a general loosening of its primitive connection with the annual or seasonal cycle. This, in some cases, allowed it to take on a much larger concept of the cycle and its spiritual meaning, and thereby transform itself into a story in which the 'Summer' was a happiness of long ago, the 'Winter' a time of trial in this material world, and the 'Spring' some future salvation. This sublimation of its primitive meaning is discernible widely in religious uses of the myth in the ancient world (most visible, for example, in the salvationist adaptation of the 'seasonal' Persephone story in the Mysteries of Eleusis), in Christian symbolism and its ritual calendar, and in much of our older literature.

*   *   *

My first example of the myth's medieval development is Chaucer's *The Franklin's Tale*. A fitting choice, because the story is based (at least so-claimed by Chaucer) on a Breton *lay*, and therefore, like many of that story-type, is likely to have had its roots in primitive myth, even specifically 'Nature' myth. Some scholars doubt Chaucer's claim, since no such Breton *lay* has been found, and yet, whatever the rights and wrongs of that matter, what is certain is that Chaucer's story shows a pattern very like that of the 'Nature' model put forward in Chapter 1.

It is going to be an important example, and so for those to whom the story is unknown or vague, I will give an outline, as follows:-

Arveragus, a Breton lord, having married his fair lady, Dorigen, decides to conduct his marriage to her by the same rules as he conducted his courtship - those of Courtly Love, whereby the lady is the sovereign mistress. Arveragus, for his dignity, keeps the title of master, but the real power now rests with his wife. She on her side promises to be faultless in character and conduct, - "never sholde ther be defaute in here" - which itself continues the Courtly Love idea, for in that cult the woman was ever the perfect 'goddess'.

In course of time Arveragus goes away to seek military adventure and renown, and the story concentrates on Dorigen, whose dream of faultlessness is soon found to clash with the evidence of actual life about her. Even God seems to fall short of the mark, for, discovering one day that there are destructive rocks around the coast, she wonders how a perfect deity could possibly allow such hurtful imperfections in his realm. Cast down at what seems life's real faultiness and cruelty, she grows melancholy, until her friends, hoping to lift her spirits, lead her into pastimes and amusements. One of these is a visit to a local pleasure garden. Here a second unpleasant discovery is made.

A local squire, Aurelius, having been much smitten by her charms and for some time languishing in desire, approaches her in the garden with the expected request. She of course gives the equally expected rebuff, but then, by a nice piece of equivocation, also gives him hope. She promises to grant his wish if he remove all the rocks from round the coast of Brittany.

Aurelius is cast into infernal torment of desire and despair. Sleepless, careless of his well-being, he declines into a dangerous state of mind and body. His brother, much concerned, finds out the cause and suggests he employ a magician who by illusion might make the rocks seem to vanish. A magician is engaged, who agrees to the task for a very large – indeed ruinous – fee.

The rocks disappear, and Dorigen is caught in a quandary of her two conflicting promises – that of perfection made to her husband, and that of compliance made to the squire. Keeping either must break the other, and so break also her perfectness of character. In despair she thinks of suicide, reflecting on the example of ladies who, rather than give up their virtue, gave up their lives. Her husband, returning home, finds her in this plight. Discovering the cause, he insists the second promise be kept. It is a matter of "trouthe" that must be upheld, for without it all other worthiness, even life itself, is empty. So she sets off for the garden to keep her promise. Aurelius, meeting her on the way, is told what her husband said and what she felt compelled to do. He is so dashed by this nobility of sacrifice, and so abashed by the contrast with his own villainous intent, he releases her from her promise.

She goes joyfully home, and he goes far less joyfully to see the magician, for he faces financial and social ruin. The magician, however, hearing the whole story and being moved at the nobility of all concerned, decides himself to be nobly sacrificial. He says the outcome has been payment enough, and so writes off Aurelius's debt …

It is one of those fascinating medieval romances that within apparent simplicity hide facets of meaning able to keep the reader wondering for days. Yet for us at present it is an example, more simply, of an old story-form surviving into a medieval version. Indeed, apart from the original male role being now played by three personages – husband, lover, and magician – in a way later to be accounted for, the older 'Nature' story is recognisable at almost every turn. For instance, there is still a noticeable first weakening of the 'king' (Arveragus's abdication of authority) followed by the expected change in the 'queen' to a resistant or uncompliant role (Dorigen's intent to keep herself faultless). Again according with the pattern, this is followed by what seems very like a 'frustrated' derangement of the male energies into 'wintry' violence, shown in

Arveragus turning to warfare, in the emergence of threatening lust (Aurelius), and in the equally threatening force of 'ravishment' – death (the destructive rocks).

But perhaps the most remarkable survival from the older story is the tale's climax, in which there are still visible the linked ideas of sexual consummation and mutual sacrifice – the 'sexual death'. That is to say, the 'queen' once again, through the scathes and strains of a world turned hurtful to her, weakens to surrender, and receives thereby the equivalent of a 'virility' that has emerged in the male energies and is finally released as he too 'dies' from his debasement of character.

The returned 'virility' in Chaucer's story is hidden in the term "trouthe", the power that Dorigen must yield to in order to be saved, like the light of the returning god that once loosed the Queen from the dark bonds of winter. This we shall see better, along with other correspondences between the two stories, as we now look more closely at this medieval version and the developments it has undergone. I will begin with Dorigen becoming the 'winter-queen' – the unchangeable Miss Perfect.

In the primitive story, as we have seen, the Queen dangerously frustrated the male life-energies by a frosty non-compliance, and thereby darkly changed their character: from a force of life's vitality to one of destructiveness (the demonic winter-king). Dorigen's story shows much the same thing (though with a different slant of meaning), starting with her opening vow to be faultless in character and conduct. In what way, though, is it the same? Because, first, her assumed perfection, in denying the need for change (for what change does perfection need?) must thwart the masculine energies in life responsible for change and renewal. Similarly, since perfection clings to an illusion, a pretence, it must equally try to thwart the creative 'masculine' energies that ever seek the realisation of truth. And then what happens? Exactly as in the primitive myth: these energies warp in denial from the creative to the destructive. Arveragus's warfare, Aurelius's rebellion and lust, and the force of Death (the black rocks) are thus better seen as this tale's equivalent of the ravaging demon-king of winter.

In all, we can see that the 'angel' has done a pretty good job of creating her own 'devil', leading us to ponder the hint in Chaucer's description of Aurelius - "He langwissheth as a furye dooth *in helle*" - and to ponder what further meaning might lurk about this point, since one of the 'primitive' heresies of medieval art, as we shall see better later, was that our long-ago 'summer' - that is, Paradise, or even the realm of heaven itself - began to collapse not through the coming of 'Evil' (Satan) but through the coming of 'Good' that reactively then gave rise to 'Evil'.

However, sticking for now with the simplest ideas about Dorigen's situation, we can say that however we interpret her resistant or negative stance, and the kind of 'evil' she thus creates, what is clear is that her final surrender is no more than what the logic of her situation, and its error, demands. That is, having by a sort of 'virginity' turned the male life-energies into various forms of the 'ravisher', she can only turn them back to their true creativity of character (and thereby find her own true fruitfulness) by giving up that 'virginity' - as adumbrated in her final tryst with Aurelius.

We can easily pick out in this not only a survival of the old Nature myth, that climaxed likewise in the Lady's surrender, but a similarity with so many folk and fairy tales in which, preserving the same idea, some Wilful Beauty also restores the 'Prince' (and her true happiness) through a yielding to the 'Beast'. (A yielding that in many cases, as here, kept the primitive 'ritual' idea-combination of death and sexual consummation.)[1]

Whatever 'folk' versions Chaucer himself may have had in mind, one major variant he seems aware of - judging by the way he conspicuously links Dorigen's pleasure-garden with "Paradise" - is the overall biblical version of the myth. As I briefly pointed out in the last chapter, the compilation of scriptures we call the Old Testament was arranged in rough agreement with the old myth-cycle. By this, the original 'summer-marriage' (in Eden) was shown to collapse when the feminine spirit (Eve) took on self-will, and was only restored when that 'feminine' self-will, as in the stubborn hearts of the people, was broken by the painful humiliation imposed

---

1   Aurelius and the "black rocks" ('rape' and 'death') are therefore linked as
      Dorigen's threatening adversaries.

through the wrath of the long-ago forsaken 'husband' (Jehovah), who then took back his people like a chastened 'bride'.[2] There is a fairly obvious parallel there with the 'myth' of Dorigen for Chaucer to pick up on.

He gives Dorigen's ordeal a New Testament connection as well. In the Gospels, the equivalent final pain and humiliation that symbolically restores the long-ago 'marriage' (that of God and human nature, of heaven and earth, of Second Adam and Eve, and so on) is the Crucifixion, which has a particular link with Dorigen's story. In medieval religious art, the garden of Paradise, in which the feminine spirit (Eve) first took on self-will, was symbolically linked with the garden of Gethsemane in which, just before the Crucifixion, the 'feminine' self-will in our fallen nature was finally surrendered (by Jesus, in obedience to a higher demand - "... not what I will, but what thou wilt"). As much as he dare (in caution against a blasphemous analogy) Chaucer seemingly uses the same symbolism of the garden as both Dorigen's "Paradise" and the place for her final surrender to a higher demand ("trouthe"). [The idea links further with the Gospel story of Mary, who, as the chastened and obedient 'Eve', also surrendered her will to a higher demand (that of the angel) and thereby conceived the Messiah - a symbol, as in the Old Testament, of the restored 'marriage' of life.]

Medieval literature is often thus difficult for our having now lost much of its network of mythical connection. Almost as difficult for us now is the term used for the higher demand to which Dorigen must sacrifice herself - "trouthe". The convenient translation - 'truth' - robs it of much of its meaning. Its full meaning begins to shape when we reflect that the factor to which Dorigen must yield herself is one that she primly first refused, and then recall that this factor included the 'creative' urge for *truth*. As this was linked with the masculine energies of change and renewal, we realise that 'truth' in the sense Chaucer uses it is not just a static mentally recognised fact, but something also active or dynamic, even something like the basic life-force itself. And by this we can see that the monstrous

---

2   The Old Testament cycle of destiny is more clearly examined and explained (in connection with *Hamlet*) in Appendix B.

things that Dorigen has made of the masculine energies by her resistance - warfare (Arveragus), the urge to violate (Aurelius), and even the force of Death (the "black rocks") - are themselves the various aspects of a darkly twisted power of 'truth' (a 'God' turned 'Satan') which her acceptance will finally change back to its real character and power - the "trouthe" as a transforming life-energy, a force of renewal and 'procreation' upon her.

With many suggestions of biblical meaning in Chaucer's tale, there is something else to be noticed. Truth, in the sense outlined above, appears also in Christian thinking - a male force to quicken and liberate the barren soul, the "truth that will set you free". And this meaning was itself illustrated by way of coital symbolism in the Christian equivalent of the myth's final 'sexual death' - the Crucifixion. It is quite visible, for example, in the imagery of the divine energies released orgasmically at the point of Christ's dying, bursting through the Veil of the Temple (a symbol of barren virtue) as if piercing the hymen of a hitherto resistant virgin. Much the same divine truth is brought upon the 'virginally' stubborn heart in what the Old Testament prophets saw as the final climax to their people's destiny, and likewise to restore its fruitfulness as in a woman hitherto resistant to the divine power - "Behold, a virgin shall conceive". And it is the same 'truth' that is restored to the hero in the high-point of both *Hamlet* and *King Lear,* in which a force of transforming energy or vision is finally generated from a wrathful masculinity and brought to bear on something resistantly 'feminine'. When we come to examine these plays, we shall better see that their stormy climaxes are in fact simply different renderings of the final 'sexual death', into which are woven both biblical meanings and features that remember the most primitive accounts of the climax to life's sexual contention.

However, in case the larger point is being lost in this spread of examples, I had better repeat at this stage that these are all cases in which an ancient story has evolved into a form of religious meaning. In the original story there was a period of contention in which a life-energy (masculine), meanwhile deranged into destructiveness, at length resumed its creative potency and by this - as in a final sexual act - broke and revitalised the resistant or wintry spirit in the feminine character of life that had first deranged it. This story-form, probably 'fertilistic' in meaning, took on in later versions a spiritual perspective in which the resumed 'male' potency became to some extent a divine force of transforming truth, able to break and revitalise something resistant in the 'feminine' heart or spirit in life, and so bring about the religious equivalent of Spring. In the case of the two Shakespeare plays cited above, that 'Spring' is very short-lived - if 'lived' at all - the reason for which we shall later consider.

★   ★   ★

Myth - and we must include in that term much of medieval romance - is very complex. Part of its complexity is that, as with a crystal, we pick out a shaping of idea one way, and then, turning the crystal slightly, pick out the same idea in a different colouring and form. This is true of *The Franklin's Tale*. Let us turn its crystal a little, and look again at the fascinating lady at its heart. The things we shall see are all further characteristics of the primitive winter-queen now translated into the terms of medieval romance.

One thing sure about Dorigen in her change to a ruling power in life is that she has taken on a powerful erotic aura. Hence the besotted antics of Aurelius. In this she links with many enchantresses in medieval romance, who likewise often centre the whole story and wield an astonishing sway upon the hero. Sometimes they are baleful in effect - the 'witch' or femme fatale, whose power the hero must defeat, as by a victory over fleshly lusts. At other times though, they are figures of forbidding purity, more in keeping with the icy sanctity of the winter-queen. But as often as not, they combine both characters, like Dorigen - sensual allure and forbidding sanctity. It seems that the medieval artistic imagination was here quite the equal of modern psychological ponderings, and was fully aware of the odd paradox to feminine sexual power: the ambiguity of taboo that gives rise to the enticing stare of Aphrodite and yet the chilling glare of Artemis.[3]

---

3   Compare this, for instance, with Freud's relating woman's sexual power to the paradoxical image of the 'Mother' in the male psyche: the 'sensual Madonna'.

It was an understanding shared by Shakespeare later. When Ophelia, for example, is set to entrap Hamlet in the 'nunnery' scene, the dialogue makes it plain that she combines the fleshly seductress of the source story[4] and the undefiled, untouchable femininity. Likewise with Isabella in *Measure for Measure*. Her aura of sexual purity in its power upon man (Angelo) is hardly distinguishable in effect from that of the more obvious daughters of Eve in the nearby brothel.

There is another feature to Dorigen we need to note. As well as exercising an erotic spell, she denotes something already suggested in the earlier mentioned idea of 'self-will'. This is pride, which is implied in her commitment to faultlessness. In this she once again links with the larger body of medieval romance, in which are many examples of a central 'goddess' both shimmering with glamour and playing the role of Pride - in one case actually specified by name: *Orgueilleuse* (in the *Parzival* story of Gawain).

This brings us again to the psychological subtlety of writers in the Middle Ages regarding the feminine nature. In reading their stories we many times come across this idea of a link between the erotic power of woman over man and the power exercised by pride in the emotional (or 'feminine') side of his make-up, as if they were recognised as kindred feminine forces of allure and control, or even in some way the *same* force. By this view, a man's lusts for an alluring woman, or, for that matter, any outward object of vain self-realisation - success, fame, wealth, and so on - were seen as to some extent simply attempts to fulfil the dark queen of the self, or pride, that already inwardly possessed him.

It is a strange notion to modern readers, except perhaps for those primed by Jungian lectures on the *anima,* and it will be later returned to. For now, by this understanding we shall better realise what Dorigen signifies in Chaucer's tale and what power she wields upon Aurelius - why, in fact, she can be both an object of his lust and yet a figuring of his own possession by the Self. We might equally see why in Shakespeare's work later, particularly in the tragedies, the subject of the dark selfhood (pride) and that of unreal

---

4   *Historiae Danicae* (Saxo-Grammaticus) and *Histoires Tragiques* (Belleforest).

desire (lust) so often show up sharply together, and sometimes with a feminine connotation.

Whatever else, we are slowly adding to the picture of how a primitive myth developed into a mixed religious and 'psychological' drama. In the first, a queen of life had for some reason altered into a force of wintry denial and control, deranging the king and his powers to destructive wildness, and then keeping him thus so that he could not find in those powers the true virility needed to break and inseminate her, and so restore her summer nature. In the second, the queen's wintry aspect had increasingly become the inter-reflecting force of an outer erotic spell and an inner pride, or selfhood, but still of the same great power to derange and control the mind and energies of man, and still intent to foil his search for their true spiritual energy, the 'virility' of vision, by which she could be broken and her inner 'Spring' of kindly joy and grace restored.

The old myth of the loss and return of the king, circling round the central mystery of the loss and return of the queen, had become one of man's quest for his own true character, centred on a lost femininity of soul, whose shadow meanwhile keeps him the dangerous fool. This myth is found in many variants in the Middle Ages, and then in Shakespeare's plays.

★   ★   ★

But the myth in its development had also become heretical. Indeed, there were a number of things implicit in its original story-line which later versions sometimes brought out in ways quite opposed to orthodox religious teaching. Some of these things we shall see at various stages of this study, particularly when we come on to the subject of the Grail romances in connection with Shakespeare's plays. For now, I shall deal with just one matter of heresy – and that briefly, for other matters beckon.

It has been suggested in this chapter that the figure of the winter-queen evolved with the myth through various forms of witch, enchantress, and femme fatale, into a figure denoting pride. It has also been suggested that just as the winter-queen caused her male partner to turn mad and destructive, so this 'feminine' pride within the human make-up was seen in some later versions to derange the 'masculine' mind and creative energies into fantasies of unreal desire - 'lust' - and also into destructiveness in their thirst for her shadowy fulfilments.

So far, so orthodox - in the main. The Church would have nodded agreement that this pride or self-will, like an 'Eve' to our nature, had indeed caused the fallen state. It would have agreed, too, that this pride, as the mother of sins, was the main hindrance to be overcome for our salvation. But those nods of agreement would have grown hesitant, and then stopped altogether, when it was found, as in the case of Dorigen, that this Lady Pride was being linked by poets with assumptions of goodness, virtue, and even holiness. For it was being told that its own heavenly ideal was simply the 'Eve', the femme fatale, now dressed in more ethereal vestments: an icon of pride still inspiring lust, though now otherworldly in its urge, and still inciting cruelties and destructiveness to life. And it was being told that its own revered purity, holiness and so forth, was itself the bewitchment that needed to be broken for our return to the 'Spring', the Paradise it so much preached and promised.

But there was far more than this to disturb the Church. The myth had often shown that this eventual breaking of that feminine power was like the deflowering of a virgin in the sexual act - her final consummation towards the 'Spring'. Horror! The very core of orthodox religious ideas of virtue - and perhaps of all male idealism - is obsessively fixed in feminine purity: the immaculate 'mother', icily pure in the inner sanctum of its mystery (and of its heart). Could it possibly be countenanced that this holy goodness was not only the winter-queen of spells, but a power that would have to submit to the rawest outrage to open the gates of Paradise?

The Church had trouble enough with its own Gospels, in which the same heretical import lurked. For example, among the symbolic details of the Crucifixion - Christ's energy at last tearing the hymen-like Temple Veil - is the same suggestion of holiness as a barren thing that needs a 'ravishment' into true fruitfulness. Much the same idea lurked in the already mentioned story of the virginal Mary and the Angel. Indeed, even the design of a medieval church building held something of the same implication. The placing of the Cross (the 'Rood') and Christ's orgasmic release of restoring energy right within the 'womb' of the building, as if bringing 'her' at last from the cold and barren dark of holiness into fruitfulness… Altogether, the Church had heretical skeletons enough in its own cupboard, and welcomed no reminders of these in secular stories. And it had some very unpleasant means of discouraging such reminders!

This is why Chaucer is careful to blur the sexually symbolic implications of Dorigen's final meeting with Aurelius, making out that no such 'sacrifice' actually took place, but leaving the shadowy suggestion all the same. It is also, I think, partly why the idea of a sexual consummation was all but erased from the Grail romances. The feminine gender of the Grail itself was veiled, and only hazy symbolism was left to suggest that her true nature of fruitfulness would only be found when her holiness, as barren as the wintry hag, received the potent drops from the male 'weapon' hitherto destructive.[5]

In Shakespeare's work also "the truest poetry" still sometimes had to be "the most feigning". Protestant England was quite as sensitive on certain matters of morality. When the holy and virginal Isabella, therefore, must finally submit in *Measure for Measure* to the lust of Angelo, a legitimate substitute (his earlier betrothed Mariana) is conveniently found. Likewise in *Hamlet*, Gertrude might suffer something quasi-sexual in her chamber, but for her linked personage, the virginally pure Ophelia, there are only hints - and then in supposed madness - that she has suffered the same 'tumbling'.

Madness was a useful cover. Shakespeare used it again in the climax of *King Lear*, and to obscure much the same idea. In the 'Nature' model the King finally reached a crisis in which his wrathful energies were sacrificially and quasi-sexually transmuted into a virility with which to break and inseminate the winter-queen. In *King Lear* likewise, as Lear reaches the climax of his wrath, his hitherto dark energies are converted to an astonishing 'potency' of life-transforming vision (Act 4). But, as the 'winter queen' has in this case become the virtuous Law (represented clearly as a feminine

---

5   The Grail romances will be examined in Chapter 8

power of pride and chaste control), the idea of her 'ravishment' has
to be blurred in the near incoherence of Lear's supposed madness.
Particularly blurred is the imagery that could have made obvious the
idea of 'virtue' receiving at last a necessary violation - the imagery
that links the ideas of the hero's climactic dying into the underworld
("hell") and his entry into the "pit" of the vulva.[6]

*   *   *

As the shift of attention to *King Lear* suggests, this play is my
next example of the primitive myth become a later religious version
of man's cyclical destiny.

There are a number of general ways in which this play could he
introduced in connection with *The Franklin's Tale* - their sharing a
Celtic origin, for instance (even something vaguely 'Arthurian'), or
their both showing a link in their opening phase (by their authors'
intent) with the Paradise theme of a sexual harmony going awry
and leading to sorrow.[7] But for a first examination perhaps a more
tangible similarity would be more useful. One is readily found, in
fact - in the opening events of both stories. Like Arveragus before
him, Lear, weakening in directive control, surrenders his power to
something feminine that seems to promise moral perfection (his
'virtuous' daughters, in this case), and likewise on the condition that
he keep for dignity's sake the title of ruler.

The more this resemblance is examined, the more definite it
grows. We see, for instance, that this new feminine rule, like
Dorigen's, is linked with the idea of pride or selfhood, which begins
to govern all behaviour. We also see that it shows a rigidity of nature
which, having ousted the feminine nature of more kindly flexibility
and compliance (Cordelia), begins the very same 'frustration' of the
masculine energies of life - a masculinity that then, and again by a
sort of reaction, darkens from the healthful urge for truth (Kent) and
the urge for change (Edmund/Edgar) into a character of
destructiveness and rebellion.

Lear's own darkening in this 'frustration' is most telling. A whole

---

6   "Behold yon simpering dame ...pah, pah!" (4.6.120-50).

7   For Lear's kingdom as a collapsing primal world, see Chapter 4.

Act (Act 2) is given to the process, showing the force of feminine control and denial slowly deranging the hero. Further, the whole process, as in *The Franklin's Tale,* is given a noticeable sexual colouring, as if a sort of 'chastity' is intent to curb or chain the creative male life-power,[8] driving it to wrecking madness – the eventual storm of rage in which Lear rends all apart, and plunges down into the 'wintry' ordeal.

Once again, though now more powerfully depicted, we see a case of feminine 'good' creating its own 'evil' out of male creativity, its own 'Satan' out of a 'God'. And, in this, Shakespeare shows an awareness not only of the old Nature myth – the summer-king turned into his destructive wintry double against a resistant Queen – but of other myths that preserve the same idea: that of Samson, for example, turned to wrecking fury under feminine bondage, and – more strikingly – that of Hercules, bound likewise by feminine nets (the garment of Deianeira), riving them madly from him like his own flesh – "Off, off, you lendings!".[9] But also – and heretically – Shakespeare in depicting Lear's rage shows an awareness of the same idea hidden in a number of Old Testament accounts of divine destruction: a Jehovah turned into his own 'winter-king', madly wiping out his own 'summer' paradise, his own nature – or even, in a sense, his own 'wife'.[10]

The play's equivalent of the winter ordeal in the Nature myth – the period of pain between the stormy collapse of the first state in Act 2 and the climax of Act 4, which should have led to the return of 'Spring' – will be mainly dealt with in a later chapter. For now a partial account will suffice.

Just as the winter-king of our primitive model began to work against the queen that had debased him, seeking a lost virility by which she might be changed from her dark nature, and he himself freed from the monstrous distortion of character she had induced him to, so Lear undergoes an ordeal of similar significance. This

---

8   See Longer Notes at this chapter's end.

9   3.4.111

10 The heresy of the 'fallen god' in the medieval literature will be dealt with mainly in Chapter 5 in connection with King Hamlet.

'virility' sought, now become more a power of truth or vision, as in Chaucer's tale, slowly begins to return to Lear, like a light growing in the fires of his twisted energies. It allows him to perceive first that his monstrousness (and that of man he represents) is due to something darkened in the feminine character controlling him - like a pride, or self-righteousness, that turns all creativity destructive and cruel to the true femininity: anything 'kind' or natural. Secondly, it empowers him towards a final conquest of this interim feminine darkness, like a light to shatter her hold, a force of potency to enter and change her back as from a rigid barrenness, or - in the Christian terms already mentioned - a force of truth, or vision, that will at last transform her barren pride to natural kindness: the bride of Spring returned from within the broken body of the Witch.

This brings us to the play's climax - the unleashed spiritual virility that liberates the true femininity. In my first (and provisional) look at this, I will focus on only some of the images and allusions Shakespeare uses to convey his meaning symbolically, for which he borrowed from both pagan and biblical myth, as if he saw them as much the same in essential meaning.

It is a complex part of the play but it is basically made easier to follow if the reader throughout keeps hold of the central idea of the 'sexual death' that so often features in the climax of the myth: the critical point at which the masculine and feminine 'characters' in the fallen life's contention undergo a violent transcendence of their interim baseness (sacrificially and/or coitally imaged) to realise again, as in a rebirth, their original fineness and happiness.

There is, however, a particular point of connection between the acts of mortal sacrifice and coitus that, once grasped, makes the climax in *King Lear* (and in many other examples of the myth) easier still to follow. This point of connection appears in what happens to the male in both events. Let me explain. The history of ritual male sacrifice, or execution, attests clearly the belief that in such an act there was realised in the male frenzy of dying a vital power of life-renewal. It was as if a hitherto dull, debased, or violent power in the male - whether criminal or beast - was transmuted in that agony to a quickening charge: a life-power wrung paradoxically from the agony of dying. It takes no unusual imagination to grasp, of course, that in coitus, at the equivalent point of 'dying', a similar transmutation occurs in the male, as the formerly destructive virility of lust is converted into a burst of life-power.

By this connection in idea, we can deduce exactly, among other things, why in myth the death of some figure denoting male baseness or monstrousness so often comes just before the 'rescue' of a feminine figure into happiness. Base masculinity has, as it were, reached its final 'coital' change to fertilising potency, releasing her from a barren or otherwise negative state.

Likewise, when the hero in such stories slays the dragon, monster, or giant, we might equally pick out that it is really himself now achieving his true masculine potential by a dying transcendence of his former baseness, which explains why this also is often followed by the release or restoration of the feminine character. Even the child-adapted *Jack and the Beanstalk* keeps something of this idea, for the giant's death still coincides with a change in the feminine nature - from the hitherto dominant 'mother' or 'giantess', keeping the hero an inferior thrall of immature manhood, into the hero's true and happy partner.

It is, in a way, very much like Oedipus at last getting it right - sacrificing the 'giant' in himself (the brutal 'father') in the same act as he 'sexually' transforms the controlling 'mother' into the true nature of partnering femininity. By this idea, we might also ponder how something similar occurs in the 'queen's chamber' climax of *Hamlet,* but it certainly helps in *King Lear,* for we should now see, for instance, why the mortal combat with "a giant" in Lear's sacrificial climax of Act 4[11] (coinciding with a giant's death in Gloucester's matching 'suicide')[12] appears alongside symbolic suggestions of the sexual act, in which, as it were, a 'giant' also dies into a life-giving hero for the vital alteration of the lady.

Another pagan-mythical link at this point in *King Lear* - and showing the same coital analogy - is found in the allusion to "Swithold".[13] This story-fragment is probably a survival of an earlier

---

11 4.6.91

12 Act4 Sc6. See Longer Notes at this chapter's end

13 3.4.123-28

account of a hero's victory over, and transformation of, a dark feminine nature (a witch). As such it is a weighty pointer to the meaning of Lear's own coming 'victory' in Act 4, which likewise breaks a dark feminine power and converts it, as if coitally, from a hard barrenness of baneful control into the fruitful, kindly nature – the return of Cordelia.[14] In addition, as Swithold was a folklore type of Odin,[15] the earlier account that this fragment remembers might have a connection with the Norse-mythical stories of Odin's final rescue of the true feminine nature, as related in the winning back of Idun (the kindly nourisher of life) and the 'feminine' mead or life-blood.[16] And as these are the Norse equivalents of the finding of the Grail, the true nature of life, the 'Swithold' story is most fitting to Lear's own 'Arthurian' search across the 'waste lands' for his lost lady.

The idea of Lear as (in part) an 'Odin' seeking to reclaim his 'bride' will not seem so strange when we later find in *Hamlet* that the ghost of the former King has both the same intent and an unmistakable likeness to Odin.

Another important pagan-folklore connection in *King Lear* is found in the allusion to 'Child Rowland',[17] whose heroic rescue of Burd Ellen exactly fits the meaning of the play's climax, for there again a lady of dark powers over man is broken of her charm and restored to her true nature. Moreover, most versions of this story preserve some idea of the final 'sexual death', as in the hero's entering 'the dark mound' to win back through a slaying the fruitfulness of life.

At the same time, and likewise by allusion and imagery, Shakespeare connects the play's 'pagan' climax with its Christian equivalent – the Crucifixion – as most fitting to what has become a religious myth of destiny. And, looking at the Gospels, we realise that in this Shakespeare was making no forced connection, for the

---

14 The Swithold Story will be further sifted in Chapter 4.

15 See Robert Graves' *The White Goddess* p.25.

16 In surviving Norse accounts, Kvasir's life-blood (the 'mead') has lost what I believe was an earlier feminine connotation, perhaps through a patriarchal 'masculising' of symbolism that affected many myths. A matter for a later chapter on the Grail (Ch 8).

17 3.4.186-88

Gospel writers themselves had used the symbolism of the 'sexual death' in describing this climax. The sacrificial entry of the male into the underworld, to bring life, linked with the idea of going "a second time into the mother's womb" to be "born again", carries this symbolic significance, as does the violation of the 'virginal' Temple earlier mentioned. In *King Lear,* this Christian version of the story's climax is remembered when Lear, saying of himself "I will die bravely like a smug bridegroom", recalls the title that Jesus took as he neared his final sacrifice: the "bridegroom". There are other Gospel connections in this part of *King Lear,* but these will be dealt with in Chapter 4. It is enough for now that we have seen something of a pagan and Christian blend of meaning in Shakespeare's working.

★   ★   ★

In case the main point is being lost in the spate of example and explanation, I had better now take stock of what is being argued about the climax in Act 4 of *King Lear.* As follows.

We saw earlier how *The Franklin's Tale* began with a 'feminine' pride or selfhood taking over direction of 'masculine' mind and energy, distorting them into the unreal and destructive; and we saw how it ended when that distortion was changed back to a true quality of insight or vision ("trouthe") which then, in a last critical intensifying of its power, was able to break the nature of pride and restore its rightful nature of kindly compliance. We saw, too, how that climactic point was symbolically linked with ideas of mutual sacrifice (death) and the sexual act into restored harmony. This, in all, was the original ('Nature') myth of life's King and Queen rendered into a religious myth of human destiny, from first Fall to final regaining of the happy Paradise.

Through looking at *King Lear,* I hope something of the same story and development has been shown, which a later chapter will bring out further. The play begins with the same rise to power of pride or self, imaged in the replacement of Cordelia by her sisters, with quite the same bemonstering effect on the masculine character and with the same ensuing contention, though far more powerfully and sombrely depicted. And the story comes to much the same resolution, though short-lived. Dressed again with sacrificial and coital suggestion, the climax shows a male power finally breaking from its destructiveness of energy into a mighty - indeed, stupendous - power of vision, which is brought to bear on the feminine pride responsible for the interim unhappiness. In addition to the mythic or symbolic ways already pointed out, this harrowing of the proud feminine is shown in the 'mock trial' of Act 3 Scene 6 (Lear trying to pierce the "hard hearts" of his false daughters) and in the inspired attack in Act 4 on the "simpering dame" of seeming virtue and upon the Law as a 'feminine' body of pride that causes vile cruelty in man towards his true nature, his own true bride. This 'law', this pride, is broken as through a ravishment by the male energies, and yet - continuing that analogy - is also changed into the true maternal fruitfulness of kindness and mercy - Cordelia returned.

The same point is made in the near-contemporary *Measure for Measure,* in which the stony purity of Isabella - again linked with pride and the power of the law upon life - must suffer a 'sexual' surrender to the male, to change into life's true kindness. Something similar in idea appears, in fact, in quite a few of Shakespeare's plays, one of which deserves more than passing notice in connection with this climactic transformation, the 'sexual death' - *The Winter's Tale.* Here we find, true to form, the proud Perdita (the "goddess" or "witchcraft" of control in our interim existence) at last suffering the male wrath that seems so essential in changing her nature to fruitful kindness (from 'stone' to 'flesh', in her mother's case).

By clues-in-names, Shakespeare also has this play's climax touch on other versions of the same mythic idea. For example, the name *Paulina,* another figure of feminine control upon man in the play, points to the teachings of Saint Paul, in which we find, as in Shakespeare, a link between mortal pride and the Law as equal 'feminine' forms of hard control (the "bondwoman") that needs a final transforming male power, as imaged in the victory of Christ at Calvary, to be changed into the true 'law' of "Charity", the restored "Jerusalem".[18] Another clue-in-name is *Hermione,* the cyclical play's axial heroine, for this was

18 Saint Paul's Epistles are randomly charged with this idea, but most of the point comes out fairly succinctly in *Galatians* Ch. 4

also a town in ancient Greece linked with Demeter/Persephone and possibly where her rites were enacted as well as, more famously, at Eleusis.[19] It adds to the evidence that the Demeter/Persephone story is a shadow to this play's action, and so further prompts us to ponder the likeness in symbolic meaning between the play's climax (and that of other Shakespeare plays) and what ritually took place at Eleusis. I mean, in that dark rite - and again dealing with the crucial change of a hard nature into the true 'feminine' kindness of a spiritual Spring - there was probably enacted a 'sexual death': a final 'insemination' of the hard wintry aspect of Persephone, as the male life-energies (Hades/Plouton) at last sacrificially achieved the right fruitful 'ravishment', and thus reversed the destructive rape with which the story began. A relevant likeness to some of Shakespeare's versions of the myth?

The wheeling Persephone story is very much a Greek equivalent of the biblical cycle from Eve's Fall to Eve's redemption - the loss and return of the true lady of kindness. Judging by his plays, we guess that Shakespeare knew it well.

★   ★   ★

In this last part of the Chapter, before going on to *Hamlet,* I want to return briefly to *The Franklin's Tale,* because it shows something else in the myth's development most relevant to this study - how an originally single role (the Winter-King) had taken on a division whereby two or three personages act as aspects of the same character. I think something of this division must have occurred at an early stage in the myth's evolution, but whatever the truth of that, the tendency continued and shows up in many later versions, including this 'Breton lay'.

In reading Chaucer's tale, we quickly pick out that the husband (Arveragus), the lover (Aurelius), and the magician, are all in some sense the same character. A clue to this is that all three play a destructive role, such as beset the King in the early myth when the Queen turned to a power of resistant control. Arveragus turns to warfare, ruinous to life in pursuit of 'feminine' shadows of fulfilment

---

19 See Robert Graves' *Greek Myths: 24.c.*

– honour, glory, and so on. Aurelius duplicates this, becoming a sort of violator of all things in his thirst for the fantasy of self-success. The magician is also destructive. But with a difference. What he seeks to 'ruin' or 'violate' is Dorigen's stiff pride. He works in a world of illusions brought about by her frustration of the masculine mind and desires, but works those illusions against her, intent to break both them and the resistant power that causes them. He is like an earlier Oberon.

So the magician, as an aspect of Arveragus, is really in the story from the start, and after the breakdown of the marriage, sits and watches in the shadows like the remaining 'mind' of the now absent and dispossessed husband, intent to restore what is in effect *his own* sovereignty by the defeat of the lady. We realise also that a version of this figure turns up not only in the later Oberon but, in some form, quite widely in Shakespeare's plays and in medieval romance – the director in the shadows, the 'magical' intelligence of destiny. We realise too that he seems ever to supervise the same process. As the 'mind' behind the whole story, he knows that his own desires and energies – the 'Aurelius' – have been turned into a 'monster' of fantasy by the resistant nature in the feminine – the 'Dorigen' – and that the way to restoration must be through working those 'energies' back towards their true life-power, the lost 'virility'. This power, when brought upon the eventually weakening 'queen' in the already much explained climax, will work the final magic by which the baseness or distortion in these sexual opposites will die into their own true return – and his own.[20]

So the King of the original myth who turned into a monster, and then by ordeal realised a virility by which to regain his true majesty in the simultaneous reclamation of his Queen, has now become two figures: the 'mind' of the King and the 'energies' of the King, with the former now magically supervising the ordeal upon the latter so as to restore the right 'virility'. This power, which the winter-queen tries to keep destructively futile, so that her own barren state of control be maintained, will at last be wielded by the magician, to

---

20 How their return is also his own will be shown in a later chapter on *The Tempest*.

overcome her and oust her barrenness for a renewed fruitfulness.

Though variations sometimes blur its showing, this character-pattern is common in ancient and medieval myth. Quite often we find a personage representing the surviving 'mind' of the original ruler, who, no matter how cloaked sometimes in the frightening and dangerous form of a monster (a survival of the primitive winter-king),[21] works upon another male – usually a younger figure, as best denotes the 'energies' – to carry out this very process of restoration: the bringing back of a lost male power by which the 'queen' and all her wintry realm will quicken again to joyous life.

By this we might begin to ponder just what the magical Thoth was up to with the lost phallus of Osiris (or with the young Prince of Byblus) for the eventual enrichment of Isis. And ponder also on the real intent of the spooky Grail King, shadowily guiding the hero of the quest towards the dark Grail's becoming herself the fruitful Lady. Similarly we might muse what magic Merlin really purposed upon the once bloody 'sword' (Balin) to make an instrument of power (Galahad) capable of wresting the Lady from grey maidenhood. And then, by a shift to plainer heresy, we could reflect on an ogrous 'magician' in the biblical destiny, who likewise had intent upon a 'Cain', to forge a sacrificial hero. I mean Jehovah himself, for he is another magical 'mind' reforming the character of debased man into the instrument for a last 'sexual act' at Calvary, for the release of poor, barren Magdalen and *his own* resurrection.

Such musings are met by definite answers in Shakespeare's plays. All the above, for instance, shadow his final summing-up of his work on the myth: the story of magical Prospero, who upon a 'Caliban' (Cain+Balin)[22] worked a wonder for the return of the true Lady – and his own.

But for now I shall take another Shakespearean example of the myth and, to lead us in, make a quick translation of some of the above. For winter-king, Grail King, and Jehovah, let us read 'King Hamlet'. For the younger energies, the Sword, or Cain, let us read

---

21 Often this figure appears as a giant – famously in the Green Knight of the *Gawain* romance. See the excellent survey of this story-type in R.S. Loomis' *Celtic Myth and Arthurian Romance: Bk2.*

22 And also *Caliburn,* Arthur's sword. A matter for Chapter 8.

'Prince Hamlet'. And for winter-queen, barren Grail, and Magdalen, whom these male instruments of destiny were to bring back into a radiant fullness of life, let us read 'Gertrude' and 'Ophelia'.

★   ★   ★

The 'Hamlet' story, like those already considered, almost certainly originated in what has been conveniently called Nature myth,[23] and so we are prompted once again to approach Shakespeare's version in the expectation of a surviving and developed form. By this approach, we soon realise, to start with, that the play opens in what is already the myth's fallen or 'wintry' situation – the ordeal – which, as in other cases, has followed some earlier disastrous breakdown in a sexual harmony: the marriage of King Hamlet and his Queen. We also realise, as we begin to ponder the retrospective information Shakespeare places in the text, to define or explain this earlier disaster, that the first higher happiness, the 'summer' of the story, ended – again as in the other cases – when something turned the masculine character destructive to life, which the ghost mysteriously conveys as his "foul crimes".

What is more, this "retrospective information" indicates, and still in agreement with earlier examples, that the masculine change to destruction or violence followed some sinister alteration in the feminine nature. For example, the stories that Shakespeare touches on to shadow the background of the play - Asgard's downfall, the collapse of Paradise, and the loss of golden Troy – all contain a sinisterly turned feminine character as in some way the cause of ruinous male violence.

These will be looked at in Chapter 5, along with Shakespeare's other mythic clues, but one thing might be examined a little more closely at this stage; and that is that Shakespeare includes in his play a series of events seemingly meant not only to repeat (in part) the past disaster, but to explain more accurately its cause. This series of events is the woeful story of Ophelia and Hamlet, in which an *altered* feminine nature does indeed cause a dangerous wildness in the male character. Shakespeare, it seems, is making quite certain

---

23 See *The Sources of 'Hamlet'* (Sir Israel Gollancz).

that we see a sexual disharmony as not only the basic cause of grief in our fallen world (imaged as 'Denmark') but the cause of an earlier calamity.[24]

And here we come across something of particular interest. In the blighted relationship of Ophelia and Hamlet, Shakespeare includes something that reminds us of a key factor in all previous mythic instances. Ophelia's alteration is into a character of *resistance,* imaged in her rejection of Hamlet's love. It is, yet again, that first ominous move of the 'queen' towards a wintry disposition. Moreover, the 'pure-demure' personality in which that wintriness is imaged has both a general likeness to the seemingly virtuous Goneril and Regan (alias the "simpering dame"), and an even sharper likeness to the 'saintly' Dorigen.

This is one of the things by which we are helped to realise a similarity between the situation and role of Hamlet and that of the earlier Aurelius as demented 'victims' of feminine resistance. Both seem equally cases of masculine creativity and desire turned by denial into a dangerous force, fantastical in mind and violent in intent. A 'god' turned 'Satan', once again. And it is a similarity in one case strengthened by imagery, for just as the first in his frustration "langwissheth as a furye dooth in helle", so the second appears "as if loosed from hell to speak of horrors".

Further to this, once prompted by the idea of a similarity in the roles and situations of these two heroes, we realise that it is not just the Prince in *Hamlet* that resembles Aurelius. There is a reminder also in the play's portrayal of man generally, as conveyed both by the action and Hamlet's observation. The world of *Hamlet* is full of 'Aureliuses': men impelled by the same lunacy of desire to the same monstrousness of behaviour, and all as if the true urge and aspiration in the male spirit has likewise been perverted by frustration of its real object and fulfilment into a substitute fascination with a "shadow" or a "strumpet". [25]

Taking this a little further. If we recall an earlier point about

---

24 The Ophelia/Hamlet story will be examined closely in Chapter 6.

25 Images used in the important exchange between Hamlet and Rosencrantz and Guildenstern, discussing Lady "Fortune" - 2.2.228-65.

medieval portrayals of this life's sexual predicament – how the darker feminine character might denote the inner power of the self or pride, with exactly the same effect on man as any outward erotic spell of woman – then we realise that *Hamlet* is very much a late example of the same artistic view of life as appears in the story of Aurelius. It presents the same prison, in which man is trapped by the dictates of the 'feminine' self, pursuing empty realisations of that self in outward aims, as if yearning to grasp an outer form of what already inwardly possesses him. (In *Macbeth* later, the same is even more darkly depicted: the power of the self as a manifestation of a sexual derangement. The world of the witch.)

At the same time, while seeing a likeness between Hamlet's situation and that of Aurelius earlier – a divine creativity warped to fantasy and villainy by a resistant femininity – we have to admit a marked difference. The main one, due partly to Shakespeare's play being a much more complex version of the same story, is that Hamlet is markedly more knowing. Here is no simple dupe of dark desires, nor one who is simply the instrument of a destiny that will eventually lead him to a 'sexual death' in a final confrontation with the opposing 'queen'. He has a perception of his situation, an instinctive sense of the truth. It tells him some of what long ago befell a higher world and what still befalls so easily in the darkness of this, and that implicated here is – *in some sense* – the 'feminine' nature. The power through which man first lost true manhood, true majesty, even true divinity, is the same that now chiefly hinders him reclaiming them. It is something about *Woman,* that mild yet central determinant and motivation upon all that man is and does, which once had a Lord by her side in Paradise, but now, for some reason, only a grotesque deformity of man ever capering to her weird Persephonal or Circean stare – "For wise men know well enough what monsters you make of them."

This instinct in Hamlet shows most clearly in his interpretation of the revenge mission. His first recorded deed on leaving the battlements is not to "sweep to my revenge", or even to plan for such, but to go and take a long hard look at the outward gaze of the feminine soul – the face of Ophelia. It is as if he has – in part at least – discerned that his true mission, far more fundamental than mere revenge, and more a matter of "setting right" a whole life-situation now "out of joint", is crucially hung upon that gaze in some way. We could even claim, therefore, that he has picked out from the ghost's instruction 'Get rid of the murderer' the implication: 'Change the *nature* that at present can make man murderous'.

Yet, as a note of caution, we would be wise to remember that, whatever the realistic elements in *Hamlet,* we are still partly in *myth,* and that the 'feminine' nature Hamlet feels he has to explore and contend with is, therefore, not so much actual woman as what woman images or reflects in man's own nature and psychological make-up. Shakespeare, in the weakening of the mythic character of his art, is almost forced into making his hero appear misogynistic, but *we* needn't be.

To return to the main argument. There are points raised above worth pondering in relation to other versions of the myth. For example, we may have here discovered why in some Grail romances there appears a revenge mission that likewise seems subordinate to, or bound up with, the larger mission of rescuing the feminine nature – the darkened Grail itself.[26] The same seems to be true of the *Ragnel* romances,[27] in which once again true masculinity can only be restored by solving the puzzle of something sinisterly present in the feminine nature. And by this we are pointed to the primitive logic of Hamlet's real mission ending in the Queen's chamber, for an act of alteration in which what at present ails her is cast out.

It is on this matter – the rescue or alteration of the Queen – that *Hamlet* goes deep in its insight into the human condition. Too deep indeed to be fully taken up in this first survey, though it can be provisionally dealt with now, and later returned to.

I will start on this by saying that so far in this study of the myth, I have pointed out that the first main move towards disaster in many of its versions is the turning of the feminine nature into a power of

---

26 The Grail romances in connection with Shakespeare's work will be looked at in later chapters.

27 These and Chaucer's own adaptation, *The Wife of Bath's Tale,* will be examined in Chapter 4.

hard control and 'resistance'. What I have failed to point out is why it does this. *Why* did the summer queen, or Dorigen, or Lear's 'daughters', or umpteen besides, change in this way? *Hamlet* is one of the versions of the myth that give an answer. The feminine side of our being is *contaminated*. Whether we take this "feminine side" in the old fertilistic sense of the Queen of Life, or as Woman, in some mystical sense, or in the subtlest psychological sense of the emotional or affective part of our make-up, the crucial fact of an inner contamination holds. Behind the nature causing the weakening and dementing of the masculine character or faculties in life is an illness or *poison*.

Some of the myths that show this – and *Hamlet* is one of the sharpest – represent this illness allegorically as a figure, a third factor in the 'sexual' drama, who deliberately instills a poison into the feminine nature so that, through its alteration, the ensuing weakness and derangement of the true masculine character (so much seen in this study) will allow him to take control – to *usurp*. He then maintains control by the same means, using the darkened feminine nature to keep the masculine from regaining the power, the 'virility', by which 'she' might be cleansed of her illness (blight or barrenness in fertility myth; blight of heart, or pride, in religious versions).

By this we glimpse already why in the ghost's account in *Hamlet,* purporting a murder by poison, there lurks the shadow of another story: about a king (or a god) being turned to weakness and mania through the poisoning of something bodily or 'feminine' about him,[28] just as the disaster in Eden (adumbrated in that account) began with the 'poisoning' of Eve. We glimpse too why Shakespeare's repeat showing of King Hamlet's disaster – the 'nunnery' scene – that ends with a like derangement of the hero, is preceded by a 'poisoning' of a young woman's nature.[29]

Thus the mythic role of Polonius (and, to some extent, Claudius) beneath the realistic surface of the play comes into focus, as also does the reason for Hamlet's hostility towards them. They are this

---

28 Chaper 5 will both show this and give the reason why Shakespeare has to make it vague.

29 For investigation in Chapter 6.

'third factor' in the myth, the presence that, having insidiously entered the feminine nature and changed it, works all through that altered nature to first usurp and then maintain control. Polonius and Claudius are therefore late examples of a type commonly found in myth, though in different guises - the 'Blight' or 'Death' possessing the Queen in fertility myth, the wily goblin behind the enchanted maiden in folktale,[30] the malign woman-using sorcerer in romance,[31] and finally the Devil of religious versions, whose first act was the 'infection' of Eve to gain power upon Adam.

By this last - the example of Eve - we will notice more keenly the way that Shakespeare has Polonius describe the effect of his words upon Ophelia - "...she took the *fruits* of my advice" - and also Hamlet's taunt at him as a 'pimp' ("fishmonger"), because that fellow's trade in those days was often symbolically likened to the whole art of the Devil: to turn what is feminine into a means of weakening man to brute folly and villainy.

The last few pages have taken up a difficult matter, and I will come back to it more fully later. It is enough for now that we have begun to see *Hamlet* as an example of the myth in which the basic sexual derangement and contention in life - the struggle first primitively conceived as that of the winter king and queen - is given a deeper explanation. This is, that behind the feminine character causing the contention, whether we see this 'character' as Self (or Pride), sometimes imaged as the powerful erotic side of woman, or whatever other compelling and controlling force upon the masculine spirit, there lurks in all a factor of blight or poison.

Hamlet, further, illustrates how the myth sometimes allegorically represents this factor as a character in the story, one of manipulative control through the feminine nature. This type of allegorical figure, doubtless first appearing in primitive ritual as the blighting spirit of Death, Winter, or similar, became in the latest mythic versions (including *Hamlet*) the figure of the Devil, whose 'poison' now used upon the Lady (or the 'feelings' in our make-up) is, according to

---

30 There are many survivals of this 'Rumpelstiltskin' type, including Shakespeare's own "roguish fay". See Appendix A: *Mad Tom*

31 A good example is Spenser's Archimago in *The Faerie Queen*.

such stories as the Biblical Fall, a damaging sense of fear, shame, self-hatred, causing the formation of pride as a defensive reaction. And with pride, all our further woes.

However, putting most of this aside for now, there is something else to concern us as we next turn to the climax of *Hamlet*. It will be apparent, I think, that those versions of the myth that allegorise the factor of blight into a manipulative figure in the action are likely also to show that figure prominently in the 'coital' climax. This is the likelihood whether that figure is primitively or fertilistically imagined as the 'barren demon' finally to be quelled or ousted from the Lady's person by the hero's 'virile' weapon, or whether, in a later religious version, he is conceived as the pride-causing devil whose dark illusions of sin and death are finally to be banished from the feminine heart by the 'virile' entry of divine light or that overwhelming power of "truth" so much mentioned in this chapter.

The expectation certainly proves true of Claudius and Polonius in the climax of *Hamlet,* where they figure clearly as the pernicious factor to be overcome in the hero's 'rescue' of the Queen (Gertrude and her role-twin, Ophelia). In the Queen's chamber scene, for example, amid reminders of the old 'fertility' climax, which Shakespeare seems well aware of, as if reviving the Norse myth of Skirnir and Gerd,[32] we see Polonius as the old lurking demon of blight behind the curtain, now quelled as the 'solar' hero at last converts his violent energy into a potency to 'inseminate' the lady.

This fertilistic symbolism adds to the image Hamlet used earlier in his threat to 'rescue' Ophelia from her blighting father,[33] which he seemingly now achieves as Ophelia is "tumbled" at the same time as Gertrude is 'humbled'. And it is further added to by other details in the Queen's chamber scene. When Polonius is linked with the "rat", the 'Peeping Tom', and the "old man" in "my lady's chamber", for instance, we are reminded of stories that probably bore stronger 'fertility' significance in Shakespeare's day – *The House that Jack Built,* the *Godiva* story, and *Goosey Gander.*

---

32 For examination in Chapter 5.

33 "Let her not walk i' th' sun. Conception is a blessing, but as your daughter may conceive – friend, look to't."(2.2.183-84)

But Shakespeare, needless to say, is not wishing to re-create a fertility myth. As in other medieval versions, the fertilistic elements in the old story are here sublimated into religious meaning, in particular 'Christian' meaning, as if displaying a Christ at last rescuing a Magdalen by ousting an inner devil from her. That is to say, the scene shows a power of virility now become one of transforming 'truth' that can enter our barren 'feminine' hearts (as with Dorigen earlier) and rid them of a deadening spiritual blight – the "devil" actually specified in Hamlet's words. And with this Christian meaning in mind, we might once again notice how Hamlet's thrusting of the phallus-like sword through the Queen's curtain to kill the 'deadener' (Polonius), alongside the thrusting of truth into her heart to oust the Claudius of lies, compares symbolically with Christ's orgasmic vigour tearing through the Curtain of the 'barren' Temple of pride during his Crucifixion. It denotes exactly the same sublimated sense of the old fertility myth: the hero's potency of divine vision at last overcoming the devil's blight within our proud 'feminine' nature.

This event in the Gospels is part of the Christian version of the old climactic 'sexual death'. The hero's vitalising plunge into the barrenness of Death, into Hell, in order to restore life – the resurrection – is a spiritual rendering of the older ritual idea of his rescue of the barren Queen into fruitfulness. As part of the 'sexual death' in this Christian version, as in many cases, the symbolism of coitus and mortal sacrifice are run together, because, as I have pointed out, they connote the same 'magical' transmutation of base male energy into life-energy. Likewise in *Hamlet,* the 'fertilising' of Gertrude (or Ophelia), on whatever level of meaning we wish to take it, coincides closely with the hero's execution. It was a pagan legacy in the source-story which Shakespeare fitly embellished with allusions to the Christian equivalent, the Crucifixion, as in Hamlet's parting words to Claudius.[34]

There is another interesting 'ritual' feature in this part of the play. As earlier mentioned, the symbolic link between coitus and mortal sacrifice also applied to the feminine side of the myth's

---

34 See Longer Notes at this Chapter's end.

climax. Dorigen's quasi-sexual surrender to the power of "trouthe", for example, noticeably bears also the idea of a death to her former self. The same is often found in Shakespeare's plays. So in *Hamlet,* for instance, Ophelia's being "tumbled" coincides fairly closely with her death. More than this: it should be noticed that her means of death tallies with the ceremonial drownings that were remembered of Spring fertility rites even to the time of Sir James Frazer, three hundred years later.[35]

Yet, after all this careful argument, there looms a major puzzle. In *Hamlet* the whole thing fails. It is a wonderful version of the myth, and yet the climactic 'sexual death' of both pagan and Christian traditions in this case ends in failure. There is no rebirth to new-found harmony. There is no resurrection, no return of Spring. True enough, there are signs, as if Shakespeare could not quite forsake the possibilities. There is just a hint of the divine rebirth, for instance, about Hamlet's return - arriving "naked" on the shore as if new-born from the sea like many a solar god. There is also a hint that it is the former King returned from the sleep of death - "This is I, Hamlet the Dane!". Yet it isn't so. There is no return of the Mighty One, restored in the gold of the sun and embracing the Lady new-risen from the grave. Ophelia's place in the earth is no "bride-bed" after all.

What went wrong? I can suggest an answer - though, once again, it will be only provisional. The answer begins in the possibility that Shakespeare was prophesying the failure of Christianity. I will explain, as briefly as I can, using what I take to be William Blake's reading of the matter.[36]

I said earlier in this chapter that the myth on its journey to the Middle Ages had in many cases become a religious story of man's destiny, from Fall to possible salvation - the Spring of the soul. As such, it could reflect either the cycle of an individual's progress or that of mankind in general - the whole sweep of time since the loss

---

35 *The Golden Bough* p.409-13 (Abridged edition: Macmillan)

36 In his *Four Zoas* I am fairly sure Blake is showing Shakespeare's work in a 'prophetic' light (especially *Hamlet* in his *Night* 7) but the appalling obscurity of that work denies easy proof.

of Eden (or some equivalent golden realm). The Jewish writers of the Old Testament, for example, seem to have had this latter sense of a 'historical' myth, for they treated the history of their people as a circle of destiny, beginning with the collapsed 'marriage' in Paradise and ending with the renewed 'marriage' between a God now purged of his wrath and a chastened people (sometimes imaged as a woman redeemed from pride and wantonness).

Shakespeare in *Hamlet* seems likewise to be using the myth (in part) to reflect man's historical destiny, to which the numerous echoes of the biblical books of the prophets in the Queen's chamber scene are perhaps a pointer,[37] but ending not in happiness, but in what seems to be another 'fall', as in *King Lear* later.

But why had the destiny failed? I think Shakespeare saw that man had come so near to realising what was really wrong with him, to realising why he was 'fallen'. The genius of the Jews, for example, as expressed in the Bible, had shown this, especially in the amazing insight of one named (whether accurately or not) Jesus, who, judged by his teachings, seems to have perceived that pride or self, the cause of our degraded limitation in this mortal life, is a condition of our emotional or 'feminine' side that forms as a defensive reaction to inner feelings of self-disgust and self-hatred: the poison that first afflicted Eve in Paradise, registered in her story as a horrific sense of shame and nothingness (sin and death). By the logic of this, and by the teaching of the myth from oldest time, it was clear that our freedom could only come through a sort of sexual act. That is, the pride, like a virgin, must at last yield herself, and in the light of truth, like a quickening charge to her barrenness, this inner malaise or poison of life-hatred be cast out: the breaking of the heart to a powerful healing. Such would be, as in fairy tale or romance, like the final embrace of a returned prince upon the seemingly ugly self, the blemished earth, in whose foul darkness lay the true bride hidden and waiting all along.

The Church, founded in part on this teaching, did to some extent incorporate its wisdom, and yet, like all patriarchal religions, and perhaps all post-primitive aspirations and ideals, it was itself

---

37 See Appendix B - *Hamlet* and the Biblical Storm of Destiny.

much affected by this inner life-hatred, this disgust at the natural, so
that it was itself reactively possessed by pride. And because masculine
desire beset by pride ever lusts for outward manifestations of that
'inner woman', so the Church lusted for pride's fulfilment, though
this was now disguised in the ideal, the heavenly, the pure - the
'harlot' transformed into the ethereal 'mother'. Moreover, the
violence and cruelty towards what fell short of the ideal, as is usual
with the mania of ascetic pride, were all too obviously shown.
Mother-yearning: women-burning.

What was as bad: by its failure to grow wise to its puritanical
zeal, its underlying life-hatred (a kind of misogyny), and to recognise
the real nature of its lust for the otherworldly ghost-mother of
purity, Christianity helped to promote its own eventual destroyer:
the reforming secular idealism, whose yearning for the perfect
scheme or state, as an earthly equivalent of the 'paradise', was to
reject the Church itself as a 'mother' not pure enough for its
imaginings and, in so doing, cast away as humbug so much of
traditional wisdom and forms of discipline that the Church, for all
its faults, had preserved for the nurture of true humanity.

Some of this process - Christian vision infected by its own
puritanical genius, and then giving rise to even greater lunacy - can
be seen in Hamlet's reform of his mother and in what follows. His
'reform' of human nature, like that of the Jewish prophets or the
Church fathers, falls far short of an "embrace of a returned prince
upon … the blemished earth". The hatred and disgust are all too
evident. It is a 'sexual act' as rape, and is not one to cast out the blight
of sin but one to keep it there, though under fresh garments of holy
and abstemious seeming - the pure mother as the product-image of
the reformer's own pride. And the eventual 'child' from this rape-
reformed 'Eve', as from Christianity, is not the Messiah but the mad
zealot, who emerges from the sea of time as from the womb -
Laertes. Here is one limitless in desire for the perfect realisation, the
modern idealistic reformer, in whom the real nature of puritanical
zeal is finally revealed as atheism. Whatever the slogans of his rabble-
banners - the usual froth of justice, liberty, or whatever - all must be
swept away for the ultimate dream of 'me', the final cleansed
realisation imaged in the purest of pure 'madonnas', Ophelia. Is this

the modern world, whose rejection of faulty traditions, including the far from perfect Church, has brought its eager liberation to the point of total breakdown? This matter of Shakespeare's 'prophetic' insight will be returned to in later chapters.

★　　　★　　　★

In summary, I will try to round off this chapter on the developed myth from the standpoint of the last example, *Hamlet*.

Fast in this world, the hero, like so many before him, senses that his true majesty of character is lost, and his powers degraded to stupidity in thought, the unreal in desire, and the destructive in act. He seeks again his former character, instinctively aware that crucial to his aim is the defeat of a feminine factor which, herself darkened in nature, holds the key to his present plight. This feminine darkness in medieval portrayals was imaged sometimes as the erotic spell of woman, or equivalent enchantment, and sometimes denoting the force of the possessive self or pride, alike responsible for keeping the hero - the mind and creative desires - in thrall to narrow baseness; though in the wisest portrayals it was shown to be only a character created in the true feminine nature by an underlying sickness or poison, sometimes figured as one who uses it to arrange all to his control.

By the logic of this, the true power the hero seeks, much as his primitive forerunner sought a virility to rid the barrenness of his queen, is something able to cleanse from the feminine soul in life's and his own composition this contamination responsible for the whole wintry nightmare, much as Christ, the ultimate hero to some, was to find a power able to penetrate the pride and cast out the 'sin' that lay beneath.

This 'sin' is a deep life-hatred or self-hatred, and its banisher a power of all-understanding, like a divine truth of light come to its darkness, showing its unreality. Yet if the hero is himself still tainted and controlled by this poison through pride, he cannot work the rescue, but must find all his insight and instinct to reform vitiated, giving rise to a product that simply repeats the state of error. This is shown in *Hamlet,* as Shakespeare replaces the optimism of the myth with a reflection of the usual failure in our lives. The hero does not find his bride, his paradise, his Grail again, but stays forlorn, because he has still the poison in his heart.

★   ★   ★

Chapter 2   Longer Notes

p. 27   Lear's 'sexual' frustration. Apart from the general idea implied in the daughters' attempt to "cut off" Lear's powers, we should note Goneril's excuse for the coercian of his followers, afraid that they may turn her castle into "a brothel" or "riotous inn" (1.4.250), followed by Lear's own image of sexual denial used about Goneril (2.2.175-79). The fool's comments, as ever, are most sharp to this process of the feminine taming of the male. He sees a growing 'maternity' of control that will reduce masculinity to a neutered child (1.4.180 & 243), and sees Kent's own binding in the stocks in the same light - a curb imposed for being "o'er-lusty at legs" (2.4.10). Most pointedly of all, he observes that the new moral regime is like a fishwife forcing down the lively eels (a phallic image) into a cooking-pot, to destroy them (2.4.122-24).

p. 29   The giant in the Gloucester story. Gloucester's 'death' (Act4 Sc6) that frees him from the "fiend" as through a leap down a cliff links with the story of the giant Gogmagog, who was cast down a cliff in the restoration of Albion by Trojan Brutus. The story appears in the same collection of legend and myth that contains an important version of the 'Lear' story - Geoffrey of Monmouth's *History of the British Kings*. Shakespeare's likely knowledge of the book probably accounts for the symbolic connection between the two stories in *King Lear*.

p. 43   Christian links in the climax of *Hamlet*. As pointed out in this chapter, the final male sacrifice was ritually connected with the idea of male orgasm - as denoting the same climactic change of base energy into life-giving potency. The Gospel accounts of the Crucifixion have traces of the same idea, and so Shakespeare fittingly connects the quasi-sexual climax of *Hamlet* (including the hero's own execution) with that Gospel event. This is shown in Hamlet's parting words to Claudius before he sets out for his death in England. His teasing the King as the 'worm–emperor', who simply eats up bodies, alludes to the punishment of the serpent in Genesis: that his rule over this fallen world would simply be to possess and consume its mortal fragments - the "dust of the earth". Jesus implied the same in his words about 'rendering to Caesar' things that are merely earthly or bodily, as he looked towards his own sacrifice. A similar play of ideas is found in the scene of Cleopatra's suicide in *Antony and Cleopatra,* in which she approaches death as a sexual surrender of her mortal body - the "dung" - to the "worm" emperor of this world: Caesar. Shakespeare in both cases obscured the meaning to guard against the charge of profane correspondence between holy writ and his plays' secular events.

Chapter 3
The Story of Eve

In the course of the last chapter, while trying to show some of the medieval development of a primitive myth, I found that the simple 'model' I was using, to gauge how far the original story-pattern had survived, proved inadequate. (Perhaps this is the fate of all simple models in an approach to myth?). It had posited an opening disastrous phase in the story, in which the feminine nature grew uncompliant or resistant in character, which then caused, through a sort of 'frustrated' reaction, the masculine character - the life-energies - to turn manic and destructive. Not a wrong idea but, as it proved, not accurate enough. *What,* for instance, caused the feminine nature, this queen of life, to grow thus 'wintry'? And was her new resistant character really sufficient to explain, by itself, the derangement of the masculine character as by frustration?

Fortunately the example of the myth that brought these questions to the fore was also one that provided a possible answer. This was *Hamlet,* in which appeared a figure (Polonius, doubling with Claudius) who, on the play's mythic level of meaning, denoted a malign power that had got poisonously within the feminine nature. This figure, whose mythic/ritual ancestry goes way back to primitive notions of demonic blight or anti-life, explained the Lady's 'wintry' disposition as due to a newly instilled self-hatred or life-hatred: a sense of the detestable about herself, from which a persona of rigid integrity was an escape or defence.

This idea of an illness or poisoning also threw more light on the derangement of the masculine character. His dementing was not simply due to a 'frustration' of his true role, as his feminine partner turned denying. It appeared that, in addition, he took on the same bane or infection as in the feminine awareness, by which he was tainted likewise by life-hatred, and his energies turned to an instrument of that hatred: life-wrecking, life-punitive. It was as if - and here King Hamlet's words begin to take on meaning as a background to the play - the 'feminine' body of life, once infected, passed on her infection, as through the bloodstream, into the mind and creative powers of that body (the masculine faculties), throwing them also into a deranged hostility towards their own life.

This brings us to the crucial factor in the myth, and also in the life - our present existence - that the myth often seems to mirror. We are in a 'winter' of the soul, because the feminine part of that soul has at a deep level a kind of wound or sorrow. Whether we see this "feminine part" mystically as one side of the spirit to our being, or as the psycho-pathetic or affective awareness in the human character - the 'heart' - or, to a limited degree or in reflection, as woman herself, the idea holds true of the myth. This chapter, and the one following, will explore an awareness of this crucial factor in some of those dealing with the myth in past ages, who used it to mirror both our present plight and our possible healing.

★ ★ ★

William Blake, like many mystics before him, perceived strongly that our present existence is made up of a basic sexual duality: the contrary forces of 'masculine' and 'feminine', who once had a higher or heavenly existence, and might, when the divisions and errors of this life are overcome, regain that happiness. His 'prophetic works', like some of his lesser pieces, give full scope to this idea, being cyclical destinies of the sexual "contraries". But these works also show Blake's sense that there was a mythic tradition that shared this view of a sexual destiny, a tradition that contained many outstanding writers of symbolic works, which by allusion and echo he gave reference to in his texts: secret sharers in his - the last - bardic compilations, you might say.

It is by studying these texts, adding in effect to our own intuitions of a sexual purpose and dynamic to our being, that we begin to see more strongly for ourselves so much of inspired literature of the past as witness to this single myth - works that despite their realistic features at times we seriously misread if by realism alone.

Not the least of these works of "inspired literature" are folk and fairy tales, ever recognised by the older writers of myth as ruder cousins of their art. And certainly, in their kinship to the most sophisticated older works of literature (for are not the best of

Shakespeare's plays, for instance, little but the best of fairy tales?) and by their simplicity, they provide a useful way of approaching the myth in older literature, and not least – blatantly obvious, indeed, once we pick it out – on this matter of a cyclical 'sexual' destiny, centred still on the mystery of the feminine nature. Cinderella in your kitchen, why do you flit like Shakespeare's witch about the seething Grail?

Whatever her answer to that – she will give it clearly later – and with whatever clarity of my own I have prepared this chapter so far, I think it will be guessed that I mean to spend some time with fairy tales, as a simple and workable demonstration of what the myth is about, particularly in its feminine characterisation. But despite mentioning Cinderella just now, I will begin on this with another fairy tale.

★   ★   ★

When we read the well-known *Snow White* type of story, one of our first suspicions is that the Wicked Queen, the 'witch' , is not a character separate from the heroine but simply her other self or 'double', like a shadow she cast one day that somehow became real. A like impression is given in some other symbolic stories, as in the relationship between Cordelia and Goneril/Regan in *King Lear,* or between Persephone and Hera in Greek myth. The impression is strengthened by the original Nature myth (Chapter 1), in which the winter-queen was seen simply as a changed or divided aspect of the summer-queen. And it is of interest, in passing, to recall that Cordelia's fore-runner in this kind of myth – Creiddylad – actually played *both* characters.

In *Snow White,* partnering this notion of an overlap in the feminine character is, perhaps logically enough, the notion that the original ruler (the father, husband, or king) and the more destructive personality used by the Queen to do her dark deeds (the 'bloody hunter') are also 'doubles'. So, matching the duality of light and dark in the feminine character, there appears a duality of light and dark in the masculine character. But here things go deeper. The change in the masculine character into a darker 'double' occurs, we notice, only *after* the queen has hardened against her softer personality. It is as if the masculine is almost entirely determined in his character – noble or base – by what kind of feminine nature he is partnered with, and that a darkening in the former must lead to a darkening in the latter.

The same is found in many other stories. For example, in the Zeus/Semele and the Athamas/Ino stories in Greek myth, male violence arises *after* the heroine's falling foul of her 'twin', the jealous Hera.[1] And might we not notice the same of *King Lear* – the masculine growing destructive *after* a divisive change in the feminine? Or of *Macbeth* – the change from hero to monster seeming to occur *as a result* of an infernal alteration in the 'queen'?

The same idea is supported by something that happens at the end of many mythic stories, for so often the hero, in finally breaking free of his monstrous debasement, declares that it was all due to a 'witch' transforming him in the first place. It is commonly found in fairy tale, and not uncommonly in romance – the *Green Knight* and *Dame Ragnell* stories, for example. When the idea is recognised, we can also see it implied in other versions. Who, for instance, changed the Duke of Milan (*The Tempest*) into a wrathful demon, and Ferdinand into a Caliban? By implication, yet another witch – Sycorax. With a little imagination we can see exactly the same in God's story in the Old Testament, so that, when he finally comes back to his true character (after the wrath of the prophetic books), we can picture him rubbing his head and muttering: 'All was well with me, you know, in my Garden and my Marriage, till Eve changed the way she did'.

That is assuming, of course, that our "little imagination" is as heretical as that of some of our older poets, and sees God and Adam as much the same character.

We could go on for many pages citing examples, because – quite simply – the pattern is so widespread. It is a cardinal point of the myth, and of the life it mirrors. Right from early versions of Nature-myth through into the Middle Ages, and into Shakespeare, there is found ever and again the same feature as found in *Snow White* and other fairy tales: that at the beginning of the cycle of destiny

---

1   The 'monster' that arises in the masculine character in the Persephone story (Hades) may have a similar explanation, since Persephone was the same goddess as Semele (See Graves' *Greek Myths* 27:11).

something altered the 'feminine' in such a way as to cause a destructive change in the 'masculine'. Whether we are looking at the old Troy myth, centred on the dangerously alluring Helen, or at the Paradise myth, centred on the changing character of Eve, or whether we look at a much later story such as Shakespeare's *Hamlet* or Milton's *Samson Agonistes,* we realise we are still with this basic apprehension of a fault in the sexual harmony that turns all destructively awry. And when in the interval of time between these examples we see many stories showing a like configuration of sexual character, we sense that we are looking at what was almost a tradition of poetic obsession with a truth about the human condition, from which it could not break free; as if over and over it must fix itself to an idea that comes up even in the humblest fairy-tale formula: 'When the Lady with the Witch is twinned, then the wise King twins with Beast'.

So the *Snow White* story has proved useful in taking us to the heart of a recurring myth. But it is useful in another way - this time helping us to understand what the characterisation of 'masculine' and 'feminine' really denotes in such myths, and also to understand better how a change in the 'feminine' results in a destructive change in the 'masculine'.

In reading *Snow White,* or any of its type, we realise that the outward drama, involving separate personages, can also be understood as an inner 'drama'. That is to say, the personages of hateful queen, kindly daughter, wise father/king and the 'bloody hunter' can all be seen as aspects of the human personality or make-up, whose inter-action forms a kind of 'psychological' version of the outward story. If we say, for example, that the feminine personages represent the 'feelings' or the psycho-pathetic side of that personality, and that the masculine personages represent the mind and active side, then we find the following inner 'drama' in correspondence with the outward story: -

The inner emotional life suffers a divisive change, in which hard and bitter feelings gain dominance over the soft and kindly ones; and in turn, as feelings ever will, this affects the mental outlook, causing it to lose imaginativeness and grow more negative towards whatever is soft, kindly or natural; and, as a result of this, behaviour itself becomes destructive to life.

In the same way, we can look at the start of *King Lear,* for example, and see exactly the same reflection of an inner or psychological drama enacted by the surface story. That is to say, the fateful story of Lear and his daughters, in which the hard and false replace the soft and true, partly reflects something that is happening within Lear himself – the same hardening change in his 'feelings', the feminine side, that then darkly and dangerously alters his understanding and finally turns his behaviour violent. Similarly in the climax of the play (Act 4), in the process that reverses the opening decline of Lear, we can see a use of the same reflective idea. Lear's outward attack on the hard, false law (or the falsely virtuous "dame" who images it) reflects his attack on what remains in himself of hard feelings or pride.

So we see in these myths how the outward portrayal of action and the inner 'psychological' action to some extent reflect one another. And by this we now have a subtler explanation of why the emergence of a darker feminine character in these stories leads to a change in the masculine character. What is outwardly depicted as a harder kind of woman influencing or inciting a male personage into a destructive personality and course of action can be seen as a dark change in the emotional or psycho-pathetic side of the man himself – from soft 'kindness' to hard 'pride' for instance – which equally determines destructive behaviour. So a story like Macbeth's moral downfall, for example, is equally intelligible as a man's fateful persuasion by a malign woman and as a man's alteration through an 'emotional' change in his being.

Readers of myth, and particularly readers of medieval romance, will be quite at home with this idea of an inter-reflectiveness of meaning, for they will have grown used to the sense of 'double vision', or even 'triple vision', experienced in reading such stories, in which often the outward drama is merged with at least one other level of meaning.

However, now is not the time to expatiate on that. We must get on to the next stage of our investigation, which starts with the discovery that some myths (or some versions of the same myth?) actually indicate how the malign or sinister side of the feminine personality arose. They not only show the 'witch' emerging from the shadow of the 'fair princess', so to speak, but show what caused her to emerge. One such myth, and one that was very influential in the Middle Ages, was the Paradise myth.

The story of Adam and Eve, as it is usually called, probably started its life as the first part of yet another form of the myth so much occupying us in this study. What points to this, among other things, is that it deals - yet again - with the breakdown of a primal sexual harmony, leading to the calamitous loss of a first 'summer' state. But the version surviving to us - that of *Genesis* - has undergone many basic changes to suit the needs of orthodox Jewish teaching. One change appears in the way the final catastrophic wrath, ending the first higher happiness, is depicted. The violence itself remains as scarcely more than a suggestion (the image of the cherubim with swords of flame) and the cause of it is completely changed. Gone is any idea of an incensed and mindless fury of a 'winter-king' unleashed upon his own fair 'summer' nature, and in its place we find a just punishment of a righteous God upon an unworthy creation. In this and other ways, patriarchal adaptations of the myth, in their need for a supreme and morally responsible deity, sometimes converted the first male violence to a righteous act of retribution (or retaliation).[2]

There are other features of the *Genesis* story that show didactic tamperings with the likely original, but, despite their interest, I must for brevity come to the point for which I brought this story into the discussion: that it provides an explanation of how, in Life's first fatal flaw, there arose a sinister shadow to the feminine nature, like winter-twin to summer-queen, or Witch to fair Snow White.

This explanation begins in what the Paradise story, imaginatively read, tells us first afflicted Eve, as through a serpent's venomous bite: an appalling new awareness of the emptiness of her being ('death') and its hideous shamefulness ('sin'). From this she recoiled, eager to form about herself, as in a garment of leaves, a substitute persona or character by which to gain, though infernally, a formidable new aura and power, defiant against the nothingness of

---

2   See Longer Notes at the end of this chapter.

death, and by which to hide, or even perhaps eliminate, her real self now seen as fouled by sin.

By this, but also by considering the earlier point about the susceptibility of things masculine to things feminine, the disastrous behaviour of 'God' (or Adam) is explained. Like the ruler (king or father) in *Snow White,* he fell to the new powerful charm of a changed feminine nature intent on the destruction of her true self. He became, as is still visible beneath the misleading terms of the biblical version of the story, the 'king' turned into his own 'bloody hunter' by the spell of a 'witch', who violated his own fair Paradise, his own 'Snow White'.

Perhaps the above 'imaginatively read' meaning of the story will be doubted by some, but others, I hope, will trust and follow. There will be good reason. However, for now, the vital point to grasp in the myth of Eve, both for itself and in relation to other myths of a primal 'sexual' disaster (many of which we shall see in later chapters) is its showing us a first fateful division in the feminine nature, due to a sort of poisonous self-hatred. By this division, a second and powerful character arose in malice to its true self, and used its power to captivate the mind and energies (the male) and turn them likewise against the true nature - even violently.

It may be of some significance to note, in passing, that something similar seems to occur to some extent in actual female behaviour. For here too, sometimes, as if reacting to a sense of the slight or slighted in her true nature, there develops, seemingly by instinct, another personality of secondary artifice, as if to cover or hide the first, and also to give not a little compensating power upon the male, even though this, as it did for Eve, leads sometimes to his offering a kind of 'violence' upon her nature.

As important as this. If we relate our findings about Eve, the feminine character, to the inner or 'psychological' workings of human behaviour, we shall better see why myth, including medieval allegory, is so given to the strange inter-reflection of inward and outward in its view of 'sexual' behaviour, as touched on a few pages back.

Let me put it this way. Whether or not a man is born with a sense of shame, self-hatred, and so on, it is certainly true that he becomes aware of such a sense at some point in his childhood, and that it gains strength thereafter. Now, this awareness is in his 'feelings', the affective side of his being, and so in his *feminine* side - the 'inner woman', as past ages sometimes called it - and it brings about exactly what the 'poison' did in Eve. I mean, as a reaction to the poisonous sense of fear and shame, the feelings seem to develop a defensive or compensatory 'character'- ego, self, pride, or whatever - which is coldly suppressive or abusive towards the now detested or 'shameful' side of its own nature: the kindly, physical, sensitive, the truly 'feminine'. In all, it is like the second Eve operating against her natural self, or like the 'witch' against the 'princess', but now *within* a man.

But the real subtlety arises - both in our lives and in the best allegorical portrayals - when we realise that exactly the same goes on to some extent in man's outward behaviour as he falls away from innocence and grace. For there too - in the outer world - he correspondingly starts to ignore, slight, or even abuse what is natural (whether woman, Nature, the physical, or the meek beauty of life) and pursue or cherish instead those things that seem very much like outward complements or realisations of his inner lady pride - all kinds of titles, trophies, successes, and so on, that are not only sensed as 'feminine' but are often epitomised, both in actual life and in allegory, as a falsely desirable woman.

Remote from literature? Not at all. Without some of this insight, we are lost also in Shakespeare. Commentators still puff and flounder, for instance, in the 'nunnery scene' of *Hamlet* because they simply cannot see more than the realistic surface. When we change the focus by imagination or by myth - including the myth of Eve - we shall see more, and begin by seeing more than *one* 'woman' in that scene.

★   ★   ★

In summary and reflection on the chapter. Investigation of the feminine character in myth has turned out to be important. To start with, a look at the *Snow White* pattern led to our finding that man in his behaviour - noble or base, creative or destructive - is much determined by a feminine influence. Next, in looking at the 'psychological' drama in myth, as a reflection of the outward action, it was seen that part of man's susceptibility to things feminine is due to the determining role of the 'feelings', his inner feminine state. It was also seen that there is a strong connection between the object of his desire in the outer world and this inner emotional state, both being 'feminine' and both exercising a related power over his behaviour. In a sometimes sinister way, for it was realised when looking at the biblical Paradise story that there are a number of myths indicating that the feminine nature is rootedly harmed – even 'poisoned'. There is indicated to be a terrible self-hatred, linked in *Genesis* with a sense of shame and hollowness of being, that causes it to assume a second character of compensating power and meaning through illusion, and with means to hide away, or even destroy, the true nature now perceived as vile. This then, like all feminine determinants on the masculine, tragically affects his behaviour, as through his inner feelings now poisonously turned to pride or, as it is often imaged, as through his feminine partner's being weirdly changed into a queen of spells. He becomes the dupe of her fantasy, in lust for her fake fulfilments, and at the same time casts off, spurns, or abuses the true nature, the truly feminine of seeming ugliness.

This strengthens the idea taken up towards the end of Chapter 2 about man's destructiveness to life, for it seems clearer now that his brutality is not simply due to the frustration of his creative role when taken over by a darker feminine nature, as was supposed in this study's early stages, but due also to that darker nature's directing him in accord with its own hatred.

The findings of this chapter might, further, strengthen insight into our behaviour ever since we left infancy, or the infancy of our primitive origins, and became what is called 'civilised'. Beneath all of it – our institutions, religions, ideologies, forms of effort and desire – despite the pretence of male determining and control, there lies this sickness in the 'feminine' soul that actually governs all. Man's ceaseless conflict and striving for the right ego-dream, in some form or other, is his folly still for the witch of pride and her empty promises; and the abused object, the victim – whatever is of Nature, dearly natural, or naturally feminine – that ever suffers by his manic lust, is still the witch's sad Snow White. At the governing root of our ills is misogyny. And misogyny, by the wise view of myth, turns out to be feminine.

The matters examined in this chapter could appear remote from the subject of literature, and more fitting to a religious or psychological seminar. In fact, as we shall see better as we proceed, they are at the centre of the myth underlying much of our finest literature, and central to the preoccupations of those who produced it. These writers often show awareness, even a fascinated awareness, that this life is very much bound up in the tensions of a sexual psychosis; and they often show awareness that this psychosis is rooted in something much awry in the feminine side of our being. Whether we look upon the stories of Blodwed, Persephone, or Cinderella; whether we wonder upon the doings of Hamlet, Lancelot, or the deranged, blind prince seeking his Rapunzel … in all, and more, this same matter lurks somewhere within the drama. "Hamlet, I am poisoned" should equally be the Queen's words at the start of that story, and also at the start of all its other versions. The tragedy of the Lady Grail, as of the Lady Cauldron of *Macbeth,* ever begins with her poisoning, as we shall see.[3]

★   ★   ★

A word of explanation in passing. This study so far has mainly focused on the darker aspects of the human character, as if intent to see in the myth, as well as in the life it mirrors, mostly what is sinister, mad, and monstrous. The imbalance has partly arisen from the sombre texture of most of the stories looked at, but also from a wish to keep a wide and complex subject as simple as possible, uncluttered by continual qualification. I trust it will be understood that the author sees well enough how, in both myth and life, the True Lady ever partners the Witch, with a benigner inspiration countering the sinister, and with a kindness of nature and wisdom to match the hardest pride; and equally how imagination, heroism, and creativity - the finest of the Masculine spirit in all - are ever present to redeem the character of the beast.

★   ★   ★

---

3   Other myths showing the lady's poisoning or infection will be shown later in
      this study and in Appendix C.

Chapter 3   Longer Notes

p.56   Patriarchal tamperings with the myth.

Patriarchal civilisations seem to have inherited myths that recorded a past violent calamity that had wiped out some pre-existing higher state of life. Central to this calamity was the fact that the masculine character – the *whole* character – had somehow become monstrously destructive. But the patriarchs, having conceived the idea of an exalted male god who could not possibly be implicated in such a terrible outrage, altered the myth to exonerate him. The Greeks, for instance, made the past calamity the work of the giants or titans in rebellion against the true god, whose own violence was therefore justified in retaliation. The Mesopotamians similarly had explained their supreme god's violence as simply the quelling of a chaos-dragon, Tiamat. The Jews came up with various versions. One was similar to the Greeks'. The first violence was due to a race of giants (Nephelim) whom the supreme deity had quelled. Similar to this was a version later used by Milton in *Paradise Lost* – the revolt of the rebel angels, who had to be put down and punished. In the Paradise myth, they seem to have hit on another device. They altered the original, in which Adam and God were aspects of one figure, and converted the violence into a just act of one side (God) upon the other (Adam) for the latter's disobedience.

Such patriarchal tamperings led to all kinds of logical absurdities, but a greater threat to their orthodoxy was that many myths had survived which told the truth. And many poets were ready to use the alternative tradition – including some medieval poets. This is one of the heresies they got involved with. I am much tempted to take up this matter now, because it draws in that fascinating forest of stories loosely called 'Arthurian' including the Grail romances.[4] However, keeping the matter to a note, I shall more simply say that a more primitive view of the male deity, reflecting the whole masculine character, and including demonic as well as light aspects, survived through myth and folklore into the Middle

---

4   To be dealt with in Chapter 8.

Ages. It was partly a relic of the old idea of the Nature-king, who could be both 'summer' and 'winter','God' and 'Satan' as it were, with equal logic, and therefore could be seen responsible for major devastation as well as major blessings. Something of this is visible in the giant of *Sir Gawain and the Green Knight,* who is a composite of man, god and demon, like most of the 'fairy' lords of the greenwood, and not unlike the spooky 'king' of the Grail romances.

Ever overlooked by the orthodox Church, writers who worked on the myth in which this more primitive unitive view of the divine character survived had to be very wary. Chaucer, in his re-working of the Paradise myth in *The Merchant's Tale,* for example, only *shades* the figure of January with hints of both God and Adam, and only *shades* it as a character capable equally of folly and wrath or wisdom and grace. Equal vagueness is found in the character of the ghost in *Hamlet,* who likewise combines features of God and Adam on one hand, and of the majestically divine and horribly demonic, on the other. His account of what really happened in the "orchard" of Paradise turns out to be equally unorthodox, as we shall see later. (Ch. 5)

Chapter 4
Eve Found and Rescued

The last chapter ended with the idea that some poets dealing with the myth of our destiny recognised the central importance of the feminine character to the mystery of our fallen state. This chapter will add to that idea, following the poet's intuition that within that character lurks a dark secret, in the finding of which, man, individually or in a body of humanity, will find release from this state.

The feminine psychology set out in the last chapter seems to have been generally well understood in the Middle Ages, especially the idea of a dark feminine power that operates both inwardly as the pride or selfhood, and outwardly as the allurements to man's unreal desire, or 'lust', and equally causing the male character to be stupid and destructive to life. The art and thought of that age show this quite often. Did they not see Satan, for instance, like Sammael to the Jews, falling through pride, yet equally through lust for Eve, and given to destruction?[1] And the angels likewise, the *B'nai Elohim,* were both overweening in their arrogance and lustful for the daughters of the earth, by which they begot the giants of destruction – the *Nephelim.*

Adam's own fall was sometimes similarly explained, as the violent wrecking of his paradise was seen to have come about through his succumbing to the linked powers of lust and pride, wielded by the darkly altered Eve. Chaucer treats the same idea humorously in *The Nun's Priest's Tale,* showing Chanteclere also bringing ravage upon his farmyard "paradise" through his weakness to pride and (quite remarkable!) lust, imaged in the power of 'fair Pertelot'. As Chaucer was also there mocking the chivalric hero as woman's dupe and plaything, it reminds us also that Lancelot (mentioned in the tale) was marred by the same linked fault. He failed to achieve the Grail, for

---

1   The Middle Ages had many variations of Biblical story, some arising from a blend with folktales and other traditions, including Jewish rabbinical legends. On Satan's lust for Eve, begetting Cain, see *Ancient Israel* (Angelo S. Rappoport) vol.1 p.194.

instance, because of sinful pride and earthly lust - imaged in the shimmering Guinevere - and he was also marred accordingly by a violence of spirit. In line with the same idea, romance heroes seeking release from such debasement had often to counter a powerful force of pride, or selfhood, imaged as an erotic female. A striking example is found in the *Green Knight* story, where Gawain's victory over lust (the bedroom temptation) is linked with his final yielding of self or pride.

But rather than get bogged down in numerous examples of the same, it might simply be said that when Spenser depicted Duessa (or Acrasia) in *The Faerie Queen* as both the infernal queen of false desire and mistress of the House of Pride, equally powerful to debase the life-energies of man, he was using what amounted to a truism of medieval romance and its religious psychology.

So far, so orthodox. The Church, waving its stern mete-wand of morality, would have had no quibble with any of this, for it agreed with its rather dim and dismal view of the feminine nature as the cause of man's woeful condition: the culpable Eve. But some poets took the matter further, giving this Eve of life a much better deal in sympathy and understanding. It was partly through a marked respect for the feminine which students of the Middle Ages, having peered into the cult of Courtly Love and its romantic view of womanhood, will know a good deal about. It was also partly through a poet's instinct for the truth, a perception that behind the feminine character there lay a secret. She held the answer to something as within a dark maze: something that explained her behaviour and her power upon the masculine, which the sincere seeker, like ardent lover or questing knight, braving its paths and the perils of her temptations athwart her true wishes, might find. So woman to the true poets of the Middle Ages held the fascination of a sphinx, a riddle as of Delphi or of whispered *weirdspell:* damnation or bliss ambivalently, death equally with life, smile of witch and yet Belle Esmerée. It was Eve's secret, by which both she and Adam were meanwhile bound to her dark earth-tree, and by which both together might wake to Spring.

It was not enough for such writers to accept that the feminine nature was just a bad lot, and then turn away onto the path favoured by the Church, leading to some masculised heaven in which the feminine, if it existed at all, was etherially ungendered. It was in the feminine nature itself - taking 'feminine' in a wide sense - that something had to be found, some cause of its distortion and man's consequent folly. And here the Church would not be pleased, for it was to be found that the feminine nature was not to blame, and, more dangerously, that the real blame lay in orthodox morality itself, in the very attitude sanctioned by the Church. What had long ago 'poisoned' Eve was still poisoning her, and then hypocritically denouncing the result.

One such true poet was Geoffrey Chaucer, who, in one part of his *Canterbury Tales,* not only gave Eve's own side of the story of life, but allowed 'Eve' herself to give it - the Wife of Bath, a character of genius in simple guise, and of astounding truth in roughness.

★   ★   ★

The Wife of Bath's Tale[2] is an adaptation of a well-known medieval story-type - 'The Hero and the Hag' - the best example of which, outside Chaucer's work, is probably the story of Gawain and Lady Ragnel. The type almost certainly had its origin in much older stories (and possibly rituals) of what is usually seen as a 'Nature' or 'fertility' kind, much concerning us earlier in this study.

Chaucer's version keeps a number of primitive features, the most noticeable of which is the ancient story-pattern. There remains, for instance, an opening violence (the rape), shattering to the primal harmony and happiness, which is followed by the expected period of 'wintry' ordeal, quest, or contention, culminating still in the end-climax of mixed sexual and sacrificial symbolism (the 'sexual death') that restores the 'Spring'. We could say that the only real change from the primitive form is that, as in many medieval examples, it is adapted to later religious and psychological insights. For example, the original quest probably dealt with a hero's search for a lost true power (akin to virility) whereby the Queen could be defeated in her will to remain wintrily barren (and eerily *powerful*). In Chaucer's version this has become, on one level, the quest for

---

2   For an outline of the story, see Appendix G.

wisdom by which to probe woman's secret wishes, but still touching that central mystery of her dark preference for power (over man) rather than fulfilment. At the same time, on a second level, the quest has become man's parallel 'inner' search - into the emotional state, the heart, the 'woman within' - to probe the nature of that equivalent feminine power upon him - the pride or self - and perhaps find its cause.

With this in mind, we turn back to the Wife's Prologue and realise that, despite its first impression of rambling formlessness, it actually shows pretty much the same thing - a sort of myth in the guise of realistic biography. In the story-pattern, for instance, we see that the Tale's first rape is matched by the Wife's arranged marriage at an early age, and that the final climax which through mutual sacrifice ends the conflict and distorted state of the sexual characters now appears fairly recognisably in the last quarrel and reconciliation of the Wife and her husband Jankin. The main body of the Prologue also matches with the Tale - in subject-matter - for it too deals with what amounts to a search for woman's true wishes. I mean, the Wife's monologue, in its spirited defence of woman's character and her rights, is arranged by Chaucer to circle round something almost as secret (as she herself is not fully aware) as the hero of the Tale has to discover - what is *really* troubling her and what the remedy.

But here, on this point of a remedy for her ills, things become tricky. For a start we soon realise that the remedy the Wife herself proposes - power over man ("maistrye") - is not, whatever she says and wishes to believe, her 'chief desire'. Indeed, it is if anything her chief curse, for it is a part of the compensatory personality of power and make-believe that, according to the 'Story of Eve', is adopted by her, and the feminine nature generally, in reaction to an under-sense of herself as unimportant and unworthy. Moreover, even as a compensation, this dark power is not blessed with happiness, for its effect, as we have seen, whether it operates through the feelings as pride (ego) or through the corresponding outward wiles and glamours of this life, is to turn the masculine character or elements - the creative desires and energies, for instance - to folly and brutality, for which her own true nature pays the price.

So what is her, and all women's, longed-for remedy and 'chief desire'? It is when we look behind the Wife's stance and assertions and also pick up Chaucer's hints at the 'Eve' theme (as when he has the Wife proclaim "Alas, alas, that ever love was sin!") that we begin to see her character aright and realise that what she really wants is what the spirit of Eve has ever longed for – to be free of that which forces her into this darker character of defensive pride, disguise and power-hunger: the dread and blighting under-sense of the hollow and faulty in her nature. Thus the truth behind the mere words of her Prologue is revealed, which is that a great deal of the Wife's public personality and its projections – the strenuous jokiness and noisy self-assurance, the bold claims to power and its satisfactions, and (particularly) her overplayed denials of any sense of shame in her sexuality and its affairs – are all a covering or amends for an actual sense of emptiness, ugliness and rejection: Eve's secret horror.

Confirmation follows in her Tale, in which Chaucer uses the hag-witch as a sort of surreal version of the Wife herself – and now plainly manifesting in visible abhorrence the inner truth of self-hatred and sorrow in the feminine character. Further confirmation comes in the implications of the hero's final sacrifice, and here once again connected with the 'Eve' theme, for in having to marry the hag in her coarse hideousness, the knight faces utter *shame* and *death* (imaged as 'social death') – the very things that blighted Eve and the feminine heart thereafter – and thereby proves himself for her sake of greater strength than they. Thus is their reality and power broken, the curse lifted, and thus also her control on man ("maistrye") has shown itself not her chief desire but a means to it.

In all, the darkness in things feminine and the power it gives her upon whatever is masculine has a two-fold and contradictory purpose; for in binding him, in no matter what will of witchery to enthrall and possess, she brings him at last to his actual means of freedom from the base and stupid, and also the means of her own release into the full state of kindness and grace. Like the hero of the primitive myth, at length finding a virility sprung from his crude energies to oust the Queen's barrenness (a condition still recalled symbolically by Chaucer in the aged sterility of the hag *and* the childlessness of the Wife herself), or like the later hero of chivalric romance, ready for whatever dread in ordeal or mortal combat, and thus thrilling his lady to surrender, so this later 'Gawain' (as he might be named by his character likeness in analogous stories) finds like a Christ a power of vision in sacrifice, a lost ghost-power of the god, to cast out all the twisting sense of the worthless and unworthy, emptiness and shame, Death and Sin, from our own 'lady', our mortal heart and nature, and thereby quicken her again from fearful pride into a new Spring of life.

I am much aware that this first brief survey of Chaucer's Wife of Bath has passed by many points of medieval subtlety and insight – the shrewdly observed ambiguity of the feminine character, for example, in being both domina and victim in one, both Pride and Kindness, Witch and Snow White, and so on. It might serve for now, however, that another remarkable example of an ancient cyclical myth of destiny, enriched by medieval genius, has been indicated, and that a little more has been added to counter those commentaries on the Wife of Bath that, whatever the concessions, basically assume with the arrogance of modernity to age, and of scholarship to common womanhood, that the Wife is little more than a shallow gas-bag brought on for our superior amusement.

★   ★   ★

I had thought next to move across to Shakespeare's *The Winter's Tale,* for its outline is very like that of *The Wife's Tale:* the story of a man in whose heart a consciousness of sin creates a self-righteous pride, turning him violent to his true bride, until by penitential ordeal this "witch" of controlling pride is broken[3] and he finds his true heart and bride again. Indeed, the likeness of story is sharpened by a similarity in the true lady's return, for just as the hag-witch in Chaucer's story bids the hero "Lift up the curtain, and see how it is", revealing her lost true self, so in Shakespeare's play the curtain is finally drawn from the statue to show again the lost wife of kindness – Hermione.

However, instead, I shall move from Chaucer's story back to a work that has already been given some examination in this study – *King Lear* - which, though clearly more complex and intense than

---

3   Symbolised in the angry breaking of Perdita's power of "witchcraft" in Act 4 Scene 4, 418-450.

Chaucer's tale, shows pretty much the same story-line: Man made destructive to life by pride (beneath which lurks an awareness of sin), but then freed of pride to find again his wisdom and his 'bride' – at least for a while, until the 'happy ending' is cancelled. And, as with *The Winter's Tale,* this general resemblance is sharpened by a point of particular similarity, appearing in a cryptic allusion as the action moves towards the climax of Lear's ordeal:-

> "Swithold footed thrice the old ('wold');
> He met the nightmare (the 'hag'), and her nine-fold;
> Bid her alight, and her troth plight,
> And aroint thee, witch, aroint thee! (5.4.123-7).

G.L. Kittredge rightly linked these lines to an old charm used in rural areas against supernatural ills,[4] and yet we can be sure that Shakespeare here, as in other 'folk' allusions made in this part of the play, is doing more than spice his text with random folklore. He is pointing us to the symbolic meaning of the action taking place - the inner drama or myth. How apt, then, that this 'Swithold' fragment should seem to come from the same background of *Ragnel* stories from which Chaucer derived *The Wife's Tale.* We can discern in it the same point: a hero at last coming to terms with the hag, breaking her from her witch-personality into the truly feminine partner, even as by a 'marriage' of sorts ("troth plight"). Moreover, this is spoken, like a hint, just before the part of the play where such a change does indeed come about - the "hags" Goneril and Regan are ousted by Cordelia's return into Lear's life.

Indeed, the more we ponder the likeness in what is achieved in the climax of *The Wife's Tale* and in the climax of *King Lear,* the more we may feel sure that the 'Swithold' allusion is a valid reminder of a connection between them. In both climaxes a hero once monstrous to the true nature, which has suffered his abuse, achieves by breaking the hag of pride his true manhood or kingship of character (Lear's "Aye, every inch a king!") and wins back his true feminine nature to be his bride or partner.

I was helped in realising the importance and meaning of the 'Swithold' allusion in *King Lear* not simply by its reminder of *The*

---

4   Cited in the footnote to these lines in the 'Arden' *King Lear* (ed Kenneth Muir).

Wife's Tale, but by looking at similar symbolic climaxes in Shakespeare's plays. If the reader considers, for example, the implications of Malcolm's self-humbling in Act 4 of *Macbeth* or of Hal's self-sacrificial acceptance of the crown in *Henry IV,*[5] I think he will see quite the same symbolic pattern – a hero who by breaking the hag-pride clears himself of the 'monster' that pride ever creates and thereby wins back both true manhood and the true feminine nature that has been meanwhile under abuse. In Malcolm's case, the abused true nature is symbolised by the realm of Scotland, and in Hal's case partly symbolised by England.[6]

I was helped, too, with the 'Swithold' allusion by that wonderful ballad that is thought once to have been included in *King Lear* – 'Loving Mad Tom'[7] – which contains cryptically the whole story. But I was most helped by a range of myth and folklore that for the most part, I am quite sure, was known and understood by writers such as Shakespeare. Swithold links not simply with Lear but with a great number whose destinies – by ordeal upon themselves or on a suffering representative – are towards the same end: the shedding of the old destructive manhood by overcoming the witch-personality in the feminine character and restoring her true nature. So Swithold, among many others, links with Odin, and so in turn with King Hamlet;[8] and also with the Celtic Ogyrvran, and so in turn with Oberon.[9]

And so, by a reading of *The Wife's Tale* and related myth, we are made aware of a similar pattern, so that we then look upon a play like *King Lear* with an assured focus, seeing what is essentially the same story. This is nowhere more true than in its climax, for in this word-storm of Act 4 Lear is seen to be very much in the same situation as Chaucer's hero. He too realises the enormity of the pride and self-righteousness that has earlier possessed him, and made him an ogre of condemnation upon life – upon the nature that suffers under the cruel blows of moral censure and affliction. And

5   *Henry IV Part 2,* Act 4 Sc 5
6   See Longer Notes at the end of this chapter.
7   See Appendix A.
8   A subject for Chapter 5.
9   See Longer Notes at the end of this chapter.

realising this, he also, who first was the 'ravisher' of life for the sake of pride, becomes the ravisher of pride for the sake of life. It is a reversal of act quite commonly found in versions of the myth, from its early 'Nature' form, which also began with a 'rape' of the summer and ended with a 'rape' of the winter. So Lear now finally, at the end of his 'winter', tears one way in fury at the power of pride, the hypocritic virtues, the very witch that dwells in the heart and in the moral law, instigating man's lusts and cruelties; and, another way, like Chaucer's knight, he embraces all that his pride has made him see as foul and unworthy. It is a power of vision and action almost beyond words and dramatic form, as Lear, wild with inspiration, undergoes what is really his own crucifixion, championing all that is hideous and contemned as his lost love, his true nature.

It is a case, symbolically speaking, of his finding again the one he had long ago violated, like Chaucer's hero, for at this point the true lady - Cordelia - comes back to him. But it is a case also of his having first found the key by which to work this return, as in Chaucer's story: the power to banish the awareness of sin that, as I have argued, lies at the heart of things feminine, replacing the true and kind with a hard pride that then generates the whole nightmare of fallen existence. So Lear's passionate words on the essential sinlessness of life are of vital importance - "None does offend - none - I say none! I'll able 'em. Take that of me, my friend, who have the power to seal th' accuser's lips!" (4.6.170). Is it by chance that this reminds of the Gospel story of the woman taken in adultery?

Lear's achievement fulfils, among other things, the folk-tale destiny of "Bessy", alluded to earlier in the play, who, like Cordelia, is the true kindness or nature meanwhile banished by an awareness of shame -

> "Come o'er the bourn, Bessy, to me -
> Her boat *hath a leak*,
> And she must not speak ...
> Why *she dares not* come over to thee!" *(3.6.25)*

This "Bessy" links in turn with another symbolic figure who, if Robert Graves was right, was once present in an accompanying ballad that gave commentary of the play's symbolic meaning.[10] Once

---

10 See Appendix A - The Ballad of Loving Mad Tom.

I name this figure in the ballad, I think the reader will see the point. She is called "Maudlen" (Magdalen), the woman of shame whom Jesus saved, who in this ballad is likewise saved by the hero.

[A note in passing. Some will think there has been so far in this too much 'male' saving 'female'. Avoiding lengthy explanation, perhaps I might simply promise that the idea (already shown in the Wife of Bath's story) of the 'feminine' being the one who empowers the 'masculine' in the whole process - including her rescue, and his own - will emerge strongly in later chapters.]

★   ★   ★

Chaucer's *Wife of Bath's Tale* has helped us focus on *King Lear* at its climax. It also helps us at its start, but more readily if we first review some earlier points of this study.

The original myth in its opening 'summer-to-winter' phase went roughly like this - Life-Queen entered by blight; turns into Queen of control-by-resistance; thwarted life-energies turn destructive, wipe out remaining Summer state. Some developed medieval versions, in which the story had become one showing the loss of our spiritual 'Summer' (the Fall), went roughly as follows - Our feminine nature entered by sin-awareness; turns to Pride and the rigidities of superior virtue; Male mind and creative energies go mad, violently destroy Paradise.

Clearly, medieval poets and artists dealing with this story, if they were fully honest, would upset the Church on a number of points - not least, the implication, as we saw earlier in the story of Dorigen, that 'Good' creates its own 'Evil', its own destructiveness, out of life's robust energies, and had thereby been responsible for the ruin of Paradise (or even Heaven?).

To guard themselves against Church annoyance - and worse - the poets therefore adopted techniques of 'hint-or-blur'. All Chaucer's versions of the Fall in the *Canterbury Tales,* for instance, show these - so well, in fact, that most modern readers (even experts) see no Fall! The start of the Wife's Tale is an extreme example. Its paradisal setting is disguised as a vague, long-ago Arthurian realm, and the violence that shatters it (the rape) is only hinted (and then in the Wife's seemingly irrelevant chatter) to have been caused by the blocking effect of moral restriction – the symbolic suppression of natural ('faerie') forces by the holy friars.

In the first part of *King Lear,* as yet another primal world moves towards stormy catastrophe, an expectation of a similar use of deliberate obscurity makes us watchful. And it is then we notice, for example, how pride has moved in to control and restrict, as shown in the behaviour of Gloucester and Lear, but symbolically reflected also in a change in the feminine centre of things, in the heart – the replacement of kind Cordelia by her harder, power-seeking sisters, sweet in specious virtue and good intentions.

The link with the Paradise disaster is more strongly realised when we see that this pride seems, as in other cases, to have formed in defence against a latent sense of shame and emptiness, the *sin* and *death* of Eve's story, evidenced in the first moments of the play by Gloucester's ill-disguised unease at what seems now "a fault" in his past free loves, and, a few moments later, by the ageing Lear's betraying a lurking awareness of his possible nothingness: "…while we unburdened crawl towards death". No wonder he yearns to hear from his daughters the words of sweet delusion. And no wonder he is so angry at the very mention of the word "Nothing" (from Cordelia).

So, seeing the opening situation in *King Lear* as a 'paradise' already fraught with a poisonous awareness, we might now go on to see how violence in the masculine character develops as a result. Though I have gone through some of the process earlier in this study, I will go through it again, so that events in the first two Acts of the play fall into focus.

The awareness of sin and death is a horror that drives the 'feelings' or feminine side of the human personality to crave a compensatory identity – something 'good' to counter the shameful, and something wonderful or significant to counter the meaningless. The masculine side of the human personality, as we saw earlier, is swayed in accord. The mind is taken by a need for a defensive hidey-hole in which an illusory 'good' might fend off a truth it fears.

This explains the opening behaviour of both Gloucester and Lear, whose defensive pride can be seen as both a form of frightened rigidity and a desire for self-protective illusion. But this rigid need for illusion – the character of pride – must in its very inflexibility and need for lies make an enemy of both change and truth. It therefore makes an enemy of the imaginative energies (male) that ever work towards change and the creation of truth (which is an ever-vitalised thing, not a static entity). These creative energies are therefore thwarted. They are deprived of a role, much like a lover who is denied his urge by his lady turning prim, or like the masculine life-force in our original 'Nature' model when the Queen turned resistant. And with the obvious result. These energies darken and warp to destructiveness, their life-productiveness become life-wrecking. If we look at the first two Acts of *King Lear*, we thus find honest Kent, 'virile' Edmund (or Edgar), and finally the passionate Lear, are all subject to a frustration of some kind – particularly Lear in Act 2[11] – and all turn destructive, though in different ways, as a result.

Another effect of sin-awareness is one that almost guarantees that the victim of this pent-up and darkened energy will be the wrong one. That is to say – again using Eve's story – the notion of sin chiefly targets what is natural – natural enjoyment, the bodily loves and desires, and so on – as tainted and repugnant. And so the true feminine nature of loving and giving, like Nature herself, becomes the 'harlot', and therefore the scapegoat upon which the frustrated energies may now be 'rightfully' vented. In this way – by a frustration and by a moral misdirection, due to sin-awareness – man becomes a 'rapist' against his own fair life, against all the things that the true feminine embodies – the form of life, the natural, both with its loves and desires and with its kindly limitations and order.

Cordelia's role thereby focuses. Her words in defence of natural instinct as the only basis for true obligation,[12] because they imply a freedom in life's kindness and love, render her the immoral one, the 'woman of sin'. She becomes all the things in life that man, possessed and thwarted by his own pride (his real inner harlot), now

---

11 Here Shakespeare is keen to show the part played by frustration in man's becoming a monster. Event and imagery – sometimes sexual – strongly depict the 'Samsonic' bondage and denial of Lear. (For more detail on this see Longer Notes to Chapter 2.)

12 1.1.91-93, 95-104.

vents his frustration on as deserving it. She is like the abused wife that the monster in man, created by his own possessive selfhood, makes the target of his cruelty. So whatever reason Shakespeare had to make it look as though Cordelia is married off comfortably to the wise King of France,[13] he shows clearly that it is a misleading event, and that her real fate – one that befalls scores of 'Cinderellas' in myth and folktale – is quite different. In the later action of the play, she is in fact the natural order that mania bursts apart; or the kindly form of Nature herself under the equally ravaging storm of the angry elements; and likewise she is the "naked" human nature beneath the blows of scorn and punishment. All this is summed up in the figure of the prostitute, who suffers the whip-lash of the 'moral' beadle,[14] just as she first suffered the lash of Lear's tongue. Whatever instinct Lear has for the real target, it takes time for him to realise fully which 'feminine' character truly deserves his anger. It takes time for his 'eyes' to sharpen again, so as to see within man himself, his assumed goodness, his pride, the real frustrater of the masculine role.

The Wife of Bath's Tale helps us focus upon *King Lear* in yet another way. Chaucer's story is 'Arthurian', like most of the *Ragnel* variants, and it begins specifically in Arthur's realm. It might seem strange to us that this realm – Logres, Camelot, or Albion – could have been linked with Paradise, and yet the Arthurian cycle is so like the orthodox religious or biblical one. Things darken in both upon a supposition of sin (the whispers of Agravaine or Mordred being the equivalent of the serpent's poison); and the medieval fondness for seeing Satan and Eve in an adulterous crime led them readily to impute the same to Lancelot and Guinevere. Likewise the sequel. Awareness of sin leads in both to a violent wipe-out of the golden realm, after which man must go in search through the dark wilderness of this world for the happiness lost.[15]

This last parallel most clearly brings us upon the 'Lear' story, for there too is a search through the wintry wilderness, the 'waste lands',

---

13 Loyalty to the source-story? A wish for some sort of 'happy end'?

14 4.6.162

15 This assumes that the Grail quest should logically come *after* the fall of Arthur's realm, and not as in Malory or the *Prose Lancelot*.

and perhaps there too a 'Grail' eventually found – though briefly – the lost Cordelia. Indeed, there are many Arthurian echoes and reminders in the play, making it certain that Shakespeare had that story in mind as one of his parallels. For brevity, I shall take up a few of these.

They begin early in the play, in fact. Edmund is begotten in a way that his father later considers sinful, which compares with the begetting of Mordred by Arthur (in that case incestuously upon his half-sister). Likewise Edmund, in both Satanic roles – stirrer of mischief and virile rebel – links with the same roles found in Mordred, ruinous to the first stability. More important is to see how Cordelia ties in with the Arthurian theme. When we look at her speech of defence, implying that no woman can give all her love to one man,[16] we sharply remember the situation of Guinevere, whose readiness to act on that idea led to adultery. It is fitting to remember also that Cordelia's mythic fore-runner, Creiddylad, included among the variants of her *type* one called Gwenhwyvar.[17]

However, there is something more important here than spotting mythic connections. It shapes when we realise that in her defence Cordelia is implying – and this is as near as Shakespeare dare put it – that the 'virtuous' morality of an imposed obligation in matters of love is against nature – the true 'bond' – which operates by a more instinctive freedom in obligation. In other words, there is a suggestion of 'free love'. Further, as she says this is in a 'paradise' teetering on collapse, Shakespeare's further suggestion is that man lost his 'paradise' through something that lost us the freedom of love, and gave us a dangerous as well as hypocritic morality instead. No wonder Lear, later, when freed of his moral error, should ridicule the whole notion of "adultery".

But it was a matter of heresy, and hence Shakespeare's precaution to make Cordelia's speech vague and Lear's later outburst one of a 'madman'. He is also careful later in *The Tempest* when putting the same idea. Gonzalo's imagining a "golden age" as one free of laws and their corruptions is made to include the idea of 'free love' only by a jesting interjection made by one of his listeners.[18] The

---

16 1.1.99-104
17 See Charles Squire's *Celtic Myth and Legend* p259 and 332.
18 *The Tempest:* 2.1.160

matter gives food for thought. In the opening paradisal Sicilia of *The Winter's Tale,* for example, what Shakespeare was forced to present as a mere close friendship between Hermione and Polixenes, about which the husband (Leontes) is supposed to have quite unfounded suspicions of adultery, may be meant quite otherwise. Likewise in the Court of King Arthur. May we infer that Lancelot and Guinevere were quite openly lovers until the idea of sin and adultery was formed in the mind of Arthur by the baneful words of Morgan and Mordred? And what of Eve and the serpent lover? Indeed, the net might be thrown quite wide and yet catch a similar fish. When Loki in Norse myth, for example, enters into the happy feast of life (in Aegir's hall) with insinuations of immorality, we have the like impression that the goddesses loved as they liked till minds darkened into thoughts of sin and adultery.

What is true of all these stories also is that the darkening into morality and restrictiveness eventually led to destructive disaster. In all cases, what remains of the paradisal Nature, the feminine form of life, the true bride, is finally swept violently away, ravaged, or murdered. The 'winter-queen', the witch, that had poisonously grown within her fair sister, carried into the mind of man a baneful distortion to his understanding, turning him self-righteously mad, and placed upon the life-energies such a denial of their role that they joined with the madness against her hated kindly self.

Then the process of ordeal begins, as man must find the feminine secret, and what it is that binds him in a bondage to his maddening prison of fantasies, wondering on his face that combines man, angel, and beast. So, famously, he sets out through the dark wilderness of his own being, to ask of women what they chiefly wish for, or like Hamlet, charged with a mission, goes forthwith to look at the face of a woman. "Cherchez la femme" is not only a good maxim for a Simenon novel. Much earlier, in the best of European myths, everything starts and ends with Eve.

[There is further investigation of *King Lear* in Appendix E at the end of this book.]

★   ★   ★

To sum up on what has been a lengthy and complex chapter. *The Wife of Bath's Prologue and Tale* is a magnificent analysis of man's fallen condition and his means to escape it. It concentrates on the Feminine personality, and shows that what mainly drives it to possess man inwardly as pride and outwardly as various allurements is a deep sense of shamefulness and unimportance - the 'sin and death' awareness in the story of Eve. It is by this possession that man is made a monster, destructive to anything of the true feminine nature, for upon this he vents the energies that are frustrated by his pride, directed this way by the feminine hatred of her natural self as sinful and shameful. The way out of his error and stupidity is when man grows wise to his possessive pride, and wise also to the underlying sense of shame and ugliness that brings it into being. By renouncing pride he clears himself of the monster, and gives love and understanding to the underlying suffering in the feminine nature, thus restoring it to its original kindness and joy.

This has been shown to be true of the climax of *King Lear* also, rounding off a destiny that began similarly with a sense of sin entering the realm, as it did into Paradise, starting off the whole nightmare of man's hatred and destructiveness towards his own true life, his own feminine 'partner'.

The Arthurian background of Chaucer's Tale, based on the common *Ragnel* type, prompted some discussion of the Arthurian elements in *King Lear* also - alas, too brief - including some idea of Shakespeare's own insight into what really befell Arthur's realm, as befell Paradise also - a sense of sin in the sexual sphere that denied and dangerously thwarted the once joyful flow of free love.

★   ★   ★

Chapter 4 Longer Notes

p.70   Malcolm and Hal. A climax of very similar meaning occurs in a number of Shakespeare's plays. For example, when Malcolm undergoes a 'negative confession' in testing Macduff (*Macbeth Act 4*), he is humbling himself so as to break the pride (the power of the witches) and therefore free himself from the monster that pride ever makes of the masculine character (the 'Macbeth'). He achieves thereby true manhood or kingliness, and frees the true feminine nature that has hitherto suffered abuse (the land of Scotland). Likewise in the climax of *Henry IV* pt2, Hal's breaking of his pride is shown in his rejection of the pride of kingship for its pains - a kind of accession to the Crown of Thorns or true self-sacrifice. By this victory over pride he becomes the true man or king, restoring the true feminine nature (England) that has hitherto suffered from the monstrousness in man created by pride. (This true nature restored is also partly symbolised as the "Jerusalem" of his father's quest.)

All this is registered in the sub-plot also. The pride destroyed is shown as the clearing of the harlot-power from Eastcheap; the monster cast off is shown in the rejection of the land-abusing Falstaff; and the liberation of the true nature from abuse is shown in Mistress Quickly's new-found freedom. All this is in turn tinged by traces of the old Robin Hood story (or ritual). John Falstaff ('false husband') is the equivalent of Little John, once possibly viewed as Robin's destructive double to be cast off when Robin returned. The name "Robin" is linked with Mistress Quickly's absent husband (See Ch. 6 Longer Notes) who symbolically returns in Hal's accession to kingship. Mistress Quickly is linked with the name Maid Marian (pt 1, 3.3.114) as part of the same symbolism - the abused feminine that the hero restores and re-marries - the 'England' of the main plot. Some of the same symbolism is found in the Wife of Bath's *Prologue*. It is no accident that her meanwhile abusive husband is called Jankin (Little John) or that she too awaits his change to the true husband for her own restoration to the kindly, fruitful nature.

p.70 **Oberon.** *Midsummer Night's Dream* is a version of the myth in which a fallen ruler, the 'Lord of Life', seeks to regain his true character and status by a process of ordeal imposed upon a debased aspect of his own masculinity - in this case represented by the male lovers in the Athenian wood, and also by the be-monstered Bottom. Oberon's aim involves the breaking of the feminine power that controls this male debasement, so that she herself is also restored to her true personality (Titania).

Shakespeare in writing that play was almost certainly influenced by a story in which the fairy king is actually called Oberon: *Huon of Bordeaux,* translated into English by Lord Berners (c1550). But there may be more to it. Both the writer of *Huon* and Shakespeare himself may have been influenced by another story - a version of the Welsh *Romance of Taliesin,* in which the equivalent dark lord of magical destiny, working a refinement of the male hero (and possibly as a means to his own true return), is called *Ogyrvran* (Tegid Voel). *Huon* was a 'chanson de geste', a story-type much influenced by older Welsh romances (through the Breton), in which there is often found a distortion of Welsh names. 'Oberon' seems a likely case - a sound-blurring of *Ogyrvran.*

Did Shakespeare know the Welsh romance? Robert Graves suggests that its similarity to *The Tempest* makes it likely (*White Goddess* p.432). If this is so, then *Midsummer Night's Dream,* a play very similar in story-pattern to *The Tempest,* may itself have been influenced by the Welsh romance. In this case, Shakespeare's Oberon has both an indirect link (by way of *Huon*) and a direct link with Ogyrvran, the shadowy magical lord who seeks his own return. (This matter will be followed further in Chapter 9.)

Chapter 5
Hamlet: the Ghost and his Story

A matter earlier discussed will be useful in this chapter. I have stressed the idea that in myth the first higher world is often imaged as a harmonious sexual relationship, or 'marriage', whose breakdown caused the Fall and whose continuing discord keeps us in this lower world of darkness and division. By this understanding we shall perhaps better see why in the 'myth' of *Hamlet* the ghost is so troubled by the loss of a marriage, the "falling-off" of his Queen, and why Hamlet himself, whatever his ostensible mission, is much taken up by the problem of man's unhappy sexual situation.

So let us look again at this, and this time more closely, to see if we might find more of Shakespeare's view on the fate of a long-ago happiness and the cause of our history of woes.

★   ★   ★

There is an under-story in the ghost's account that does not agree with the surface story of a straightforward brother-murder and usurpation. We are first warned to this under-story by the setting of the crime - the "orchard" - which brings to mind all the sinister ambiguity borne by the apple in myth and folklore. Did not disaster, for instance, betide the marriage of Heurodys when she slept beneath the orchard-tree?[1] And did not some ill likewise befall the feast of Guinevere when the apples were poisoned? And perhaps also, with a major reminder of the Trojan disaster in Act 2 of *Hamlet,* we might recollect that Troy's misfortune began with an apple banefully intended - in the ill-fated Judgment of Paris. But, above all, in the main biblical tradition, more evident to Shakespeare's audience than to us, there is the fruit of Paradise that European folklore ever insisted was an apple.

The Paradise myth in fact gives us our main lead into the ghost's under-story. After the mention of the "orchard" in the account of his downfall, we next notice another fitting detail. The poisoner

---

1   In the powerful medieval romance poem, *Sir Orfeo*

who stole into this orchard is, aptly enough, referred to as a "serpent". Though the ghost discounts the 'serpent' detail as part of a false explanation put about by Claudius to disguise his crime, he nevertheless uses the image – and repeats it even after saying it is not strictly true. Shakespeare in writing on two levels, realism and myth, must hold such contradictions, it seems.

But having got ourselves nicely locked on to the Paradise idea in the ghost's account, with the ghost himself as a kind of Adam, we then find a sharp divergence from the normal Paradise myth. I don't mean the suggestion made by this 'Adam' that 'Eve' and the 'serpent' committed adultery, for that was a common enough notion in medieval versions of the Fall. The real divergence is that the ghost speaks as if he is a combination of Adam and something divine, and thus relates events of the Fall as if they took place in a heavenly setting, as in this reflection on his wife's unfaithfulness:-

> "... But virtue, as it never will be mov'd
> Though lewdness court it in the shape of *heaven*,
> So lust, though to a *radiant angel* link'd,
> Will sate itself in a *celestial* bed
> And prey on garbage." (1.5.53-57)

The reader today might easily dismiss this 'celestial' detail (as well as Hamlet's general estimate of the former king as some kind of deity) as simply poetic hyperbole, but to do so, I think, would be to miss the point. When Shakespeare combines in the King's character the idea of Adam and something divine, he means to be taken seriously, just as in the similar characterisation of Lear or Prospero later.

To understand this concept of Adam as a divinity, I believe we need to look back to an older religious view of the masculine character in life's make-up, something that was held before patriarchal orthodoxy made a sharp distinction between the character and status of man and those of God.

The further we go back towards a primitive mentality, the more we find an understanding that tended to blur the distinction both between the natural and the supernatural, and between the human and divine, as if to such an understanding these forms of being shared a common and intermingled existence. This 'primitive' view survived into the Middle Ages alongside the standard, divisive theology. When we read Arthurian romance, for example, we still seem to be witnessing a life in which the world of man and the otherworld of gods (or demi-gods) are strangely intertwined. The idea survived also in some religious conceptions. For example, the medieval Jewish kabbalistic notion of the original Adam - Adam Kadmon, the all-inclusive or cosmic giant - was of a figure both human and divine.[2]

If we look at Chaucer's *Merchant's Tale,* we find another example. In this re-working of the Paradise myth, the main character January is clearly the 'Adam' falling foul of his 'Eve', and yet his wrath at being betrayed recalls the wrath of Jehovah at the failure of Paradise (and equivalent first worlds in the Bible). Likewise the final reconciliation of January and his wife points to the prophetic books of the Old Testament, in which Jehovah is at last reconciled with what the prophets imaged as his erring 'wife', the disloyal human nature.

Now, it goes almost without saying that the implication of this 'primitive' notion of a oneness in man and the divine was heretical, and for that reason the poets who followed this notion in their stories were careful to make their meaning obscure. Apart from anything else, to imply that there was a unity to Adam and God also implied that when one 'fell' from Paradise, so did the other. It implied the complex heresy of 'the fallen god'.

And here we begin to pick out the strangest thing in the shadows of the ghost's account, and glimpse in his own admission of "foul crimes" the first flickers of a more horrid truth beneath the presented surface of his narrative: that he was not so much the victim of a murder as one himself turned murderous. A strange account of the Paradise disaster it turns out to be indeed, for it involves a 'God' that was not only his own 'Adam', but his own 'Satan'.

In following this up, we could easily get ourselves entangled in the dark hinterland to medieval culture, drawing in many things of

---

2   It was an idea later used by Blake in his character of Albion, the original divine humanity.

folklore, folk ritual and belief, to which Shakespeare's fearsome 'fairy' ghost partly owes his origins, and then further entangle ourselves in the web of heresy that lay hidden there and also in the shadowy beliefs and theological speculations which, due to a jealous Church, have left less obvious traces. There are whispers there of Hud and Robin, of older loyalties and witchcraft, and of other things that flittered in the long shadow that an older pagan world cast over the Middle Ages. Instead, I will take a short cut into both the character of Shakespeare's ghost and its heresy.

Two hundred years before *Hamlet,* there was written a remarkable narrative poem, *Sir Gawain and the Green Knight.*[3] One of the most remarkable things about it is that it contains, though in hazy form, a major heresy. This heresy begins to show when we consider Gawain's final sacrifice to the elder figure, the Green Knight, and find that it resembles in idea Jesus' sacrificial yielding to the will of the father-god at Calvary. The resemblance strengthens when we see other reminders of the Christ-role about Gawain - the Pentangle symbol he bears, for instance, which was medievally linked with the five wounds of Christ and possibly also with the Star of David, Jesus' forebear through his mother (who is herself seemingly remembered by the Virgin's picture carried inside Gawain's shield).

It is here that the first part of the heresy strikes us, as we realise that this story's final sacrificial 'Jesus' was at the start its 'Cain'. That is to say, Gawain's violent ending of the opening happy feast of life equates in the biblical cycle with the violent end of Paradise that, by the medieval mind, was sometimes attributed to the figure of Cain (a rebel destroyer of life, often indistinguishable from Satan himself). So 'Cain' and 'Jesus' are indicated to be basically the same mythic figure, a kind of first and last of the male cycle of destiny.

The heresy then deepens as we realise, following the signs in the text and perhaps helped also by the many medieval examples of this 'Hero and Magical Giant' story-type, that this story's 'Cain/Jesus' and its 'Jehovah' (the Green Knight) are to some extent aspects of one and the same character - that of a fallen masculinity, darkened

---

3   For an outline of the story, see Appendix G.

by guilt and violence, and to a perpetual opposition, until the instinct of sacrifice can be changed to that of self-sacrifice. But if this is so - if the two figures are, in part, mutually reflected aspects of the same - then this 'Jehovah' also reflects the 'Cain' that 'murdered' Paradise.

It comes down to this. The medieval story suggests the idea that the divine was part of the whole masculine character that turned murderous at the Fall, and now shares in that character as it works its way towards some sacrificial realisation whereby the original character might be restored. It is a version of the old 'Nature' myth, in which the summer-king himself became his own wintry demon and then through ordeal must break free of his deformity and reclaim his original character. The only real difference, as often in myth and medieval romance, is that the be-wintered king has now divided into two figures: a frightening supernatural director and a sort of younger aspect, with the latter undergoing the redemptive ordeal for them both, much as if God is working out his restoration in the character of his son - or in that of man himself.

This, as simply as I can put it, is the 'fallen god' heresy that had survived in various mythical stories of the Middle Ages. Very widely, in fact, as we shall see when we consider the Grail romances. These, and a number of connected myths, contain the same heresy, part hidden in the obscurity (and sometimes incompetence) of their romance form, and further hidden by Church influence: God himself had become the Satan, the destroyer. And these stories contained something else quite as disturbing to orthodoxy, and so equally disguised - the Paradise violated by the deranged masculine character was his own 'body of life', and therefore his true 'feminine' nature. The Paradise (or Grail) to be sought was the Lady the searcher himself had wronged.

What I have said about *The Green Knight* applies equally to *Hamlet*, which in some respects is a Shakespearean version of the same romance, but now turned to tragedy and its destiny of masculine redemption not fulfilled. We first suspect the same story-idea when we look at the ghost and find another version of the 'winter-king', working his return to a lost manhood or majesty by way of an ordeal placed upon his 'younger' aspect, an ordeal that ends likewise in a sacrificial yielding to the axe. Like the Green Knight, the destinally directing ghost combines supernatural power, divine wisdom, and an ogrous disposition: a god meanwhile trapped in the personage of a demon, strongly associated likewise with the powers of the underworld, the world of the dead or Faery.

The same heresy is involved also – and with the same obscurity. Like the Green Knight and Gawain, the two Hamlets, father and son, seem to some extent to be a single mutually reflecting character, and likewise bound to a cyclical destiny which begins with "foul crimes" against life. Further, as we proceed, these crimes will also be seen to link not only with a true masculinity turned monstrous, but with a divinity turned to its own Satan: the destroyer of his own true feminine nature, or Paradise. By this, we might glimpse that Hamlet's real mission is not one of revenge, as the surface story presents, but (like Gawain's) one of freeing his own character (and that of the reflecting 'elder') from its infernal distortion, and of restoring thereby a lost divine-humanity of manhood.

The same story (and its implicit heresy) appears more clearly in *King Lear*. Its first two Acts show the original King of Life becoming his own Satan, a self-righteous wrecker of his realm and 'body', bringing a tempest of fury on it, as his life-energies turn to an insane and blistering wrath. The sequel also fits the same story – the demented 'god' who must through the harsh ordeal of this fallen life free himself of his demonic form and spirit, and find again his true majesty and manhood, even as in a death. The same story is followed also in some other of Shakespeare's plays, including his last: the destinal cycle of Prospero.

★   ★   ★

As the reader will know, when he recalls my earlier chapters, this present preamble to a fuller investigation of the ghost's account has not covered the whole story by any means. It has hardly touched on the feminine character, for instance, that in some versions is central to the whole drama, and not least in the first catastrophic 'fall'.

Here the *Sir Gawain* story helps us once again in our approach to *Hamlet*. We notice, for instance, that at its end the restored man or hero claims that his monstrous deformity of character was all due to the power of a woman, a witch, called in that story Morgan le Fay. By this we realise something about *Hamlet*. As soon as he is charged with his mission, Hamlet goes to take a long, hard look at the face of a woman (Ophelia). It is as if he has picked up from his father's words the idea that the whole monstrous debasement of the masculine character – and therefore the key to its liberation also – is in the hands of the feminine nature in some way. His words to Ophelia thereby take on sharp significance – "For wise men know well enough what monsters you make of them". And then we might notice another similarity in the two stories. In the climactic action of *Sir Gawain,* as if essential to the process of man's liberation, there occurs a contest with a feminine power in a private chamber (Gawain's temptation by Sir Bercilak's wife). Likewise at the climax of *Hamlet,* just before the hero's surrender to the axe, like Gawain, Hamlet has to meet and break a feminine power in a private chamber – his stormy meeting with Gertrude.

What the *Sir Gawain* story helps us here to see in *Hamlet* seems to come down to this – the idea of a feminine control over man's character for good or ill, and the crucial need for that nature itself to be changed in any quest for true masculinity. What we are back with, in fact, is the idea earlier set out in 'The Story of Eve'. The transformation of a god into a demon in the 'masculine' character is due to a darkness in the 'feminine' nature – whether as the heart or emotional side of the human psyche, or, more generally, in the feminine spirit in life – and will persist until that nature is fully restored to what it once was.

The *Sir Gawain* story, however, does not tell us what caused this dark side in the feminine nature with such monstrous effect on the masculine. It does not, unlike some stories earlier looked at, give much insight into what I have called the real story of Eve. *Hamlet,* on the other hand, gives sharp insight, and possibly its most powerful demonstration. This matter, outlined in Chapter 2, is now to be looked at more closely, after dealing first with its most crucial element – the poison described in the ghost's story.

★   ★   ★

Commentary on *Hamlet* is often snagged by Shakespeare's

vagueness about the actual poison used by Claudius upon King Hamlet - "hebenon".[4] But perhaps the vagueness is deliberate, so that the reader might consider, alongside the idea of a deadly poison, another idea that arises from the suggestion of 'henbane'. This does not usually cause death when administered through the ears, but what it does cause has perhaps more significance in the play - insanity.

So in the mythic under-story of the play, King Hamlet wasn't murdered - he went mad? If so, we might wonder in what way, and are straight away helped to an answer by something about his son. He also 'goes mad'. It is supposed to be a pretence, but we can see there is something real about it nonetheless, and, considering the deliberate overlap Shakespeare uses for his two Hamlets, we may be justified in explaining one insanity by way of the other. So what is Prince Hamlet's madness? It contains a hatred and destructive tendency towards the flesh, order and form; against nature, even Woman in general. A puritanical monster lurks.

We are further helped in this when, in looking at other Shakespeare plays, we see similar instances: a sort of sin-aware misogyny, a crazy hatred of what in the natural state seems to have fallen from the ideal into taint - as in the case of Lear, Leontes and Othello, for example. This last case seems particularly relevant, because the way the madness was induced is similarly imaged - "I will pour this pestilence into his ears" (Iago). And as these instances of masculine hatred also include violence, are we not drawing closer to an understanding of why the ghost - otherwise mysteriously - admits to "foul crimes" and to being in a "prison-house", confined to "fast in fires", till purged? An understanding also of why Hamlet, having inherited like all men since Adam, this same craziness, also feels that this life is a kind of "prison", in which something fundamentally "out of joint" needs to be put right in his *own* character.

But for more precision. While on the battlements waiting for the ghost (Act 1 Sc4), Hamlet reflects on the way men take on vicious corruption in their characters - the well-known monologue

---

4   See Longer Notes in the 'Arden' *Hamlet* (ed. Harold Jenkins).

beginning "So oft it chances in particular men…" Whatever its relevance to the immediate setting - the drunken revelry going on below - it seems also to foreshadow the ghost's account we are soon to hear, which also deals with a kind of corruption befalling an illustrious character.

A detail that sharply anticipates the ghost's account comes at the end of Hamlet's reflections - "The dram of evil doth all the noble substance often dout to his own scandal". Now, as is well known to Shakespeare's editors, this part of the text has itself suffered 'corruption', with no-one sure what Shakespeare actually wrote, but sometimes the word *eale* is claimed in place of "evil", since a possible meaning of *eale* - 'yeast' - connects with the word "leaven" a few lines earlier. Thomas Carter was one who took this reading, claiming it as part of an allusion to Jesus' warning to "beware the leaven of the pharisees".[5] The claim turns out to be quite apt indeed, if Hamlet's words are a prelude to the ghost's account, because the pharisee mentality was notorious for moral judgment on good and evil - the sense of sin. And wasn't this the same 'poison' that was first brought into Paradise?

It is surely not by chance that this suggestion in the text occurs a few moments before we hear the story of a great ancestor who (like Adam) was 'poisoned' in his garden and - by what seems to have been Shakespeare's view - suffered a fundamental change of character: from a divine hero to a monster capable of "foul crimes". The poison was one of the worst, and *does* cause madness - a hatred of life, especially in its physical or feminine aspects.

Hamlet's speech of reflection therefore logically introduces the ghost's account of what really went wrong in the 'kingdom' of Adam, causing such a change in the "noble substance" of the once true Man that it brought about a mad destruction of that kingdom.

And now to the point promised two pages back - that *Hamlet,* as part of its reflection on Adam's disaster and the fallen state of man, shows much insight into what we might call Eve's role in that disaster. Let me first give a reminder. I have argued of the Paradise myth throughout that the poisonous awareness first affected Eve -

---

5   Thomas Carter: *Shakespeare and Holy Scripture* p.360

the 'feelings' or feminine side of the human character – and that she, appalled by the now appearing sinfulness and emptiness of her nature, reactively took on a new 'dream' persona, separate and despiteful to her natural self. This, it was claimed, like all emotional states of the psyche, influenced the mind and creative energies, the masculine, which in accord fell thrall to desirable illusions and a destructive hatred of his true 'bride' or nature. Now we turn to the ghost's version of the Paradise tragedy and realise that he too hints that the poison first affected the *feminine* side of his being. Let us look at his words:-

> "...And in the porches of my ears did pour
> The lep'rous distilment; whose effect
> Holds such an enmity with blood of man
> That swift as quicksilver it courses through
> The natural gates and alleys of the body
> And with a sudden vigour it doth posset
> And curd, like eager droppings into milk,
> The thin and wholesome blood. So did it mine;
> And a most instant tetter bark'd about,
> Most lazar-like, with vile and loathsome crust,
> All my smooth body..." (1.5.63-73)

To grasp fully how it is the feminine side of his being that is here described as being poisonously attacked, I think we should have to understand how in the original androgynous unity of Paradise the feminine was the physical or bodily aspect, like the tree of life itself, that is here shown being infected and skellered into loathsome ugliness. However, putting the mystical understanding aside, we might still quite clearly see how Shakespeare denotes the femininity of King Hamlet's body by particular details. The first is the mention of "milk", ever a feminine symbol, which is here linked with the life-blood affected by the poison. The second is "smooth body", again indicating something feminine. We thus are given the impression that it is King Hamlet's 'body of life', his feminine nature, that is being poisoned. It is not only in Act 5, during the repeat of the first violent calamity, that Shakespeare is telling us the Queen is "poisoned". It is here in this account of that first murderous calamity itself.

Looking more closely at the details of this account reveals much more, and eventually gives conviction to our first impression. It involves a knowledge of related myth and symbolism, most of it lost to the general reader, but I shall make it clear, as follows.

"Lep'rous"? "lazar-like"? These details in the ghost's description bear particular meaning. In some Grail romances, the central sickness, the sense of sin, which must be relieved for the quest to be fulfilled, is shown as leprosy, and affecting a *woman* – the 'sick queen'.[6] Again there is some trace of a poetic recognition that central to our fallen condition, from which all man's insanity and inhumanity arise, is a stricken feminine consciousness: the sense of sin within Eve. The cure of this figure, and her return to radiant fruitfulness, links one way with the feminine Grail itself restored to life abundant, another way with the old Nature-myth of the winter-queen at last being transformed into fruitfulness, and yet another way with the spiritual meaning: the ridding of sin awareness from our 'feminine' nature, so that our hearts will return to radiant kindness, and our masculine side in accord return to true directing faith and strength of vision, free of the monster.

An alternative figure of the 'sick queen' in such romances is the hag or loathly damsel, whose monstrous ugliness of feature is the visual equivalent of the leprous sickness. (So Shakespeare likewise has the ghost stress the visual hideousness of this poisonous sickness afflicting his feminine body or nature.) The hag in such stories, quite as much as the sick queen, is the feminine nature entrapped sorrowfully within the tainted character of the witch awaiting her return as the radiant bride.

So, by fixing on the symbolic detail of the ghost's account and not dismissing it as mere gothic trimmings, we are able to uncover a variant of the sorrowful 'Story of Eve' – the long-ago poisoned nature which, meanwhile within a distorted character and its powers, awaits a cure for her sickness. By this we are able to focus better on the roles of Gertrude and Ophelia in the play, more clearly seeing, for example, why in the Queen's Chamber scene the two

---

6   In the *Queste del Saint Graal,* for instance, and hence in Malory's version of the Grail Quest in *Le Morte Darthur.*

figures meant to be cast symbolically from her presence, her heart, her flesh, for her salvation – Polonius and Claudius – are linked with the idea of the sterile, unsavoury or diseased. Likewise, in Act 4 with Ophelia, Gertrude's partnering character, the notion of a blighted femininity better prepares us to pick up the idea of an awful barrenness and sense of betrayal now reaching a crisis of realization.

We may also have by way of the reminder of Grail romance some further explanation for the allusion, made by Ophelia in this part of the play, to the lost dead hero or true man "on the bier", whose return could seemingly relieve the lady's woe or cursed state, for a similar male figure, likewise bewailed by a sorrowful woman, or women, is found in a number of Grail stories. However, that is something perhaps better left to a later examination of the scene in question.

Another detail worth noting in the extract recently quoted from the ghost's account is "bark'd about". It is not just a further detail to strengthen the visual image of ugly and crusted disfigurement. It images also the idea of a tree, and links with a network of tree-symbolism found in the medieval world and earlier myth, most relevant to this present topic. However, this also would involve quite lengthy explanation at this point, holding up the argument unduly. The subject of tree-symbolism will be taken up in later chapters, but the reader, if taken by my view that "bark'd about" actually connotes the idea of the original ruler trapped symbolically in a tree, will find something of interest in the opening Cantos of Spenser's *Faery Queen*. Here there is much that helps explain the myth that Shakespeare was dealing with, and also – in the story of Fradubio, imprisoned in a tree by a witch (Canto 2) – some verbal similarities that strongly suggest Shakespeare was influenced by this part of Spenser's work.

For now, we need to get back to the main track and to the main point of our search – to show that King Hamlet's real story is that he was turned monstrous by a 'poisoning' of his own feminine nature, and thus made murderous towards his own fair Paradise, his true bride of life.

Another Shakespeare play supports this reading. A few years after *Hamlet,* in *Macbeth,* Shakespeare was to show again – and this time clearly happening to a woman – a first infernal alteration that then turned the man, according with the pattern, into a monster of unreal desires one way, and manic violence another. This is the hellish transformation of Lady Macbeth in Act 1 Scene 5, which Shakespeare describes in terms that actually recall the effects of the poison on King Hamlet's body:-

> "...Come you spirits
> That tend on mortal thoughts, unsex me here;
> And fill me, from the crown to the toe, top-full
> Of direst cruelty. *Make thick my blood,*
> *Stop up th' access and passage* to remorse...
> ... Come to my woman's breasts,
> And *take my milk for gall...* (1.5.37-45)

It further helps the point of my argument to recall a story mentioned in this chapter's first page - the medieval *Sir Orfeo*. In this, the person in the orchard poisoned by a baneful awareness once again is a woman - Heurodys. The likeness of her fate to that of King Hamlet becomes stronger, indeed, when we remember that her Greek counterpart - Eurydice - was actually bitten by a serpent. *Sir Orfeo* is a story to be read with care, because it is another version of the mythic cycle of destiny, and yet another version that begins with a variant of the true 'Story of Eve' and the Paradise disaster.

In her dream by the apple-tree, Heurodys is assailed by the same poisonous awareness that befell Eve in Paradise. Not only does she dream of death, but her actions on waking denote the linked awareness of sin - a new sense of vileness to her nature. For this reason she sets about to rive and scratch at her fair face, her hair and fine raiment, in a frenzy of self-hatred. It is a violence then duplicated by this story's equivalent of the masculine character being driven destructively mad in turn - the underworld king who emerges in her frenzy to carry her off.

It turns out, however, that I need not have chased up support outside *Hamlet* for my argument, because what the ghost implies in his account of the first calamity is borne out by something in the sub-plot of the play itself. As outlined in Chapter 2, the story of Ophelia acts like a repetition or reinforcement of the ghost's own story. That is to say, when we see Ophelia's father (and brother) ridiculing her trust in love and undermining her simple faith in her natural womanhood and affections, we realise that there is a kind of 'poisonous' indoctrination taking place that matches with the ghost's indication of a first baneful alteration of the feminine nature. Likewise the outcome – the dangerous dementing of her male partner. Hamlet's enraged treatment of Ophelia in the 'nunnery' scene not only recalls the smashing of the first sexual harmony or 'marriage' in Paradise – "I say we will have no more marriage!" – it looks back to the insane crime against life, against the feminine nature, that his father has suggested was his own crime, arising from the first poisoning, the bite of the serpent. A matter for close examination in the next chapter.

We have seen that the ghost relates a past tragedy in which man's character turned monstrous. His whole account thus serves as a kind of artistic mirror in which Hamlet might see the enormity of his own character also, inherited from that woeful time. Partly for the same reason, I believe, Shakespeare includes the lengthy reminder of Troy's disaster in Act 2 (the first player's excerpt from "Aeneas' Tale to Dido"); for this disaster, too, is a witness of the murderous spirit in man's character, by which present man, Hamlet, the inheritor of its horror, can see himself.

Since the ghost's account was based on the Paradise myth, it is here useful to recall that the loss of golden Troy was in the medieval world sometimes equated with the loss of Paradise. Indeed, the Troy story appears in its literature with uncanny frequency, and sometimes in this symbolic way. It is mentioned, for example, at the beginning and end of *Sir Gawain and the Green Knight,* as if its author saw Troy a fit symbol for the first paradisal happiness of life violently lost and eventually to be restored. The same symbolic use appears in Shakespeare's last play (*The Tempest*), where a shadowy presence of the Troy myth likewise reinforces the idea of a cycle from paradise lost to paradise regained.

The Troy story of violent loss, sorrowful ordeal, and final return was chiefly known through Homer's *Odyssey,* and this version seems to have been in Shakespeare's mind when writing *Hamlet.* For instance, Hamlet's being greatly moved by the narration about Troy actually matches the Homeric episode in which Odysseus, staying with the Phaeacians, hears a court-minstrel sing of Troy's grievous tragedy, and is reduced to tears. The name *Laertes,* used for one of the personages in *Hamlet,* itself comes from the *Odyssey.* Further, Hamlet's own situation, looking on moodily at the wife and court of his absent father, debased by a usurper, has much likeness to that of Telemachus, Odysseus' own son, who awaits the return of the true hero to claim all. Fittingly, this Telemachus is also many times in Homer's text linked with Orestes, the type of avenger often seen as a sort of 'Greek Hamlet'. In all, with such details in mind, we might suspect that when Hamlet returns from the sea late in the play, there is still some trace-awareness of the story of Odysseus.

But all this may be getting us little further. Is there anything more in the Troy story that led Shakespeare to use it for a major interlude in a play shadowed by the Paradise disaster? In particular, is there anything in it to link with the main topic of this chapter – an alteration in the feminine nature with disastrous effect on male behaviour? Indeed there is.

There are three points in the Troy story that connect in idea with the crucial alteration of Eve as the first stage of calamity. The first is in the Judgment of Paris. Here the apple used as a prize has a baleful character. It belongs to Eris, who, because slighted, has grown spiteful. The well-known motif of 'the slighted goddess', in myth and fairy tale, equates with Eve's own poisoned estimation of herself, and it gives rise to the same desire – a compensatory will to power over man, spiteful to life. This ominous sign is added to by what happens in the Judgment of Paris itself – the award of the prize to Venus. It denotes the rise of the feminine power I earlier linked with the second character of Eve: the power of the ego-dream, tied both to the erotic and the self's unreal desires, as man's debased and destructive motivation.

The next stage in the story – the break-up of Menelaus's marriage – also connects with the Paradise myth. Paris, now motivated by the enthralling power of Venus, imaged in the alluring Helen, is swayed by selfish desire and takes the destructive role of 'sexual rebel', like Satan in desire for Eve. The wrath ensuing in Menelaus, as well as its imaged equivalent in the stormy seas of the lovers' flight to Cyprus,[7] looks forward to the massive wrath of the

---

7   Remembered in *Othello* in the stormy voyage to Cyprus?

Trojan War itself, This turns out to be the third point of connection with the Paradise myth.

The ruin of Troy - whether through a violence generated within it as in Atlantis or Sodom, or, as historicised, brought upon it from without (the Greeks) - repeated on a massive scale the ruin already wreaked upon the marriage of Menelaus. And the cause was the same - the baleful power of pride or self-infatuation that Helen's mind-captivating beauty imaged. It gave rise to all the havoc we have come to expect of the myth-pattern in its various accounts of a first disaster, including that of Paradise. So great was Helen's power, enthralling not only to Paris, but to Priam and the whole of Troy, we begin to think of something quite supernatural or witch-like. Indeed, some writers of the ancient world believed Helen was not real, but a phantom sent purposely to wreak Troy's ruin through her spell.[8] In the same way, Eve's sinister side appearing in Paradise is sometimes remembered in Jewish legend as *Lilith,* the witch-bride of Adam.

To sum up on the Troy story before going on. Its main relevance to *Hamlet,* like the Paradise myth, is that it gives the play another mythic dimension, like a shadowy reflection of the situation or events in the play itself. In this reflection we discern the picture of man's folly in the lust for selfish fantasy, set on by a feminine nature turned sinisterly awry, exciting dreams of a wonderful identity to be gained, in despite and cost to what is real and true. In this way the Troy story mirrors the situation of man in *Hamlet:* the dupes of "strumpet fortune", with the same lust for a shadow or a "shadow's shadow", [9] for the enticements of the glamorous illusion - success, promotion, glory, the high ideal - and all likewise pursued at the price of betrayal or destruction of what is real, even through its murder, the murder of life itself. Though no Helen is mentioned in the play, or any altered, baneful Eve, Shakespeare is clearly showing the same power to be at work as the incitement or lure to self-centred fantasy, even to the extreme of a monstrousness capable of repeating the first "foul crimes" by which some higher state was

---

8   See Graves' *Greek Myths* 159u and note 1.

9   2.2.260-63

murderously ravaged.

★   ★   ★

While thinking on mythic parallels in *Hamlet,* we might be struck by one thought in particular. If Shakespeare remembered the Troy story as relevant to his play, then he would be likely to remember, as of equal relevance, the story of a past calamity from the same background as the play - Germanic or Norse myth. Let us look into this. If Troy could give us a means of fresh focus upon *Hamlet,* then perhaps the story of Asgard might do so too.

Asgard's ruinous fall in a great war was to Northern Europe what Troy's was to the south. Indeed, there are such similarities in their stories - even both having a horse by which the besiegers gained entry - that it seems likely their mythical elements had in part the same ancestry. Among the more important similarities is the fateful female role. Just as 'phantom' Helen appeared in Troy before the disaster, so in Asgard appeared the supernatural woman (or women),[10] probably connected with the arrival of Freyja, who was of like magical beauty, and one of whose names - Heid - actually meant the same as Helen: 'the shining one'.

There is more to this feminine connection than that, but I will work towards it by way of another line of thought. *Hamlet* begins in the smoke and clangour of a great Baltic war. Whatever its connection with the pseudo-historical war recorded in the story's Scandinavian source, it is possible that Shakespeare is using it more as a reminder of that other Baltic war, in which Asgard perished - a war that some might deem, like a first Ragnarok, the Norse equivalent of the long-ago cataclysm remembered in many mythologies.

In this 'event', if we judge by Norse myths and the likely medieval view, the fate of the god Odin was seen as yet another case of a disastrous primal change in the masculine spirit, from heroic

---

10   The reader will find, as I did, a very good collection of the Norse myths, with excellent notes and commentary, in K. Crossley-Holland's *Norse Myths.* Other myths and legends not included in this collection are to be found in old favourites like H.A. Guerber's *The Norsemen* and D.A. Mackenzie's *Teutonic Myth and Legend.*

majesty to monster, which thereafter remained like a ghost of fury in the male psyche, a kind of grim Erlkönig stalking its darkness, the genius of war and vengeance, ever hungry for punishment and blood. At the same time, like many ogres in myth and romance, what he ever really seems to seek is his lost character, his lost majesty, and, as needful to this end, tries to find the true feminine nature, some Idun or Gerd or Freyja, who is meanwhile held in a like darkness or debasement of character, as in an underworld or supernatural prison.

The reader will by this have marked a similarity with the figure and story of King Hamlet. He also was once a figure of godlike majesty, who then rises like a terrible demon from the darkness of war, still armed for bloodshed, still demanding murder and vengeance, a dark shadow of the character of man, as of Hamlet himself. And he too might be seen as seeking to reclaim his true character, by means of one who will understand what true mission stands cloaked in the demand for murder – a kind of sacrifice not of life but of what is monstrous in the character of man himself. And he, too, seeks as part of this the reclamation of his fallen bride, her rescue from her present darkness; for without her change from the witch responsible for his monstrousness, he will never find his own true character.

In all, just as Lear (or Arthur) seeks again his character and kingship through the winning back of something truly feminine (the Cordelia, the Grail), and just as the ogrous god Jehovah sought to return as the true lord and husband by the breaking of the feminine heart from her obduracy into her true nature, so Odin and King Hamlet, whether directly or by surrogate, seek their return through a death to what is monstrous and through a concomitant wresting of the feminine to her former nature.

This points once again towards Gertrude as the real target of Hamlet's mission, the central factor in a life gone "out of joint" that he feels he has "to set ... right".[11] It is no surprise therefore to find that her name probably comes down – by way of 'Gerutha' in the medieval source – from *Gerd,* who in an original Norse story is actually one who has to be rescued from her supernatural character

---

11 1.5.196-97

of winter-queen.[12] The details of her rescue are also interesting. Skirnir, an emissary of the god, or perhaps the god himself in disguise, wins through to her chamber in the supernatural winter-castle, to break her from her fallen character, which is most resistant to being altered. He storms at her, threatens her with a sword, and points out that the alternative to the true marriage offered her is to be sexually enjoyed by a sub-human. Finally she yields and consents to become again the true bride of the god. This story, originally a Nature myth most likely – the winning back of the wintry earth to the embrace of the sun – I believe was incorporated, in adapted form, in the Saxo-Grammaticus version of the 'Amleth' story and so eventually appeared as the Queen's Chamber scene in *Hamlet,* with its significance fully realised by Shakespeare. He seems quite clearly to have grasped that beneath the surface of a revenge plot, which he was mainly tied to, was another story in which the real mission of Hamlet was the restoration of a divine sexual harmony.

Norse help in our focusing on *Hamlet* does not end there. There are other things, though in showing them I shall have to touch on some of the material to be used in a later chapter on *Macbeth,* in which, as we shall find, there is a good deal of Norse influence. One Norse story has particular relevance. It is one that I believe influenced Shakespeare in the earlier mentioned scene in which Lady Macbeth, in her eagerness for infernal power, invites a demonic possession of her nature, with – yet again – a monstrous effect on the masculine character.

The story in question is that of Freyja and Brisingamen.[13] It will be given in full when we come on to *Macbeth* in Chapter 7. For now, only its opening is relevant. It tells us how the Lady Freyja, ominously lonely, went seeking power from the realm of darkness. She called upon the underworld beings, the swart-elves, who offered to make her a magically powerful, golden ornament – the 'brisingamen', probably a necklace or torque – on condition that she

---

12 Not the only link between Gerd and Gertrude. Gerd was possibly a variant character of Freyja, whose medieval christianized form was Saint 'Gertrude'. (See Guerber's *Norsemen* p.137)

13 A version appears in *Flateyjarbok,* written in the time of Chaucer, but doubtless there were other versions.

let them enjoy her sexually. In other words, somewhat like Lady Macbeth, Freyja in desire for an infernal power, imaged in the story's equivalent of the "golden round" so much craved by Shakespeare's heroine, allowed her nature to be entered and altered by dark forces. Equally similar is the sort of power that resulted in Freyja. She became a witch-goddess, a supernaturally mighty queen of man's demented desires, inciting him to destructiveness and battle-madness, as is well attested of her more sinister character in Norse accounts. She became in fact one of the darkest examples of what I have claimed to be the second, or altered character of Eve - the phantom of man's unreal desires and the attendant destructiveness to what is natural, even to life itself. This is shown in Freyja's effect on her hitherto illustrious partner - Odin (or Od, or Hod) - who, much like Macbeth indeed, becomes a monster, calling for massive warfare on earth to satisfy his mania for blood.

The general resemblance in the two stories suggests at least the possibility of Norse influence in Shakespeare's writing of *Macbeth*, a possibility that will be strengthened when we later find a good deal of Norse influence in that play. But what about the earlier *Hamlet*? Does the same story lurk somewhere in the ghost's own Odin-like shadow? Something to explain the opening warfare - the equivalent of Odin's own first violence, wrecking to the primal world of Asgard - and something to explain also why Gertrude (alias Gerd, alias Freyja) can only be restored to her true nature by the ridding of a sub-human presence in her heart and flesh?

Definite proof eludes us, as in most cases of artistic influence in so remote a period, and yet I will try at least to add a little more substance to the possibility.

When we come on to *Macbeth*, we shall see that the feast in Lady Macbeth's castle on the night of Duncan's murder is a symbol of Lady Macbeth herself. Like the cauldron (badly placed in the existing text) this feast suffers a poisonous alteration roughly coinciding with her own change of character - from one of life's joy and bounty to one of hellish influence upon the mind and energies of man. It is as if the dark intoxicant in the wine of the feast mirrors the poison that has entered the feminine bloodstream.

Now, as the reader will know, there is also a drunken feast in

Hamlet – the one taking place when Hamlet awaits the ghost on the battlements. What the reader may not have noticed is that this feast is placed as if deliberately to coincide with the reflections of Hamlet ("So oft it chances in particular men...") and the ghost's account, both of which deal with a monstrous corruption that overtakes the masculine character, as through a poisonous "leaven" or "eale" ('yeast') put into the 'feminine' bloodstream. This was earlier argued to connect with the Paradise myth – the blasting of Eve that had baneful effect on the energies of life, turning them to the equivalent of King Hamlet's "foul crimes". But is it also a reminder of another feast of life that went badly wrong? One that Shakespeare was later to enlarge on in symbolic conjunction with Lady Macbeth's sinister alteration into the eagerness of man's now madly intoxicated soul?

I would not ask such wild-seeming questions were it not that in Norse myth, and perhaps connected with the Brisingamen story of sexual calamity, are fragments of myth dealing with a drunken feast resulting in murderous violence. These fragments may once have been part of a single and more definite account that persisted – as the Brisingamen story itself may have done – in a source now lost, or an English folktale version, known to Shakespeare. The first tells of the wise and kindly god, Kvasir, who attends a feast and is treacherously stabbed to death by the swart-elves, who drain him of his blood. This kindly golden blood of life, I believe, was originally of a feminine connotation, and its theft the equivalent of its poisonous alteration. King Duncan's own similar fate in *Macbeth* – stabbed to death at a feast and drained of his blood, the "wine of life" – is likewise linked by Shakespeare with the idea of a poisonous alteration in the feminine bloodstream, giving rise to murderous violence. As such, the first fragment links with another Kvasir myth, which, under its surviving guise, might suggest a similar alteration of the kindly bloodstream by a poison – a 'yeast' in fact, that is spit into his feminine body.[14] Both the Kvasir accounts seem to link in turn

---

14 The story is remembered in a bizarre and misleading fragment, which is supposed to show the gods creating Kvasir by spitting into a pot and mixing him into being. But Kvasir already existed, and spittle as a natural source of yeast suggests that these were not gods creating, but demons poisoning, Kvasir's blood and flesh.

with the story of another feast – that of the gods in Aegir's hall. This likewise is poisoned, and in a way that recalls the "leaven" of Hamlet's reflections and the "poison" of King Hamlet's account. Just as these were linked with a baneful sense entering the feelings and giving rise to life-hatred and violence, so in Aegir's feast the poison is that of a darkening moral awareness – the insinuations of Loki about the gods' behaviour, and not least that of the goddesses in their sexual freedoms. This also may have led to massive violence – perhaps the same as is found in the Brisingamen story and, as hinted, in King Hamlet's account: the end of the divine world as in a kind of first Ragnarok of wrath and life's wrecking.

Now, all this might seem very tenuous, and I wouldn't have mentioned any of it had it not been for a strong hunch that there is meaning in Shakespeare's placing of the riotous feast in *Hamlet*. It is like a reminder of something, some first calamity that in the main biblical tradition turns up in the poisoned 'feast of life' in Paradise, and in pagan tradition – including the Norse – more fragmentarily or uncertainly remembered.

★   ★   ★

In summary. Following the idea of 'The Story of Eve', I have in this chapter tried to show how the ghost's narrative in *Hamlet* cryptically tells us of a dangerous derangement in the masculine character, due to a dark alteration in his feminine nature, warped by a virulent awareness. Man and God, as one, were turned into a mad monster, wrecking the first state or paradise. This malady persists in this life till man restores fully his true feminine nature, and thus himself. I have hoped to show in this how in *Hamlet* Shakespeare, aware of many myths that share the same idea, used them like shadowy parallels in his story. There are more to come as we next look at the true story of Ophelia.

Chapter 6
Ophelia's Story

We began this study with the idea of a cyclical myth, which arose in the primitive world and then recurred through variations of structure and meaning, until finally it arrived in the Middle Ages to take on some of its finest forms. These show not least in the work of Shakespeare, who, both by inheriting its pattern in traditional material and by his own genius, brought out its meaning in unparalleled dramatic and poetic versions. Of all these, *Hamlet* stands pre-eminent, both in the sustained power of its poetry and in the power to mesmerise with a sense of an all-life story, its realistic form trailing shadows of meaning that give the authority of a central archetype in the human imagination.

Yet it is precisely here, in the very source of its power, that the play is nowadays found so puzzling. We do not know myth, we do not read mythically, and so those shadows of meaning remain as shadows, and we tend to concentrate instead on the realistic presentation, seeking to interpret by what is in effect only half a text. It is not surprising, then, that so much of the commentary on the play, with which we load our shelves and minds, turns out to be unsatisfactory. Something has been missed by the scan of modern intelligence, leaving a hole at the centre of its meaning which, I suspect, was not there for even the simplest of Shakespeare's audience. Nor is it surprising that the parts of the play that remain most puzzling are those in which the mythic shadow, the sense of an 'inner story', is most noticeable, including the two scenes in which Ophelia appears as a major figure - the 'nunnery' scene and that of her 'madness' in Act 4.

In approaching these two scenes, I think it would be useful simply to review the myth of which *Hamlet* is a late and very complex example. By this, a general perspective on Ophelia's role will begin to form. It will mean repeating, though briefly, much of the matter of Chapter 2 - the myth's development - but it will be worthwhile.

The basic myth showed a derangement in the masculine and

feminine sides of life, and in their harmonious relationship. For some reason the Lady darkly changed, and the Lord by this was turned frustratedly and dementedly into a distortion of his majesty and his wondrous life-powers: a monster of unreal desires and ravaging to his own nature, as if by the spell of a witch at his heart now bidding him spoil her summer self as hateful. But then he realised from his madness and his wrecking energies something of his old light, his former potency, by which the slowly weakening witch or winter-queen might be shattered of her power and her true nature restored. It was then for both a final death to their wintry selves, as in a sexual act by which both sides yield into the power to be born anew.

This myth in some versions showed a third factor, something that explained the whole sorry dislocation of harmony and the following dark ordeal. In primitive versions it was a shadowy goblin or demon elf, who banefully entered the Lady and turned her to the queen of fascinations, the dementer of the true man, and thereby gained control of the now wintry life, which he maintained through the same mischievous arts - the plying of the shimmering queen of spells upon the man, to keep him bemonstered, lunatic, lost and futile to his true power by which the goblin himself might be found within the queen and cast out for her rescue.

In later versions, this demon elf became a malign enchanter or wizard, but with the same tricks and playing the same manipulative game,[1] and in more orthodox texts he became the Devil. He still worked through the feminine nature, usually personed in story as an actual woman corrupted phantasmally, the femme fatale, the vampire, but in subtler versions this was related 'psychologically' to the feminine generally, including the inner 'feelings' or heart of the human make-up. These, when darkened by his contamination, took on the nature of pride or selfhood, whose character and force matched those of an erotic fascination, but within, like an inner shadow to the outward. These versions include the Paradise myth, in which Eve as the victim of the 'serpent' is open to this subtler interpretation - the feminine or psycho-pathetic awareness being

---

1   A good example is Spenser's Archimago (*The Faerie Queen*).

infiltrated by a stark hatred of herself as valueless and shameful ("death" and "sin") and thus turned, in reaction or compensation, into the 'inner' equivalent of the femme fatale: a power of pride, able to subvert and derange the 'masculine' qualities of mind and creative energy into fantasies of self-realisation and the same life-hatred as her own.

In these subtler versions of the myth – we might call them religious or psychological versions – because the 'poisoner' has become a spiritual power, then the corresponding 'potency' that the hero must find to counter him also becomes a spiritual power – a vital force of divine truth, for instance, able to defeat what is now a cause of barrenness in the feminine soul or heart of the human character.

By this review or overall survey of the myth, I feel sure we can approach *Hamlet* with a stronger focus, able to offset or augment the realistic portrayal of character and action with a mythic meaning, much as would the Elizabethan audience itself, having been weaned by countless stories to symbolic associations and shades of meaning that the modern audience usually lacks. Claudius, for example, now focuses clearly on the mythic level of the play as the devil or subhuman goblin who, having first poisoned the feminine nature into a means of debasement and control upon the masculine, as we inferred from the ghost's account in the last chapter, must continue that policy. He must neutralise anyone in whom a power of truth still lingers and might grow to a strength fatal to his rule. This includes Hamlet, a man "picked out of ten thousand" who, by whatever sense of divorce from the devil's merry-go-round, by whatever sense of alienation from its habitual pleasures and blurs of delusion, has found a detachment, and in that detachment an instinct to what is really going on. It is like a voice from the past that tells him what happened long ago, and what still happens. The voice of a ghost within.

Already we draw near to the real meaning of the 'nunnery' scene. It is Claudius's attempt to neutralise Hamlet, and, as it uses the same means by which the character of King Hamlet himself was 'neutralised' – the tainted feminine nature – it actually repeats that event, like a dramatic recreation of the Paradise disaster lurking in the ghost's account. This is why Shakespeare includes in the scene a number of reminders of that disaster, one of them being in Hamlet's teasing of Ophelia:

"Are you honest…are you fair?…if you be honest and fair, your honesty should admit no discourse with your beauty…for the power of beauty will sooner transform honesty from what it is to a bawd than the force of honesty can translate beauty into his likeness. This was sometime a paradox, but now the time gives it proof. I did love you once." (3.1.103-5)

This apparent parody of a moralist's advice to women - to guard their "beauty" lest it corrupt their "honesty" (their 'virtue') - hides a deeper comment on the superior power of the *feminine* ("beauty") to subvert the *masculine* ("honesty", in the sense of 'truth'); and it is linked to the Paradise story (where this power was first disastrously proved) by Hamlet's "This was sometime a paradox" ('This was once an impossibility'). He means that in Eden there was once such a balance or harmony between feminine and masculine, the "fair" and the "honest", that neither side could possibly exercise a baneful power upon the other. (Until, that is, something gave Eve an infernal strength of 'beauty' quite overwhelming to man's mere 'honesty' of mind.) The idea of a Paradise allusion also explains Hamlet's closing comment, "I did love you once". It is the same 'once' as above, in Eden, when there could have been such a thing as love - before it was ruined.

Yet in Claudius, the watchful villain in this scene, there are contradictions of character. At times in the play he is clearly in the mythic role of Devil - poisoner, corrupter, manipulator - and not least in his first approach to Hamlet in the Court scene of Act 1, where his argument is very like that put to tempt Christ in the wilderness - to forget the 'father' and, instead, comply self-advantageously with the worldly system. At other times, though, he seems as much a victim of the poisoned state of life as any man. This comes out strongly in the scene where he tries to repent - at his prayers - in which he is shown to be the victim of fantasy himself, the dupe of the devil's merry-go-round: the same chaser of the self's dream, now pathetically hanging on to its remaining tatters - "my crown, mine own ambition, and my queen".

It brings up a complex matter that appears in fact in a number of versions of the myth. There is a recurring confusion between the figure of the devil behind the whole fallen state and the figure of the male desires and energies which that devilish power has selfishly deranged. Over and over we find this, and not least in the Paradise myth itself, in which Satan's role is open to two contradictory interpretations often found in older literature: the poisoner of the feminine nature and, in another light, the creative energies which that feminine nature then seductively perverts into selfish fantasy and destructiveness. It is as if the patriarchal mentality behind this version of the myth, as in so many others, was blurring the story for its own purposes. That is to say, being favourable to 'elder' qualities in life and to 'elder' stability as its idea of good, and being equally unfavourable to 'youth', the energies of change, it conveniently rigged the myth to equate the 'serpent' of venomous evil with the 'serpent' of life's virile energies. The reader will find this evidenced in so many of the myth's post-primitive or patriarchal forms, from the portrayal of Loki in the Norse, or of Set in the Egyptian version, right through into Milton's Satan in *Paradise Lost*. However, as I said, it is a complex matter. The point for this present chapter is that the confusion about the nature of Satan seriously blurs the portrayal of Claudius - a 'poisoner' who is yet a victim or product of the poisoned system.[2]

Shakespeare was happier with Polonius. As his own character-creation he could portray him on the play's mythic level unambiguously as the 'blighter' behind life's fallen state: the devil who, in partnership with Claudius, maintains control by the weakening and debasement of true masculinity, including the power of truth itself. And his means, as already much argued, is the feminine nature, whose corruption as into a phantasm of spells can degrade, and keep degraded, the male mind and creative energies,

---

2   The same confusion shows in other Shakespeare plays. Though in *Othello* and *Cymbeline,* for instance, he distinguishes the characters of the devil and the bedevilled male (Iago and Othello, Iachimo and Posthumus, respectively), in other plays the roles are run together - e.g. Edmund (*Lear*), Angelo (*Measure for Measure*), and Macbeth. The same is true of Caliban (jointly with Antonio) in *The Tempest.*

just as was first practised in the Adamic "orchard" of King Hamlet.

In this light, we can make full sense of Hamlet's taunt at Polonius as a 'pimp' ('fishmonger'),[3] the dealer in feminine fantasy for his own power and gain, or - less directly - as a 'puppet-master' behind the feminine play of shadows.[4] We can make sense, too, of his being charactered as the "rat", the Peeping Tom and the "old man" in the Queen's chamber scene, since these three figures appear in stories ('The House of Jack', 'Godiva', 'Goosy Gander') that probably survived from fertility rites in which the equivalent of the biblical devil - some cause of barrenness or illness in the Queen - was eliminated by the 'solar' hero.

So we listen more carefully to his counselling of Ophelia. Though on the realistic level of the play his advice (and here should be included the advice of her brother, as of the same stock)[5] might seem prudent guidance into caution and self-regard, needful to a young woman in a faulty world, it shows under mythic focus something more sinister. Something in fact as damaging in its way as what was poured into the ear of King Hamlet; for it instils fear, mistrust, a sense of the shameful, the sinful, into the faith of a woman's love. Here indeed is the moral 'leaven of the pharisee', injected into a nature that receives it like a poison, as did her counterpart in Eden. It is not by chance, then, that Shakespeare has Polonius speak of his work thus - "...she took *the fruits* of my advice..." (2.2.145).

We look with more interest, now, at how Ophelia appears as she is set in place in the 'nunnery' scene itself. If all is going according to the story-pattern, and not least that of the Paradise myth, then we might expect to find an 'Eve' much changed by the 'serpent', now to be plied disastrously upon 'Adam'. We are not disappointed. The dialogue at this point records exactly the aura of a darkened femininity about Ophelia, such as often shows in medieval portrayals of the femme fatale: the strange sin-spell of taboo that paradoxically combines the pure, untouchable sanctity with the sensual allure. As

---

3   2.2.174

4   3.2.241

5   For the advice of Laertes and Polonius, see Act 1, Scene 3.

Polonius places her demurely reading some devotional text, we thus find point to the comments he makes and those of Claudius:

Polonius: "We are oft to blame in this...
'Tis too much prov'd, that with *devotion's visage*
And pious action we do sugar o'er
The devil himself."

Claudius: "O 'tis too true...
The harlot's cheek, beautied with plast'ring art,
Is not more ugly to the thing that helps it..."

And yet, in proceeding to the examination of this scene, we should not become so fixed on the idea of actual persons involved that we miss the allegorical story. As I said earlier, to the medieval mind very often, the power of the femme fatale as a manifestation of a poisoned or darkened nature was only half the picture. It was only the outward showing of an inner change, in the 'woman within', the 'feelings' transformed to pride or selfhood, which was equally seductive and disastrous within the masculine. So that we get a full perspective on this scene's re-enactment of what befell King Hamlet, and led also to his wrathful rejection of his nature, his 'marriage', as part of the devil's trick to destroy him, I need to re-state the main points of this 'Story of Eve'.

The key point is what results from the poisonous awareness invading the feminine or 'feelings' side of our being, which Shakespeare shows in the 'counselling' of Ophelia and which *Genesis* showed in the poisoned fruit of the serpent: the awareness of her hideous shamefulness ('sin') and bleak unimportance ('death'). There arises from this awareness a division, out of which develops a pride hostile to the nature now detested as ugly in its loves and instincts, a pride with yearnings for a compensatory identity of purity and status. This has a disastrous effect on 'masculine' mental outlook and action, which the inner emotional state ever governs. As we have seen earlier, this pride both frustrates the creative side of our being, turning it destructive, and also infiltrates the mind with its own detestations of nature, particularly of what is naturally feminine, and with its own yearnings for the contrary dream-ideal, the pure, the perfect.

This is exactly shown in Hamlet's behaviour in this scene, for one way he rejects as unworthy the whole apparently sordid nature of life, particularly its feminine or physical aspect - "Why would'st thou be a breeder of sinners?" - and another way yearns for its ideal or sublimated form, imaged in woman as the pure figment: "Get thee to a nunnery!". It is like a diseased mind rejecting its own body, its own natural union - "I say we will have no more marriage!".

In all, what we are shown is that Hamlet, now possessed by an altered feminine life, a 'second Ophelia' so to speak, is caused by that pride and self-righteousness to direct hate and wrath against the natural feminine, the natural Ophelia. In the same way, Lear, when possessed by the changed aspect of 'Cordelia' (Goneril and Regan) directs his wrath against all that the true Cordelia represents - the form of life, the true nature with its loves and desires, now appearing loathsome.

Though puzzling to those limited to realism, the 'nunnery' scene, from its opening desire to escape or violate the natural body (Hamlet's contemplation of suicide) right up to the final renunciation of the natural feminine, is not Hamlet's own independent behaviour. It is the outward expression or result of what has divisively taken place in his feminine life. Through him, one 'Ophelia' is rejecting and trying to destroy the other. It is the same not only in the myth or symbolic drama of *King Lear,* as already pointed out. It is the same in the drama of Lady Macbeth, who *through* the Masculine destroys what is truly natural or feminine. Likewise in *Othello,* what drives the hero to murder Desdemona is what has arisen in him through his 'feelings' being poisoned by an insane moral awareness - the pride or the ideal, against which the natural must appear a loathsome imperfection.

We thus see how the 'nunnery' scene, at least on one level, shows a re-enactment of the disaster that, as I have argued, befell the original King Hamlet, which also began when something poisonously hateful entered the feminine life, and also ended with a destructive breakdown of sexual harmony. And as that first disaster in the play was contrived by the poisoner - the serpent in Paradise who sought to gain control through a manic self-destruction by the true man - so this re-enactment is contrived by the same figure (duplicated in Claudius and Polonius), now seeking to keep the control he has gained by using the contaminated feminine nature to neutralise any man that might regain the original power of truth by which his rule will be shattered.

Because it is a re-enactment, we might be reminded how in our own lives also the Fall actually repeats itself, for we too sooner or later fall foul of a poison, part inherited and part activated by life's conditions. That is to say, our innocence is sooner or later blighted, and our feelings hardened into selfhood, by which we too begin to believe in fantasy realisations, like the ghostly memory of a lost wholeness, and ever at the cost of truth and true life, which we ignore, reject, or even trample in our dream-desire. How strange it is, then, that though we venerate works like *Hamlet* for their remarkable insight into the human condition, we think it nowadays improper or 'uneducated' to deal any more with concepts like the Devil, the Fall, the awareness of Sin, or even believe that they in any sense exist. Is our veneration, then, no more than useful bowing, a groomed respect for something we in fact neither understand nor wish to?

★   ★   ★

To round off this first part of the chapter, I shall add two points of reflection about the 'nunnery' scene.

The first is about something that I think the reader will have gathered. If we view this scene in *Hamlet* from a mythic point of view, we come up with quite a different meaning from that suggested by its realistic surface. That surface tells us that the whole scene is arranged by Claudius and Polonius to find out just how dangerous Hamlet is to Claudius's position. Is there something that makes him a threat? Does he perhaps know something, or at least suspect something about Claudius's doings that renders him a person to be closely watched, or even eliminated? Ophelia, in line with this, is simply used to prompt some possible disclosure or unguarded comment from him. The device fails, because Hamlet by and large discloses nothing tangible. He even seems to be aware that the whole thing is a set-up - "Where is your father?" - and is therefore careful to give the impression that his brooding enmity is due to Ophelia.

Viewed mythically, on the other hand, Claudius and Polonius are fully successful. Just as the 'devil' destroyed the true majesty of man in King Hamlet, subverting his mental strength and creativity through a contamination of his 'emotional' life, so they destroy a potential of the same in the Prince, and by the same means. Man cannot defeat the devil if his own 'heart' is deeply poisoned, but must remain a prisoner to self-fantasy and to a hatred of his own feminine humanity.

My second point is perhaps related to this. When we observe Ophelia's part in *Hamlet,* it seems clear that Shakespeare saw her as a hapless victim. She is turned into a dangerous falsehood quite against her natural self and wishes. The implication is that Eve also – indeed the whole character of things feminine, including the heart and feelings in each one of us - is powerless to do other than she does, whatever her true desires and hopes. Once the 'poison' is there, something else takes over. She must go for power, even though it means the betrayal of the 'truth' - the god that should share her nature - and of her own real happiness.

Why then was Shakespeare inclined to be severe with the 'lady'? I do not mean just in this play, but generally. For instance, he never again shows the whole sorry corruption of her nature, by which she might be exonerated in her behaviour. With Goneril and Regan, for example, there is only a hint at what might have twisted them - "... for he did ever love our sister most". With Lady Macbeth it is worse. He plays down the idea of her being the victim, and instead stresses her knowing desire for an infernal power. And in his last play, when we might expect a final graciousness, something of the chivalrous 'The Lady has no blame', he in fact treats Sycorax as a complete monster whose evil is unexplained.

It is as if Shakespeare, unless simply careless or playing to male prejudice, is suppressing his own wisdom. Was it that a clear recognition of her blamelessness would have broken the spell of his whole artistic fascination, in which a strange love-hate with the feminine was involved? Or something deeper? I suggested at the end of Chapter 2 that the tragic failure in *Hamlet* was possibly Shakespeare's reflection on humanity's own failure to break with the underlying cause of its fallen state: a latent life-hatred that is much bound up with a sort of misogyny. Perhaps the failure reflects equally on Shakespeare himself. Sifting a writer's work for his own character is a doubtful business, and yet the later retreat from the insight shown in *Hamlet* may point to Shakespeare's own retreat from what he had shown about himself.

★   ★   ★

The 'Ophelia-in-madness' scene (Act4 Sc5) hardly needs a claim to be read mythically. Most commentators would agree that a realistic reading alone would be unjust to the depths of meaning Shakespeare seems to have intended. Indeed, Ophelia's comments appear similar in nature and intention to those of Mad Tom (Edgar) in *King Lear* – a sort of cryptic commentary on the 'inner story' to the play.

Before dealing with the scene, however, I must say I realise that it is not a part of *Hamlet* that most readers will have kept clearly in their memories, made up as it is of random fragments, allusions and asides. To make good any haziness, I shall first give an outline of Ophelia's part:-

1.   (21-43) A verse lament for a dead man, whose loss was not mourned even though he was the "true love". She partly indicates herself as a betrayer of the man, Hamlet, with possible reminder of the 'nunnery' scene, but also includes Gertrude, her partnering character, in the role of feminine betrayal, and so the dead man, the "true love", is equally interpretable as King Hamlet. Likewise the closing allusion to the folktale of "the baker's daughter", who played false with the hero and suffered sorrows and regret, is meant to apply equally to herself and Gertrude.

2.   (48-66) The 'Valentine's Day' song. This reverses the roles of betrayer and betrayed, for now a trusting maid is sexually enjoyed and then forsaken by the man. Indeed, it comes across as a sort of male revenge for the above betrayal of man by woman.

3.   (68-73) Another mention of the dead man, who is now linked with Polonius. He hardly fits the character of "true love" or 'true man' in any sense, but Shakespeare wishes us to connect the slain Polonius with the earlier slain King Hamlet perhaps to reinforce the role of Laertes now as the new avenger.

4.   (164-171) Another mention of the man's death and funeral, and again linked with treachery - "It is the false steward that stole his master's daughter" (denoting Claudius).

5.   (173-183) The distribution of symbolic flowers - (a) rosemary (remembrance) and pansies (gloomy thoughts) to Laertes, now taking on the earlier Hamlet role that was much charactered by 'remembrance (for his father) and dark thoughts. (b) Fennel and columbine to Claudius, probably, since they denote trickery and adultery. (c) Rue of regret and remorse to herself and Gertrude, who also receives a daisy. (d) There are no violets, the emblem of true love, to give out, because true love perished with the death of the true man who is ever in her thoughts in this scene, though now once again confused with her father.

6.   (184-196) An allusion to "bonny sweet Robin" (as the true love), but the lighter note is finally quelled by a last mention of the man's funeral again, the impossibility of his return, and the heroine's resignation to death in turn.

★

Well, starting with the easiest threads in all this, we can say that most of the commentary relates to the story of Ophelia and Gertrude who, as linked figures, have both played false to the true man and have suffered something like the man's revenge (see point 2 above). This is clearly so in the case of Gertrude, who has borne the quasi-sexual storm of Hamlet in her chamber, which has altered her nature much as might an actual sexual act. Shakespeare, with the tie between Gertrude and Ophelia in mind, has Ophelia also admit, as if in imagination, to a sexual ravishment - "tumbled".

Next we might say that Ophelia and Gertrude also represent the character of woman through the ages, a kind of eternal Eve who - taking the dimmest view, as in this play's "frailty thy name is woman" - has been inclined to ignore or betray the true love and then realise the penalty: a life beset by guilts and the rough or deceitful treatment of a less worthy male, and his abuse, leading her to long for the true love somehow to return.

It is when we thus start extending the scope that we find we are moving the whole thing into symbolic or mythic terms: the story of the feminine nature generally, including that which dwells in each of us. For we all, by inheritance or by the pressures and persuasions of life, seem in our feminine hearts to have the same weakness for betraying what we know is true, and in our pride or selfhood ignore or repress it, until the blindness even becomes habitual, like Gertrude's. We all then in our pride find also that we suffer the blows of life – disappointments, cruel mischances, sickness, pains, and finally death – which seem very much like that truth getting back at us in twisted and demonic forms, somehow seeking our surrender.

Moving this perception of the feminine character in life fully into the framework of myth, we next might see that we are still looking at the winter-queen of the original myth, the lady who also changed her true partner for the threatful winter-king, and suffered his abuse as the price of her power. And pretty much the same stayed in all the evolved versions of her character we have looked at. Did not Dorigen of *The Franklin's Tale,* for example, do likewise, and then become herself a lady of sorrows, beset by the male life-energies turned monstrous? And Eve? And countless others of the type – the multitude of Proud Princesses that find their sway, their self-will, ever produces a monster gruelling or scathing to them, like a Grisly Beard to their heart, or a Beast to their Beauty.

The only difference is that myths of this sort usually have a happy ending. The winter-queen in her surrender – the final 'sexual death' – finds her lost fruitfulness and joy, for her harsh adversary was the life-king in disguise all along, who, sharing the last 'death' with her, sheds his monstrous form and returns as her lover. Likewise with Eve, for her last surrender as the 'harlot of Judah' allowed her to conceive the Messiah of renewal, and allowed the return of her long-ago forsaken husband (figured as Jehovah). And in this way, the penalty set upon her in leaving Paradise – to endure the ravaging blows of man – turned out to be her salvation: "In sorrow shalt thou bring forth children". Likewise with Dorigen and all other Beauties and Proud Princesses, whose sorrows turn at last to joy, fruitfulness, or salvation. But it is not so when the myth is used as tragedy, nor in our lives that we tend to live by a tragic spirit. Most seem to go to their graves like Ophelia, taking the last blow of the god as no loving act but as a violation, and with no readiness of the pride to surrender to a new-found vision.

But what particular versions of the myth does Shakespeare have Ophelia touch on as story-shadows to her fate? One is the story of Robin – "For bonny sweet Robin is all my joy". This almost certainly had its roots in the primitive myth dealt with in this study, and therefore, as certainly, was a distant relative of the similarly derived 'Hamlet' story. It survives to us in little more than the poor rag-bag of tales about the part-historical (?) Robin Hood the outlaw, and his lady (best known as Marian); but in Shakespeare's day its folk and ritual survivals were more widespread and better known: especially distinct in the May festivities – the 'May Games'.

Perhaps if, alongside known details of these Games, we used related stories that survive with greater clarity, we might make a better guess about the Robin story known to Shakespeare, and so make Ophelia's allusion more useful. A good example to choose might be the Welsh story of Llew Llaw Gyffes, a hero that Robert Graves thought a sort of Celtic 'Robin' (*White Goddess* p.318). In this, according to type, the lady – Blodeuwedd – betrays her husband (Llew Llaw), and takes his slayer as her love. The husband at length returns from death to reclaim his rule, and the guilty pair are punished. What brings the story closer to Ophelia (and Gertrude) in this scene, and possibly therefore to the Robin story she alludes to, is that Blodeuwedd was associated with flowers (a kind of Celtic Flora) and her punishment of guilty regret is imaged as her being turned into an owl – the image Ophelia also uses of her plight (See on).

The above version of the 'Robin' story would certainly fit well with this scene, but the May Games version, which Shakespeare also seems aware of (See on), would not, especially in their ending – restored lovers' joy (summer) after sacrificial surrender of their 'wintry' roles. Two 'Robin' stories? Well, not exactly, but it does bring us to an important point about the myth in general and the changes affecting it. Whereas the primitive form of the myth, as I have generally claimed throughout this study, probably showed the first disaster in the cycle as a matter of mischance – the Queen being turned by a blight or poison into the involuntary cause of her partner's monstrous change – some later versions slanted events in this disaster in such a way as to make the Queen culpable. In these, she does not change her summer lord into his 'wintry' character, but incites a rougher 'wintry' male (a separate figure entirely) to take his place. Many factors can be guessed to have affected this fundamental change of story-line, but a major one surely was a greater readiness to see the feminine character in a gloomy light – treachery, adultery, or even incitement to murder – very much in keeping with the misogyny of patriarchal societies.

Marian therefore, along with most of her type – the various forms of Blathnat (Blodwed), Delilah, Clytemnaestra, etc. – eventually turned up in versions of the story as a character of betrayal (the fickle wanton) and with something far more grievous to bewail than ever had the primitive Queen when the truth about her nature came bleakly home to her. And this darker Marian story, along with the later misogynistic flavour to the myth generally, seems to be the one that Shakespeare had in mind as a parallel to the story of Ophelia, as she, with clear reminders of that unhappy heroine,[6] hints in her madness at the taint of betrayal in woman's character and the tragic power of murderous incitement.

At the same time, it should be noticed that Shakespeare does much to right the misogynistic imbalance, and even restores something of the primitive sense of the Queen's innocence – the idea that she herself was first the victim of a 'poison' that banefully changed her nature. I will bring this out more strongly as I proceed with the argument, and – a timely promise – as I apply that argument more closely now to the 'Robin' story in *Hamlet*.

There are a number of later 'patriarchal' versions of the myth that, despite the misogynistic bias, preserve at least a trace of the lady's original excuse – some equivalent of the blight or poison responsible for her 'fickle' change. Eve, for example, has the serpent to blame, and Delilah has the insidious Philistine authorities. And Marian has something similar. In the 'Kirklees' story of Robin's betrayal, in which the lady's treacherous role is played by Robin's

---

6 Ophelia's giving out flowers in her 'mad' scene is sometimes linked with Marian's practice in the May Games. (See H. Jenkins' Longer Note to 4.5.184 – Arden edition p.542.)

kinswoman, the prioress, the authorities suborning her to treachery seem likewise to be a remembrance of the original 'poison' that influenced the Queen. And here we come to the main relevance of the 'Robin' story to *Hamlet*. Recognising that Ophelia's being set up to betray Hamlet is generally similar to the treachery at Kirklees priory, we begin to look more curiously at Ophelia herself. Her strange aura of frost and flame, of pure untouchable and fleshly spell – hasn't this appeared in the myth from earliest examples of the winter-queen, through various witches and femmes fatales, and through ambiguous saintly/seductive figures such as the intoxicating Dorigen? And who else does the series include? The clue is that Ophelia not only has the authorities in the shadow of her now morally 'infected' nature. She also carries a prayer-book. The prioress? Possibly, and a possibility strengthened by Shakespeare having his hero include three mentions of "nunnery" in his tirade. The scene seems shadowed by the 'house of nuns' wherein the folk-hero met the same fate: the 'death' of his true manhood or majesty and, in some earlier version perhaps, the emergence of his destructive double.[7]

There are some other primitive features preserved in the Kirklees story that are of interest in connection with Shakespeare's work. They relate to the hero's blood that is drained in his 'murder'. When we have chance to link this with other versions, with King Duncan's death in Macbeth, and with Norse stories that seem to have influenced Shakespeare in that play, we shall see, first, that the hero's blood may have held some *feminine* significance, and, secondly, that its theft or loss may symbolically have signified the same as its poisoning and sinister alteration. In other words, the loss of Robin's blood and the baneful alteration in his feminine nature (imaged in the cold prioress), could be the *same* event. There is something possibly to ponder here, if the 'nunnery' scene does indeed repeat the earlier tragedy of Hamlet's father. As we saw in the last chapter, his *feminine* blood was poisoned.

The mention of Norse myth might usefully make our

---

7   Though surviving hard evidence about the Hud cult, and of the Old Religion generally, is meagre, the area of Huddersfield and Kirklees shows one or two possibly related features, including the curious name of an inn near the old priory estate - *The Three Nuns*.

pondering longer. In the last chapter, when I was examining the symbolic last storm or 'sexual death' taking place in Gertrude's chamber, I linked the event to the Norse story of Gerd, who suffers the wrath of the god in order to be made fruitful again. This Gerd as well as being a likely mythic fore-runner of Gertrude, was also possibly a variant form of Freyja, who had likewise earlier betrayed (or caused to be monstrously changed) her true lord, and must sorrowfully await his return.[8] The name of her true lord was Od, or Hod, the lost character of Odin who, though meanwhile monstrous, would one day return in his true form. The name 'Hod' seems to connect with the Hod, or Hud, of the English story, the 'Robin' who also suffered betrayal and would some day return in his true character. In depicting Ophelia's sorrows (and Gertrude's) was Shakespeare aware of both treacherous Marian and her distant Norse 'cousin', Freyja?

However, as the reader will guess, I am here in this background of mythical influence on Shakespeare's work probing at a mixture of fact and hypothesis. Much of the evidence has faded into obscurity and legend. Even so, it might be claimed - in the case of Robin Hood at least - more evidence remains than is usually supposed, and some of it right under our noses in leading works of older literature.[9] And some of it, perhaps, in the memories and thoughts of folk not usually consulted by scholars.

★   ★   ★

I will finish the chapter by exploring another folktale allusion made by Ophelia in the scene of her 'mad' commentary - "They say the owl was a baker's daughter" (4.5.42). It seems to be another case of Shakespeare pointing to the inner (or mythic) meaning of his play by mentioning what was once a well-known symbolic story. Unfortunately for the modern audience, eager for Shakespeare's meaning, the folktale here alluded to survives in only a few

---

8   A Norse myth with this implication is the *Brisingamen* story. Another that might be guessed to have the same implication is the story of Freyja's lover (now called Svipdag) who is turned into a dragon of wrath. Freyja in her true side ever longs for his return and meanwhile searches and weeps in sorrow upon the earth.

9   See Longer Note at the end of this chapter.

imperfect versions.

Ophelia mentions it just after her opening lament for the "true love" whose death, because not genuinely mourned, is implied to have involved treachery in some way. The *Baker's Daughter* story, since it is one of feminine wrong towards the true man, is therefore connected in idea. Its surviving versions give this general outline:- Jesus went to buy bread. The baker's daughter, thinking to cheat him, put short measure of dough in the oven, but Jesus caused the dough to increase and swell mightily, whereupon the baker's daughter cried out in alarm - Hoo! hoo! - and for her deceit was turned into an owl, a bird of sorrows.

Now, I think the reader will straightaway notice in this story an idea-resemblance to *Hamlet,* and one that goes quite a way beyond the general theme of feminine deceit. For instance, its idea of denying the true man also figures in *Hamlet,* as does the final sorrow of the woman (the owl of rue) in realising what she has done. Perhaps most striking of all, though, is the sexual symbolism of the dough in the oven, which connects with the quasi-sexual punishment of the feminine character much in evidence in *Hamlet* as the end of her resistance and false nature.

It would have been very interesting if a fuller version of this story had survived. It might well have made Ophelia's allusion more enlightening. Well, perhaps by using the outline of the version above in connection with the text of *Hamlet,* we might be able to reconstruct that very story. We are after all dealing with a lost myth, so why not a lost 'baker's daughter'? Let us try out of interest - but also in the hope of discovery.

What main features have we to go on in the *Baker's Daughter*? - (a) a medieval fondness for mixing biblical theme with folktale; (b) the making of abundant bread; (c) a cheating woman; (d) presumably a baker, as her father, lurking somewhere; (e) Jesus as the hero.

But there is something else here useful to recall: the fondness that earlier ages had for symbolically linking Jesus with Old Testament figures.[10] Whom was Jesus often thus linked with? Joseph.

---

10   Inter-testament 'typology' lasted well into Victorian times, as witnessed by the 'John Brown' Family Bible.

That's interesting, because in the Joseph story we find the theme of the shortage and abundance of bread, a baker, and a cheating woman.

The possibility here emerging is that the *Baker's Daughter* was influenced by the Old Testament story of Joseph. A discovery of some importance in the context of *Hamlet,* because the pattern of the Joseph story resembles that of the play. Indeed, if we strip from the Joseph story the likely priestly veneer by which Joseph was made the unblemished hero (see later), we realise that his temptation by the wanton wife of Potiphar, leading to a charge of rape against him, shows traces of the old disastrous first stage of the myth as seen clearly in *Hamlet* – something sinister about the feminine nature that turns the true masculine character (god, king, or hero) violent. Also in parallel – and with no need of adjustment – is what happens to the hero afterwards, for in both stories he suffers harsh bondage (the 'prison' symbolism of Joseph's ordeal is matched by the imagery used of both Hamlets, father and son) that should lead to an eventual regaining of the lost power of majesty and a return to happy prosperity (tragically scotched in *Hamlet*).

Other likenesses to *Hamlet* are found in the folk versions of the Joseph story that were popular in the Middle Ages and may have influenced the *Baker's Daughter* more than the *Genesis* version. In these, Potiphar's cheating wife (usually called Zuleika),[11] is cast into sorrows and beggary when her wickedness is revealed, but is eventually found by the liberated and regally promoted Joseph, and uplifted back to happiness as his wife. The commonly found *motif* of the 'woman of sin and sorrow' at last discovered and married by the hero returned regally from disgrace or ordeal (the "maiden all forlorn" marrying the man erewhile "tattered and torn") is visible also in *Hamlet,* in Ophelia's commentary of Act 4 particularly, except that – once again – tragic influence cancels the natural happy ending.

But the real importance of the 'Zuleika' versions of the Joseph story, for us in our study of *Hamlet,* lies in what they tell us about the 'baker' in the story, and why he is finally hanged, which is left

---

11 An interesting collection and investigation of the medieval Joseph/Zuleika
    stories is readily found in A.S. Rappoport's *Ancient Israel* – vol.2.

unexplained in the biblical version. What the 'Zuleika' stories tell us
is that he is a poisoner! Indeed, his crime is an attempt to *poison the
king*. It may be not surprising then to find that Claudius in *Hamlet*
is connected with the image of poisonous blighting that occurs in
the Joseph story - "like a mildew'd ear blasting his wholesome
brother".[12] And by this, something of a parallel in the two stories
begins to sharpen. Perhaps in the Joseph story this 'baker' could be
guessed to have engineered the whole first disaster, much like the
"serpent" Claudius in *Hamlet,* as we saw in the last chapter, and
much like the equally poisonous Polonius, as we saw in this. Perhaps
this 'baker' could be seen likewise as having poisoned the human
heart, the feminine nature, and thereby having driven the true man
violent (the alleged rape), causing him to be bound until he works
out a way to cleanse the poisoned system - the feminine - and make
it once again 'fruitful', like Zuleika or the land of Egypt. The final
hanging of the baker in the Joseph story would thus equate with
Hamlet's casting out Claudius and Polonius from the Queen's
chamber or person, to cleanse her nature and make her once again
spiritually fruitful.

There may be yet more to it, which we begin to see when we
realise that the 'poison' in both stories is the same. At Joseph's last
feast with his brethren, he cast all vengeance and accusation from his
heart. He thus, symbolically, cleansed the heart and the blood of
life's feast of its poison. Likewise at the Last Supper, in a symbolic
foreshadowing of his sacrificial victory, Jesus, Joseph's New
Testament counterpart or *antitype,* cleansed the wine (the blood) of
the feast of life. That is to say, as the malign Judas represented the
Devil, the first poisoner of life's feast (or Paradise), then Jesus' passing
him the sop from the wine-cup was symbolically giving back the
poisoner his poison, and thus cleansing the cup, the human heart, of
sin and accusation. (Is it simply by chance that *thirteen* has
traditionally linked the Devil and Judas - and the 'baker'?)

Now we see more clearly the point of some of the symbolism in
Hamlet. In the last chapter while examining the ghost's account, I
showed how the feast of life, the blood, was first infected by a 'yeast',

---

12 Compare with Pharoah's dream - Genesis 41.

which by various means I linked with a sense of sin, the 'poison' that entered Paradise. This, like an infection in the body's wine of life, its feminine heart or feelings, drove the hero to be violent (like Joseph, at least by accusation[13]), for which he too serves in a "prison-house"[14] until able (through his son) to cleanse the feminine heart, the infected blood of life, of the poison - Hamlet's cleansing of Gertrude, and the casting out of the devils from her presence - which is also linked with Hamlet's own journey to a 'crucifixion'.

Yes, it would have been interesting if a full version of the 'baker's daughter' story had survived, but perhaps this search for it has begun to prove as useful as any surviving story. It has pointed to a possible folktale that may have formed a close parallel to the symbolic 'inner' story in *Hamlet* - a first poisoning of the feminine nature which led the masculine to be destructive, out of which character by process of ordeal he finally breaks free, restoring the feminine nature and his own kingship.

★   ★   ★

There is another matter of interest raised by the Joseph story. Exploring it will further help our awareness of the network of myths Shakespeare may have been touching on as shadowy parallels to the story of *Hamlet,* and will lead us to a clearer understanding of the topic I brought up at the end of Chapter 2 - *Hamlet* as a reflection of a failure in the cycle of human destiny.

Our exploration begins in an apparently trivial detail. The story of Joseph tells us that the hero wants his brothers brought back to Egypt, and for this purpose he has a precious drinking vessel, a goblet, secretly hidden in the sacks of corn they are carrying away. It is a pretext for their arrest on a charge of theft, ensuring their return. But why a precious goblet? The answer begins to form when we look at the feast that Joseph arranges for a final act of forgiveness on his treacherous brothers. The idea of his finally casting out bitterness and

---

13 In all versions of the Joseph story, the hero is guiltless of the alleged rape on his master's wife, and yet perhaps an earlier story had shown a crime that his illustrious status as a religious hero later could not allow to be shown.

14 1.5.14 Both the ghost of King Hamlet and Hamlet himself are shown in the text to be symbolically imprisoned.

accusation from his *heart* explains the symbolism of the goblet
restored, especially when we link this event with something in the
story of Jesus with which it tallies. As mentioned a few pages back,
Jesus, Joseph's counterpart or *antitype* in the New Testament, also held
a final feast, but in this case the bitterness in the human heart to be
finally ridded is clearly imaged as its removal from a wine-cup or
goblet (and given to Iscariot as his lot). In both cases, this wine-cup
seems to be a symbol of the human heart that is now to be cleansed
and made the vessel of the true wine of life's nourishing and
gladdening. But what has been suppressed in both these patriarchal
accounts is that the goblet, the vessel of life-blood, the 'heart' of life,
is a feminine symbol. It is therefore the poisoned feminine nature that
is in both cases being restored to its natural joy and life sustenance, its
lost bounty. 'Eve' who was first 'poisoned' into the underlying bane of
life is thus cleansed back into life's service and fruitfulness.

As this chapter has shown, the same myth of Eve, whatever its
variants, shadows the story of *Hamlet,* the climax of which is meant
to be the same final rescue of the feminine nature – Gertrude's
"heart" being broken and purged of a negative presence by a final
'inseminating' act. This is the play's equivalent of the feminine
'goblet' of life at last being cleansed and restored to its true radiant
beauty as the vessel of life.

But there is something deeper to this, which, though it will be
followed up more fully in a later chapter, deserves our attention
now. The 'goblet' also figured very powerfully in the Grail romances,
and again – despite carelessness or suppression – as a symbol of the
feminine nature, meanwhile darkened, poisoned, or barren, but also
to be restored at last to true bounty and fruitfulness by a male act.
One of its alternative figures is the sick queen, the blighted or
wintry damsel, and another is the woman (or women) who
meanwhile mourns by the "bier" of the dead hero.[15] Now, isn't this
one of the main subjects of Ophelia's 'mad' commentary in Act 4?
Yes, and it has the same symbolic implication. Her hope is that the
true man, long ago betrayed in some way by the feminine nature,

---

15 A useful survey of this mournful figure in Grail romances is in J.L. Weston's
    From Ritual to Romance (p.48-50).

will return for her sorrow to be turned to joy, because he alone has the power to cast out from her nature, her heart, the poison that blights it. The Grail must be made 'fruitful' again by the lost male power returning, which in fully spiritual terms is the Christ of vision casting out the life-hatred that possesses our nature and centres our present bedevilling sickness.

But this is what Hamlet was meant to be doing in the cleansing and 'insemination' of Gertrude, and in Ophelia's "tumbling". Why then is Ophelia still longing for it to take place? In answer to this, we could simply point to the equivalent events in parallel myths and say that there, too, the feminine nature laments in grief at the apparent failure of the hero to achieve his mission by sacrifice. Whether it is the women who weep for Thammuz or Adonis, or the Magdalen who sorrows at Jesus' grave, or even the Marian of grief, it could register the sense of apparent failure, for until the 'resurrection' takes place, the hero seems to have gone to his death for no fruitful purpose.

Well, we could simply do this, but in this case we would be wrong, because in *Hamlet* the climax, the 'sexual death', actually has been a *failure*. As I argued at the end of Chapter 2, Hamlet's reform of the body of life, its feminine nature or heart, like all idealistic puritanical reforms, simply alters the externals into a finer form in conformity with its ideal. It fails to remove the latent poison in fallen life - the life-hatred, the underlying disgust at our nature, which is at the very base of reforming idealism itself. It is a denial of Christian truth: the ousting of sin, the blighting presence in the heart of our sickness and sorrow.

And this failure of Hamlet to 'achieve the Grail' is not just a reflection of a failure of vision in idealistic reform. It may reflect also the failure of Christian Europe. Again as I argued at the end of Chapter 2, Shakespeare may be using his play to show man's historical destiny - the cycle of the myth in its historical enactment - as ending in failure. The truth in Christianity had not been realised. The power of vision that might have transcended fallen mental limitations and pierced healingly to the poisoned heart, restoring it to happiness and grace, had been ignored. Christianity became almost entirely just another holy-holy religion based on a

latently persistent life-hatred: the awareness of sin, fostering still the
contempts and accusations of life, especially of its natural or
'feminine' aspects. The modern world it was 'giving birth' to in
Shakespeare's day would therefore be a false enlightenment, a mere
pretence of liberated humanity, under whose obsession with its own
goodness and self-congratulation lurked the poisoned heart, a
poisoned Grail. For all its boasts and banners, it would nurture a
monstrousness to life, and perhaps eventually a calamity to *repeat* that
of the Fall.

And this idea of a repeat Fall of Man explains the grim shadows
to events in the last Act of *Hamlet*. Notice, for example, how Laertes'
stormy return is described in imagery reminiscent of a long-ago
calamity,[16] and how he is linked with the name "Paris", as if
deliberately to remind of Troy's long-ago equivalent calamity, which
was then sometimes linked with the Fall. Likewise Horatio's last
words to Hamlet - "... and flights of angels sing thee to thy rest" -
recall the death of Lancelot in Malory ("... and I saw the angels
heave up Sir Lancelot unto heaven"), so as to remind of the British
version of the first bloody catastrophe - the collapse of Arthur's
world - now repeated.

And then there is something about the figure of Fortinbras, who
finally emerges as the supreme power. The armoured god of war -
haven't we seen this before? Why, of course - the ghost earlier in the
story. Fortinbras denotes the same. It was not only Troy or Albion
that long ago perished as man's character turned to manic violence.
Another of the same was Asgard, the golden equivalent in Norse
records, whose loss marked the emergence of the monstrous Odin
as man's fallen character in life. The play has come full circle.

And yet, most significant of all, as if to centre the whole of this
finally repeated *Götterdämmerung,* we see the Queen holding in her
hands a poisoned goblet.

★   ★   ★

In summary. In the first part of the chapter I argued the need to
distinguish between the realistic and mythic levels of *Hamlet,*

16 4.5.98-105

especially in the portrayal of Claudius and Polonius. On the mythic level, both these villains are the power that rules this world through a poisonous awareness in the feminine nature that has converted it to a force of selfhood. By this, the masculine is swayed into lust for fantasy-goals, dream-ideals - the queen of shadows - and into a hatred of the true nature as soiled and worthy of rejection. This devil's method repeats the one used at the Fall, where a sexual harmony was wrecked, and so the 'nunnery' scene to some extent repeats the real tragedy of King Hamlet.

Later in the chapter, I took Ophelia's 'mad' words as cryptic commentary on the mythic level of the play, arguing that the feminine character now sees the price she pays for power over the masculine. Having turned the prince of life into a force of violation and hatred - the twisted life-energies that come against her painfully - she rues his loss and longs for his return. This is partly conveyed in the 'Robin' myth, and also in the story of *The Baker's Daughter,* which, connected with other biblical stories, gives insight into the play as 'myth' - from first betrayal in Eden to what should have been a restored lost 'marriage'.

Chapter 6   Longer Notes

p.119   Robin.   Much of the evidence of the old religion connected with Hud, or Robin, has disappeared, and yet perhaps more survives than is usually recognized.   As well as in some accounts of folk festivals, like the May celebrations, it may linger shadowily in some leading works of our literature.

The first is the Prologue and Tale of Chaucer's *Wife of Bath.* The name of the wife's abusive husband - Jankin (Jonkin) - literally means 'Little John', perhaps used to denote the grosser aspect of the true husband. She herself, symbolically speaking, is therefore 'Marian' in her wintry aspect, the fallen feminine personality who holds "maistrye" over the male but only at the price of submitting her kindly natural side to the abusive character she has created in him. The final full return of this kindly side - the return of the 'summer-queen' so to speak - coincides (as ever) with the return of the true man. That is to say, their true characters return when both in a final climax - imaged in the myth as a death or a sexual consummation, and in the Wife's Prologue imaged comically as a final exchange of blows - are broken free of their 'wintry' or debased characters and transformed back into their true selves and their lost harmony together: the 'Robin' as the true husband, and the loving 'Marian'. This true Robin may link further with the Christ mentioned right at the start of her Prologue, the harlot's rescuer, who also finally returned after a sacrifice of his fallen, mortal character (the Crucifixion). The *Wife's Tale* itself more or less repeats the same story, with the 'rapist' finally transformed into the true prince by sacrifice, and with the wintry 'hag' transformed into the radiant 'summer queen'.

Shakespeare has at least three plays that touch on the 'Robin' story as a sub-theme. One of them, as pointed out in this chapter, is *Hamlet*. The play's overall story is the same as the old 'Nature' cycle, of which the 'Robin' myth was a likely variant. The true lord is betrayed (or turned into his destructive double) by his 'Marian', who then controls the male character - but, again, only at the price of submitting her true nature to his wraths, ravages and abuse. This true nature within her therefore bewails the power her wintry or fallen character wields, and longs for the return of the true man. This return, quite in accord with the usual story-pattern, can only come about through the death of her wintry power and that of his own wintry character, which ritually (and in this play) could be both sacrificially and sexually imaged or enacted: the final consummation before the return or rebirth.

The same symbolic story is found in the Bolingbroke cycle (*Henry IV*). The debased male (Falstaff - 'False Husband' - Little John) masquerades as King of the fallen or 'wintry' world of Eastcheap, under the power of the fallen feminine nature (Quickly/Tearsheet, linked at one point with "Maid Marian"), whose true nature he abuses and wrongs. The true man meanwhile is imaged as the lost "Robin", the former landlord of the Rochester inn, who equates with the rnissing husband of Mistress Quickly - the "honest man". His dark intelligence remaining in the background of events - the commonly found shadowy figure in Shakespeare's plays - is partly represented by Bolingbroke, the directing power arranging the return of true kingship. This return, as expected of the pattern, comes about through the sacrifice of what is debased and 'wintry' in man's character. This is shown in Hal's final renunciation of base motive (coupled with his rejection of Falstaff, the 'Little John' who images base motive and destructiveness) in his acceptance of true kingship as a sacrificial act – a kind of 'crown of thorns' – in his dying father's presence. This final sacrifice by Hal, like a victory over the darker self in the masculine character, coincides – again, according with the pattern – with the 'sacrifice' of the fallen or 'harlot' power in the feminine nature: the clearing out and drubbing of the trulls in Eastcheap. The new king and his restored bride – "England" (or the achieved "Jerusalem" of his father's quest) – are thus equatable with the returned true Robin and Marian of the folk religion, and perhaps with the risen lord and his redeemed "Jerusalem" of the Christian myth.

Not surprisingly, the story-pattern of *Henry IV* matches closely that of *Hamlet,* in which the "Robin" symbolism is also found. We can see this readily if we translate Eastcheap into Elsinore, Quickly/Tearsheet into Gertrude/Ophelia, Falstaff into Claudius, the directing Bolingbroke into the restless, commanding ghost, and Prince Hal into Prince Hamlet, who finally through death to his fallen nature achieves quasi-sexually the return of the lost true lord – the rebirth from the sea. The destiny, however, in *Hamlet* fails.

Another play with the same story-pattern and with reminders of the Robin cycle is *As You Like It.* The wood of the outlaws – Arden – is ruled by the darker feminine personality (Rosalind/Phebe) equating with 'wintry' Marian, whose power is ended, and her true self restored and fulfilled, when the 'true-love-Robin' figure, Orlando, faces mortal sacrifice – the fight with the lion – in a climax that also includes the lady's surrender to marriage.

In addition, *Midsummer Night's Dream,* as well as – again – fitting the story-pattern, has reminders of the Robin story and may be, indeed, the nearest we shall ever get to one of England's versions of an ancient ritual drama.

Chapter 7
Macbeth

I have spent much time in this study examining the first part of a myth that I believe survived in some leading works of our literature. This first part tells of a poisonous change in the feminine side of a higher and happier state of life, causing a wrecking and ravaging spirit to emerge in its masculine elements and to bring a violent doom upon that state.

Strangely, the crucial factor in this calamity – the sinister change in the feminine nature – seems not to have drawn much comment in studies of myth in general, and certainly in studies of the later 'literary' versions of this myth, as found in Shakespeare's work for instance. Why is so weighty a thing neglected? Are scholars as poor in heed to the lady in myth as to women about them, or as they are to the thoughts and whispers in that feminine realm, their own hearts?

Well, whatever the full answer there, it has to be admitted that, as far as myth is concerned, it is not all the scholars' fault, for very often the vital part the lady plays in the myth is not obvious. Sometimes, for instance, we must infer much of it, as in Chaucer's *Knight's Tale,* where we realise that the mad desires and rages of the two lovers in rivalry for the fair but unattainable Emily is meant to epitomize the whole lunatic state of man; or as in *The Winter's Tale,* where we deduce Leontes' illness to rise from poisoned feelings, the inner 'lady' now become the heart of darkness. At other times, the lady in myth appears in disguise – as a symbol, for example – so that what ill befalls her, of dire effect on all, may be missed or misconstrued. I mean, the cauldron, or the bloodstream, or the heart, or any of a number of feminine symbols may be shown to be poisoned or infected in some way without the reader realising that this is in fact befalling the lady of life and woefully altering the whole spirit and fabric of existence.

There is, besides, another trick in mythical presentations that might further excuse the reader missing this factor of the banefully shifting feminine nature. I'll generalise on this for brevity. In myth, very often, when a lady is lost from the happy or higher world, or stolen from it, or when something of feminine connotation is lost or stolen - a golden necklace perhaps, or a crown, or the golden apples of life, and so on - it denotes, in part, her *alteration* in nature. A sinister alteration. This is especially so when the stealer or means of her loss is a malign being. As an example, when Idun, Persephone, and Eurydice are snatched away from the happy world, their 'loss' bears - to some extent - the sense of 'lost from their true nature': that is, changed into something worse. Ladies of this mythical type, therefore, often suitably take on the character of Queen of the Underworld (or Faery), or the witch, or the winter-queen, and so on. But the point I wish to make here is that this shift of character, or place, because it is to something lower or darker, is an alternative rendering of the lady's sinister alteration by - in other versions - poison or infection, and with an equally grim effect on man's behaviour.

I seem to be hammering at something unimportant here, yet when we get into *Macbeth* in a moment or two (and into Norse myth, so influential in that play), the reader will see importance enough. Perhaps already? I mean, thinking on *Macbeth* in the light of the above, does he now not glimpse more of a link between the golden blood being 'stolen' and the lady's 'wine' being contaminated, or her nourishing body entered by something foul and thereby altered? As if they are Shakespeare's symbolic variants of the same event?

As I said in the last chapter about the Hud myth, the stealing of the hero's 'feminine' blood and the baneful contamination of the lady have an equivalence that is also shown in King Duncan's fate and, as we shall see, in Norse or Germanic myths.

★   ★   ★

In the chapter's preamble above, a number of feminine symbols were mentioned. One of them was a cauldron. I will approach *Macbeth* by way of this symbol, beginning with a story by a writer Shakespeare is known to have studied closely - Ovid, the author of *Metamorphoses.* In this work we find the story of Athamas, as follows:-

The goddess Hera, embittered against Athamas and his wife Ino, went to the underworld to employ the Hecate-like Tisiphone for her purpose of revenge. Tisiphone ('vengeful destruction') at Hera's bidding prepared poisonous snakes, but also in a cauldron concocted a witch's brew of insanity, into which various hellish ingredients were poured. The details of this concoction are worth noting. It was "compounded of foam from Cerberus' jaws, and the venom of the Lernaean hydra, mixed with vague hallucinations, blind forgetfulness, tears, crime and madness, and lust for murder. These she ground up together, moistened with fresh blood, and cooked the mixture in a bronze cauldron, stirring it with a green hemlock stalk."[1] This mixture, and the snakes containing it, were then applied to the sleeping bodies of Athamas and Ino. Athamas, thus afflicted by the venom of madness, despair and murder, killed one of his sons and drove Ino to cast herself with her other son from a cliff into the sea. There was a divine intervention at this point, converting the disaster into the potential of future blessing, but that need not concern us.

Now, I think the reader will have guessed two things. The first is that I see this story of disaster as hiding within its particular form yet another version of a first baneful change in the feminine character, out of which arises a destructive change in the masculine. In other words, it is a kind of Greek version of the 'Story of Eve' or Paradise myth.[2] By this view, Hera, Tisiphone and Ino are to be understood as basically one character into which a poisonous awareness enters and, according with my earlier argument and the usual pattern, causes a division - the 'wicked queen' and the 'fair princess' - affecting in turn the male to act destructively for the former against the latter.

The reader's likely second guess - going by the nightmare ingredients poured into the cauldron - is that I believe this story to have influenced Shakespeare in writing *Macbeth*. Indeed, I see his 'cauldron' scene (Act4 Sc1) as one of three ways in the play that he

---

1   Quoted from Mary M. Innes' *Penguin* edition, p.107

2   Indeed, in early studies of mythology, Athamas was sometimes linked with Adam.

himself shows the crucial change in the feminine character. In the first, he shows Lady Macbeth undergoing a hellish infiltration into her being - the famous "Come you spirits" scene (Act2 Sc5) - making her hostile to the true nature, and affecting her husband to act in accord. Later in the same Act he shows the feminine character as life's feast, which suffers the same poisonous infiltration (the drugging of the drink) and likewise causes the male mind and behaviour to alter - the warping into fantasy or lust (hence the importance of the Porter's words) and into a murderous hatred against life (Macbeth). In the third, the same thing is all shown as a poisoning of the feminine life-cauldron, which then gives forth a monster of destruction as from a poisoned womb.

But there is a major snag to this line of thought, no doubt already spotted by the reader. Shakespeare's cauldron appears in the play long after the destructive madness, such as assailed Athamas, has entered the world of men. Indeed, its appearance at the start of Act 4 comes on the threshold of the restoration, and the future that emerges from it, in a spectacular foreshowing, is only 'hellish' to Macbeth (who does not want to see portents of his own downfall). To the audience, the portents are generally good.

The hellish cauldron therefore seems to be in the wrong place in the text. It should be near the beginning of the play, where darkness gathers, where suggestions of encroaching evil and infernal fantasy are shown, and where there is a suspicion of men having tasted the "insane root". This is where the idea of a dark poison entering the source of life much better fits. And there it would tally also with the alteration of Lady Macbeth, in which she is seen more or less calling hell into her body and bloodstream, as into the natural cauldron of life. There too it would tally with the symbolism of the feast, for Lady Macbeth, like the cauldron of life and nature, is the mistress of the feast whose bounty is likewise shown to change as by an intoxicating bane, changing the restorative powers of nature and sleep into the mother of nightmare, from whose shadows emerges the mad monster, the man of blood.

We need then to re-site the venom-entered cauldron in the play, to take it from a scene where it stumbles into contradiction and mere gothic melodrama (Act4 Sc1) and put it instead into the first

major witch-scene (Actl Sc3). We might even make a case for
exchanging that scene's present opening - the story of "The Master
of the Tyger" - and putting that in the later scene, where it would
in fact better fit, because it symbolises the harsh process in which
the masculine character is purged from its debasement (Macbeth)
into the true man (Malcolm): one of the subjects of Act 4 indeed.

A wild tampering with Shakespeare's 'sacred' text? Not really.
Most Shakespeare scholars would agree that the text we use today
is imperfect and reconstituted, particularly the witch scenes.

So Ovid's story of Athamas, centred on a hellish cauldron, has
proved of some use as an approach to *Macbeth*. There is another
story that seems to hold within it the same idea of a poisoning of
the feminine nature and seems also to connect with *Macbeth*. It is a
Norse story of a warrior's dealing with witches that, as far as I know,
has prompted no interest in commentaries on the play, even though
one detail in it might well have done. The foggy air in which
Shakespeare's witches first appear, and in which presumably
Macbeth first meets them, is not mentioned by either Holinshed or
Stewart (the play's usually cited sources) and yet appears in this
Norse account found in the narratives of Saxo-Grammaticus:-

Höth is Balder's enemy in a major Baltic war, fought partly over
an alluring lady called Nana. One day while out hunting, Höth loses
his way in a fog and comes upon three maidens in a forest hut, who
tell him that they decide the fate of battles, whereupon they vanish
into the air (as in Macbeth), leaving Höth alone on an open field.
He sees them again later, preparing a food which sustains the might
of his rival Balder, in which they are mixing serpent's venom. He
asks for and is granted a taste of this food for himself, along with
their battle-favour, and so defeats and slays Balder.[3]

Now, allowing for distortions that affect old myths - especially
those that survive in revised versions long after their currency -
there might be seen in this account an older meaning such as we
have seen in the Athamas story and such as survives in many myths:
namely, that it was the feminine nature herself that first took in a
'venom' - hence the poison in life's food or sustenance - whose

---

3   The above is a summarised account. A longer version is readily to be found in
     K. Crossley-Holland's *Norse Myths* - p.226-27.

effect then passed into the masculine and created, according with the pattern, a destructive character. In this example, however, as in many versions of the myth appearing in warrior-societies of male supremacy, the destructive character now appears as a 'double' to the original hero, and the victim of destruction is no longer the true feminine nature but the original hero himself.[4]

However, apart from the 'fog' detail and the story's provenance in Saxo-Grammaticus, there is little to support the view that Shakespeare knew the story of Balder and Höth when writing *Macbeth*. I shall leave it simply as a possibility, and for its general interest. If he had read this story, with his usual perception, it would have helped confirm his own intuition while writing *Macbeth* that behind all real violence lies a 'poisoned' feminine nature.

Also confirming this intuition – and a story more likely to have been known to Shakespeare – may have been another Norse myth, which I first mentioned in Chapter 5 in connection with a poison affecting the 'feminine' nature of King Hamlet. This is the story of Freyja and Brisingamen, which seems to shadow Shakespeare's description of Lady Macbeth's infiltration by hellish spirits, and her change then into a 'witch' inciting a monstrous alteration in her masculine partner. The known sources of *Macbeth* make no mention of Lady Macbeth's remarkable self-damnation whereas Freyja's story shows an interesting analogy, both in the demonic invasion of her body and in the darker character that then emerges. This character, for which Freyja was well known in Norse accounts, was that of witch-queen, mighty in incitement to male lusts, erotically and in war, a kind of dark Venus and Bellona in one. However, to give the story:-

Freyja in loneliness went to the underworld to visit the swart-elves. She craved the gold brisingamen, a necklace of their making (that would give her great power over man?).[5] The swart-elves were agreeable but only if she yielded her body to their lusts. Freyja

---

4 This form of the story is very widely found in myth (the main Balder story, for instance, and those of Osiris and Adonis), in romance too, and commonly in Shakespeare's accounts of male rivalry and violence. (This topic will be further examined in Chapter 8, dealing with the Grail romances, and in Appendix F: *The Male Rivals*.)

5 My own surmise by analogy with the magical girdle of Venus.

agreed and gained the magical adornment, and then returned home. Unfortunately, the malign Loki had seen all this, and he told Odin (possibly Od, Freyja's husband). He demanded proof, and so Loki, using his shape-shifting powers, entered Freyja's chamber while she slept, took on the shape of a flea and bit her, causing her to stir and so enable him to reach the clasp of brisingamen. When he later presents Odin with this proof of her sinfulness, Odin's crazed reaction is such as to suggest that here was the cause and the beginning of the terrible character well attested in Norse accounts – the ogrous punisher, destroyer, shadowy lord of war and human sacrifice. In this story, he calls for massive warfare on earth, using Freyja herself as the glamour to battle-madness in the minds of men and gods.[6]

This medieval rendering of older material seems to combine three myths telling the *same* story from a different angle – the story, once again, of the poisoning of awareness in the 'feelings', the feminine side of life, as the cause of a calamitous male violence. In the first of the three (Freyja and the swart-elves), we see the feminine awareness malignly entered and tainted – imaged coitally, as in some accounts of Eve's corruption by the 'serpent'. In the second (Odin and Loki), the dark awareness becomes – again as in Eve's story – a sense of the sinfulness of life, nature, 'woman', now infiltrating the ruling 'mind', with Loki playing the part of Mordred to Arthur (about Guinevere), Iago to Othello, or Iachimo to Posthumus (*Cymbeline*). In the third (Loki in Freyja's chamber), we see the same infection carried out as if by a bite to the sleeping lady. All three lead equally, as in so many myths of a primal feminine alteration, to a violent change in the male character.

However, the *Brisingamen* writer's intuition that all three somehow belong together is not matched by his grasp of the myths involved, and serious distortions arise. For example, he doesn't show why Odin can be so incensed against Freyja and yet use her as an ally – the incitress of men's lust for war. It is left to us to deduce the explanation from parallel myths – that there are in fact *two* Freyjas.

---

6   The Brisingamen story is most accessible to the general reader in Kevin Crossley-Holland's *The Norse Myths* - p.65-69.

The infernal incitress, the 'witch', is the second aspect of the feminine nature resulting from the poisoning, who, as ever is the case, makes a victim of her kinder self now abhorred - the life-form or nature to be punished by male wrath and violence.

As another example of distortion. Loki's taking the necklace to Odin, to prove Freyja's fault, almost certainly falsifies an earlier story in which the lady's change of character - here dimly recalled as due to a poisonous bite on her body - was shown as the loss or theft of her true 'gold' or true 'necklace', denoting the loss of her true nature. We can guess this from the connected Norse story of Idun, in which the fair Lady of Life, imaged alternatively in her golden apples of health and sustenance, is snatched away (stolen) to the underworld as a result of Loki's malign persuasions. There, in clear form, is the 'Persephonal' story of loss and infernal replacement (or change) suffered by the feminine nature, which the Brisingamen romance distorts. We can guess the real story also by deduction from another connected myth, in which the heroic Heimdall has to fight with Loki to *regain* the lost necklace (again imaging the true feminine nature),[7] much as in parallel myths the questing hero has to rescue either the lost lady or her equivalent symbol, including of course the Grail.

We might even deduce some of the true meaning behind this medieval romance by way of the name of the necklace itself. As the term *bris* probably denotes the idea of 'fire', we glimpse that somewhere in the symbolism of the necklace is hinted the change of light into its more destructive form of flame and burning, thereby suggesting the alteration in the feminine character, and in its influence upon man, from one of higher inspiration (light) to one more sinister (fire). Likewise, gold itself, from which the necklace is made, often in myth images both the feminine character and also its ambivalence of power over the male mind. Its being changed, or stolen by some evil underling - goblin, swart-elf, and so forth - so often involves this same change in man's 'feminine' nature and guidance - from the human (or divine) to the infernal.

This leaves us with the story's most glaring distortion of all. As

---

7   Found in what is called the *Husdrapa* fragment.

indicated in the above argument, Freyja never went voluntarily to the underworld in search of an infernal power. The underworld, if anything, came to her. As we have seen in parallel stories of such as Heurodys (*Sir Orfeo*), Persephone, and Eve, the true lady or life's fair queen became the victim of darker forces, causing her nature to divide sinisterly against itself. The *Brisingamen* story, I am fairly sure, is one of a number of cases of a misogynistic bias seriously altering the myth.

My straying a fair way from Shakespeare in dealing with the Freyja story I hope will be allowed by those interested in myth and pardoned by the rest. But now, by this matter of an anti-feminine distortion of the lady's role in the myth, we are brought back in any case to Shakespeare, because what could be taken as his own version of Freyja's fate is equally misogynistic. Lady Macbeth appears just as willing - even eager - to accept dark forces into her being and body, to work infernal change in her nature and in her power over man.

That Shakespeare was influenced by the Freya/Brisingamen story can scarcely ever be proved, but what makes it more likely is that he seems to use other Norse elements in *Macbeth,* which we will now look into.

★   ★   ★

Of the other Norse features in *Macbeth,* one will start to show when we recall the earlier mentioned symbolism of the feminine nature as life's sustaining 'feast'. Mythology provides us with many examples of this feast of life's joy going poisonously awry, two of which are in Norse stories. One of them tells of Kvasir, a god-figure of kindliness and wisdom, whose blood was seen as the wonderful wine or mead by which life was sustained and made joyful. One day he attends a feast, invited by the eerie swart-elves who, though later claiming that he has mysteriously gone away in a mood of great pride, themselves stab him to death and drain him of his blood, to make for themselves a rich mead. Thus the Norse poets pictured the loss or theft of the divine mead or wine of life, their 'Grail' fluid of vital joy and sustenance. Reading this might remind us how the kindly King Duncan in *Macbeth* attends a feast that likewise turns treacherous and murderous, dealing him a similar bloody end. But more than this, notice the imagery that Shakespeare uses for the crime, as if in mind of Kvasir's fate - that of life *stolen,* followed by "…the wine of life is drawn, and the mere lees is left this vault to brag on" and "…the spring, the head, the fountain of your blood is stopp'd, the very source of it is stopp'd".[8] It is also of interest that in a possibly related Norse myth the slaying of an original god (Ymir) turns the seas to blood, because this too figures in Macbeth's reflections as he visualises that his bloody hands will "…rather the multitudinous seas incarnadine, making the green one red".

There is something else in this blood symbolism to consider. Despite the attempt of many patriarchal users of the myth (including the Christian) to make its divine symbols and features wholly 'masculine', this primal blood, like the cauldron or the later Grail, sometimes kept traces of feminine connotation. In Norse accounts, accordingly, the loss of Kvasir's blood is noticeably paralleled, in its significance and be-wintering effect, by the violent loss of Lady Idun to the underworld. Shakespeare similarly uses of Duncan's bloody death images of woman-violation (2.1.55) or woman-murder (2.2.35-9) - and possibly, indeed, by recognizable Norse influence since one of the attributes of the kindly nature that Macbeth imagines he has slain exactly matches with Idun - "chief nourisher in Life's feast" - and, further, Idun's associations with gold seem to be remembered in the imagery of gold used of Duncan's blood.

There is yet more to this imagery, about which an earlier point is worth repeating. Gold is often an ambivalent symbol in myth, connoting the higher/divine and, as readily, its infernal counterpart: the glitter of base-mindedness or lust. As a symbol of man's aim and inspiration to action - whether nobly or basely - it links with the feminine as the factor of instigation in all his behaviour. The loss or change of the primal divine gold of Idun or Freyja in Norse myth therefore marks a sinister alteration in that feminine nature and the kind of instigation she exercises. Likewise in *Macbeth,* the blood of King Duncan, claimed (above) to be both of a higher feminine nature and of a higher 'gold', seems to contrast with the gold of lady

8 2.3.93-97

Macbeth's infernal eagerness – the "golden round" of power – as she herself transforms darkly into a witch-power over man's ambition. This is the equivalent of Freyja becoming "The Hag" or the gold-hungry *Gulveig* of man's baser desires.[9]

A like ambivalence is found in the symbolism of the blood of life, the wine or mead of a higher nature, with which the 'gold' is linked. Its being stolen or debased by the lower beings, in the Norse, seems to denote its change into a lower kind of incitement or inspiration, as in drunkenness – a 'poisoning' of the higher blood of life that brings darker fantasies to the mind – just as was claimed to happen to the feminine cauldron itself: a poisoning that in turn infernally darkened man's whole cast of thought and desire. The drunkenness on the night of Duncan's murder accordingly may be part of the whole picture of a change in the feminine 'blood' as the motivation of self's fantasies. The same idea may have been used by Shakespeare in the drunkenness of such as self-seeking Falstaff, Stephano (*The Tempest*), or in that of Cassio (*Othello*), which is arranged poisonously by the devilish Iago and reflects on the larger picture of Othello's own darkened fantasies of lust and murder. The same symbolism applies to the drunken feasting of Claudius in *Hamlet,* for this too seems to be a reminder of a past murderous debasement.

Touching here is another Kvasir myth, recorded obscurely, and maybe incorrectly, dealing with an account of the gods creating Kvasir in a pot by spitting into it and forming thereby the god who became synonymous with the divine mead. In the possibility of something here mis-recorded, even of two stories muddled into one, we might see, by the realisation that saliva is a natural yeast, that it is actually giving yet another account of a 'poison' entering the primal bloodstream, the mead of life. It therefore explains what really went wrong at Kvasir's feast, as with Lady Macbeth's, or as in the feast shadowed in the context of Hamlet's speech about the "eale" or yeast, closely followed by an account of a poison in the

---

9   In the story of Asgard, Freyja's changed and sinister character is called 'Hag (or witch) of Ironwood' and 'Gold-Hungry' (Gulveig). As such, she roused the madness that ravaged Asgard, just as the shimmering power of Helen set on the ravaging of Troy.

bloodstream and a long-ago monstrousness.

There are things in *Macbeth* (and in *Hamlet*) that are not in usually recognised sources and seem to have been Shakespeare's own adaptation from some Norse derivative. We can only guess what existed then in tavern-tale, mariner's yarn, folktale - like the Jack-and-Jill and Jack-and-the-Giant stories - for the likelihood is that we shall never know. So we will go on being goaded by the odd suggestive detail or puzzling similarity. Why, for instance, do the stealers of power in those myths (the swart-elves or 'dwarfs') seem to be remembered knowingly in Shakespeare's description of Macbeth - "dwarfish thief"? Or why does Macbeth's journey to the oracular cavern, not found in known sources, resemble Odin's journey to the underworld to know the future?

This last-mentioned detail in fact leads to a point of interest. The way it links Macbeth and Odin sparks the possibility that Shakespeare knew not only an 'Odin' story now lost but one more accurate than the account of Odin's journey that survives. Either that or it is a case of inspiration proving staggeringly acute. But to explain this. The Norse myths show Odin, as Balder's anxious father, going to the prophetess (Volva) in the underworld, hoping to avert his son's death, or, as some think, seeking Balder's release from Hel after his death. Whichever, it is far different from Macbeth's purpose for the visit - hoping to gain foreknowledge and so avert his own downfall. And yet other stories about Odin, not least that of his monstrous change in the Brisingamen account, show him as a blood-thirsty god of war and sacrifice. Indeed, this is his best-known character. Shakespeare may have come across a story showing Odin in this light, and therefore matching his character of Macbeth - perhaps even one showing Odin not as the concerned father of Balder but his slayer, and not going into the underworld in fear of Balder's death but, like Macbeth, in fear of the hero's return.

★   ★   ★

The Norse presence in some of Shakespeare's work is hard to fix and evaluate, and yet ever beckons to us for recognition. Let me review some of this:-

The ghost's account in *Hamlet,* we saw earlier, combines the idea of a virulent awareness of sin (implied by the 'Fall' theme) and the symbolic idea of a poison entering the 'feminine' blood and body, with monstrous effect on the masculine character. Just before this, Hamlet reflects on a corrupting presence in man's make-up ("So oft it chances in particular men...") like an "eale" (yeast), which again, by way of the Gospels ("the leaven of the pharisees"), links with the idea of a dangerous and damaging sin-awareness. Further, not only do the ideas of the two Hamlets seem to connect; they seem, though obscurely, to connect also with the event going on at the same time – Claudius's feast of drunken revelry – as if this, too, illustrates the effect of a poison or 'leaven' in the blood (as in the wine), turning it from a power of health to one of malice. As it did perhaps in some calamity long ago?

Some clarification on this seems to come when we realise that a similar linkage of ideas and events appears in Norse myth in the context of feasts turning foul (and perhaps causing some primal catastrophe). In one, subhuman forces emerge and turn murderously against the divine Kvasir, who was elsewhere shown to have his blood (the mead of joy) marred by a yeast, which perhaps explains why the feast itself turned bad. Another (a version of the same?) takes place in the hall of Aegir, the guardian of life's cauldron of joy and sustenance. This feast was also fouled by a poisonous factor – Loki's baleful accusations of fault and sin in the lives of the gods and goddesses present – which possibly brought on a calamitous violence.

Shakespeare returned to pretty much the same pattern of symbolism and meaning in *Macbeth,* five years later, with what seems a more definite Norse presence. This shows in the linked symbolism of the gold, the blood, the wine, the feast and the cauldron, which Shakespeare seems to apply to yet another story of a femininity suffering dark alteration and bringing a catastrophic change, in turn, to the masculine character. The femininity of these symbols is partly confirmed by their all being centred on the sinister alteration of the play's major feminine personage, Lady Macbeth. Also partly confirmed here is the Norse influence in the play, because this episode is similar in idea and outcome to the equally sinister and fateful change in the nature of Freyja.

★   ★   ★

END NOTE

On the night of Duncan's murder, Shakespeare matches the horror inside the castle with a description of wild events outside. By this is conveyed the violence of the Fall, as often occurs near the start of his plays. What blurs this meaning is that there is much disorder and violence in the play before Duncan's murder – the opening battle scenes. It is another case of source material clashing with the pattern of 'myth' that Shakespeare intends. So, in a number of ways, he helps us imaginatively to connect the opening violence with the later murder, as the same event, symbolically viewed. For example, he markedly links the first Cawdor – the rebel of the opening violence – with the second (Macbeth) who centres the later violence. Likewise he starts the play with a witch scene followed by massive slaughter, to foreshadow the witch-like change in Lady Macbeth that precedes equal violence.

★   ★   ★

Chapter 8
Of Titania and Sycorax, and of the Grail

One of the remarkable things about *Midsummer Night's Dream* is that this relatively early play so clearly outlines a story-pattern that Shakespeare, whatever his sources and sometimes despite them, was often to follow throughout his career as a playwright. Another remarkable thing is the way this play, both by its pattern and mythic composition, foreshadows particularly his later romances. When we compare it, for instance, with his final summing-up of both his career and his dramatic art, *The Tempest,* and see the marked similarities, we have a sense that much of his mature artistic period was a sort of perambulation about the same story-wood, by which he returned finally to the same spot. And on that spot he reaffirmed, where he had first affirmed it, an allegiance to myth as the magical mirror in which could be formed the cyclical destiny of life.

It was a myth that, moreover, was dealt with by many before him, perhaps in a tradition that went back to the earliest mystical and religious conceptions of life, in which Nature, the divine, as well as Man, were seen to trace together the cycle of sorrow and eventual blessedness, when the 'sexual' forces grown contrary, and having plunged themselves into this terrain of fantasies we call life, would at last change from their distortions, as from the costumes of a tragi-comic drama, and find again their long-lost Summer and its Marriage.

★　　★　　★

As is now to be expected of the story-pattern, the opening of *Midsummer Night's Dream* deals with the breakdown of a first golden state of harmony, as the mind and energies of man turn dark and destructive to the life they should sustain. As equally to be expected, the change is due to something that has altered in the feminine side of life's composition, later mainly figured in the play as Titania, the Queen of the Night. There is no need to know of Eve's story, as examined earlier, for us to see this. Simple fairy tale will suffice: 'When the Lady with the Witch is twinned, then wise King twins with Beast'.

As soon as Theseus, the ruler, appears in moony preoccupation, which he supposes being in love, we know what is to come. This fateful self-absorption in the ruler, whatever the variety of ways in which it shows in Shakespeare's plays, is ever the first step towards violence and the loss of the first, higher realm. We see the ruling mind already enmeshed in emotionally darkened attitudes, as within the embrace of something balefully feminine – call it pride, or self, or whatever other fantasy seems best to explain a weakening in the directing mind, and its loss of sharp, true vision. Theseus is in love, but with himself, as surely as Lear is at the start of that later play. Whatever the ostensible name of his bride-to-be, we might say the real mistress of his heart is called 'Titania', a power that will bring on disaster as this emotional darkness in the ruler inevitably spreads to all.

And, sure enough, almost immediately the rule of *the-self-in-all* is proclaimed, as Egeus and Lysander enter with their conflicting demands of truth and right – *my* feelings as truth: *my* feelings as right – fantasies to be chased or affirmed, at whatever cost to life, nature, or kindness, that by contrast seem unimportant or unworthy. We are already in this first scene within a few steps of Titania's wood, where the lovers later behave likewise – on one side, the pursuit of a dream-realisation, as if in lust for a "goddess", to complement the dark queen already in their hearts; and, on the other, a cruelty to any real truth or kindness. The victim of the witch, through the behaviour of man, is ever her true nature.

Shakespeare in this play does not show how the feminine nature took on this power of dark control – how she twinned with the powerful witch. He does not indicate a first 'poison', like a self-hatred or a life-hatred, as he was to do in some later plays, but he shows clearly enough its outcome. Man falls under a powerful feminine sway, like the "boy-child" we hear of later, who seems to image the whole masculine character in Titania's determined embrace. The same determination of control shows also – in a perhaps misleadingly comic way – in her power over Bottom, whose transformation into a beast also images the effect of the witch's spell upon the masculine character. I say "misleadingly comic" because we are likely in the farcical context to overlook the serious connections of this 'ass' image. Once we realise, however, that the 'ass' in Shakespeare's plays connects with the murderous Claudius in *Hamlet*,[1] and with the destructive Caliban,[2] and when we further remember how it figured the character of Satan in medieval symbolism,[3] and also Set, Osiris' destructive double, in Egyptian myth, we then see more of the point. The pictorial image of the beast, as often in myth and fairy tale, denotes the transformation of the masculine character by the 'witch of self' into something subhuman and life-destructive.

Life-destructive. This is the most tragic result of the fateful plunge of the masculine spirit into the darkness of the self. It is shown in many of Shakespeare's plays, most frighteningly in *Macbeth,* in which a far more hellish 'Titania' turns man into a far more terrifying 'monster'; but the clearest illustration of the actual process of transformation is found in *King Lear.* Here we see how the accession of the self as the ruling factor (imaged partly in Goneril and Regan - the "hags") is due to an underlying life-hatred, which, both in itself and through a hardening of life's free flexibilities, frustrates and inflames the creative energies, the masculine spirit, into a destructive force - the murderer of his own life-form, his own 'wife', the original Paradise.

This brings us to the massive derangement of life described in Act 2 of *Midsummer Night's Dream* - the wild upheaval in Nature that features in the "debate" of Titania and Oberon, augmenting on a large scale the theme of discord already seen in the Court of Athens. Often in Shakespeare's plays, and in accord with the story-pattern I first outlined in Chapter 1, there occurs an event of marked disruption or violence, to denote the end of the first higher state and the plunge into this mortal world of ordeal. In my idea of Nature myth, this first violence connects with the Fall (Autumn) and the first onset of wrecking Winter, which survived in later religious myth, when the idea of a spiritual 'fall' was equally linked

---

1   3.2.278

2   *The Tempest* 5.1.295

3   Satan was linked symbolically with the ass, upon which Christ eventually rode in triumph.

with some event of violence. As this event was often pictured as a natural calamity - eruption, storm, flood, etc. - and not least in the Old Testament, we are warned to look more closely at this description of natural upheaval in *Midsummer Night's Dream.*

In looking at this, it quickly becomes clear that Shakespeare is not merely remembering some unseasonal weather in the early 1590's. There is significance hinted at in the detail of his description, starting with the reminders of Ovid's account of Deucalion's Flood.[4] This classical Flood account would have been equated in Shakespeare's day with the biblical account (Noah's Flood) - such being the practice of linking pagan and biblical stories. But, more than this, Noah's Flood was then linked further with other instances of universal calamity recorded in the Bible - including the one befalling the first happier state or Paradise.[5]

This, in fact, gives us a true focus on Shakespeare's description of the elemental upheaval in Act 2, in which it is fairly clearly revealed that he is not only thinking of the Fall but thinking of it - as in some other of his plays - in a quite heretical way. The violence is not, as glossed in the Bible, that of a justified deity upon sinful nature, but one perpetrated by the masculine life-character that has become destructively deranged. As ever in the myth-pattern we have considered, a 'sexual' disharmony has resulted in the masculine side of life becoming life-wrecking. The 'summer-king', the 'Theseus', has become the 'winter-king' (one aspect of Oberon) by a change in the 'queen - or, in the fairy-tale terms used earlier, the 'king' has been turned into a 'beast' by the alteration in his feminine partner: the coming of the 'witch'.

By this consideration, much of Titania's description of the chaos in Nature falls into place. With the Fall in mind, for instance, we see why this quarrel of the Fairy King and Queen reminds us of the one in Chaucer's *Merchant's Tale,* in which a version of the Fall was being

---

4   As noted in most editorial commentary, Shakespeare in writing this play was much influenced by Ovid's *Metamorphoses.*

5   The equating of Old Testament life-obliterating disasters - usually involving God's wrath upon his creation - is not simply a quaint medieval practice. Modern scholarship is sometimes in agreement. See, for example, S.H. Hooke's *Middle Eastern Mythology,* particularly p.105-8 & 139-43.

written. We also see more point to the seasonal dislocation described. It is the chaos of the seasons which was thought by our forebears to be the intermediate stage between the uni-seasonal harmony of Eden and the cyclical, seasonal compromise of our fallen state.[6] Perhaps above all, though, something that Titania says at the end of her description now shapes as a clear reminder of Adam and Eve - "And this same progeny of evils comes from our debate, from our dissension; *we are their parents and original*" (2.1.115).

We realise also that the chaos of life-energies she describes connects with the destructiveness we have generally seen affecting the masculine character in other mythical accounts of the Fall. In the case of this play, the one who mainly represents the 'man-gone-wild' is Oberon. Indeed, as the dark, demonic lord of the wood - a type of Herne, Hud, or Robin's darker 'twin' - he is quite recognisable as a folklore version of the original winter-king, the earlier Nature myth's destructive aspect of the summer-king, who survived in some developed forms of the cyclical myth as a figure combining ogrousness and destinal intelligence - The Green Knight in the *Gawain* story, for example.

As Oberon is fairly obviously a demonic 'twin' of the original 'summer' ruler, Theseus, we can understand why he is so angry with Titania for turning Theseus into a rapist - "Didst thou not lead him through the glimmering night from Perigouna, whom he ravishèd?"[7] It is *he* who has been thus transformed into something violent, and the rape - often in myth denoting the first violence - is therefore part of the whole picture of destructiveness in the male that in this part of the play is shown to befall life.

To sum up on this point. Titania is the central character of *Midsummer Night's Dream*. She is the dark will that enslaves and operates through all masculine behaviour. Her captivation and be-monstering of Bottom, her hold on the boy-child, her presence in Hermia and Helena as the motivation of the youths' insanities of 'love' and hate, her possession of Egeus in self-righteous tyranny and of Lysander in rebellion, her transformation of the original ruler into a demon of storms and destruction ... all these are

6   The same idea is found in the Demeter/Persephone myth.
7   2.1.77-78

manifestations of her power. It is why her defeat by the magical remnant mind (an aspect of Oberon's character) and her reclamation through surrender are so important in the restoration of sanity and human wholeness.

★   ★   ★

In the same way, though she is supposed to have died before the play begins, Sycorax is the central character of *The Tempest,* right from the first calamity in Milan up to her final surrender as the powerful Venus in Act 4.[8] Strange though it may seem, someone who never actually appears, as such, in the play is nevertheless of major importance.

To see some of this, we might look at the first disaster in Milan, which ended in a destructive storm – for, if rightly viewed, Prospero's storm was not a later event, as the surface of the story makes out, but the calamitous violence that, as often in the myth (and, not least, Shakespeare's versions), finally wiped out the first world.

So what happened in 'Milan'? And what had it to do with Sycorax? Prospero tells Miranda how, long ago, in pursuit of "secret studies" he had neglected his duties as Duke of Milan, and had made his brother (Antonio) the acting head of state. Upon this, Antonio had grown ambitious and gradually replaced him. About this replacement Shakespeare uses two interesting images:

"…That now he was the ivy which had hid my princely trunk, and suck'd my verdure out on 't." (1 .2.85-87)

and: –

"… my trust , like a good parent, did beget of him a falsehood… he did believe he was indeed the duke…" (1.2.93-103)

The point to the first quotation is that it involves what we might call 'Sycorax in disguise'. We can see this by fixing on the *ivy* image. This image of vegetative entrapment was used by Ovid in the story of Hermaphroditus: the story of a male becoming enslaved to a sinister feminine power. Moreover, Shakespeare had used the same image to show Titania's power earlier, and for the same meaning –

---

8 4.1.86-100

the entrapment of Bottom to her world and will - "So doth the woodbine the sweet honeysuckle gently entwist; the *female ivy* so enrings the barky fingers of the elm".[9] The hero in that case was changed by the captivation into an animal.[10] What we are thus told by the image in *The Tempest,* in agreement with the other myths we have considered, is how a sinister feminine force transformed the masculine into something inhuman or monstrous. Symbolically speaking, Antonio is not so much the Duke's brother, as realism presents, but the Duke's own darker self - the transformation that ever arises in the myth through a feminine power.

The second quotation carries this idea further. In so many myths of the first masculine transformation from the human (or divine) into the beast, from the wise into the destructive, the process is sexually imaged, as implied here in the image of 'begetting'. In these myths, instead of the ruler falling for feminine enslavement (his pride) and turning into a monster, the process of falling in love with himself is shown as his seduction by a femme fatale and his 'begetting' his own monstrousness. It is commonly found. Arthur's turning destructive, for instance, is alternatively imaged as his begetting a destructive character - Mordred. Likewise Satan in legend is shown to beget Cain, or (in Milton) to beget the ravaging character of Death. Equally the angels in lust for the daughters of earth begot the destructive giants, the Nephelim,[11] and likewise Bergelmir (Farbauti) in the Norse story sired the demonic Loki.

And in Shakespeare's work? Gloucester's story (*King Lear*) images sexually this same change from ruling mind into destructiveness - he begot Edmund. Likewise in the above description of the first Duke of Milan being changed in character Shakespeare uses the image of a begetting. This explains why

---

9   4.1.41-3

10 Bottom was actually changed into an ass by Puck - yes, but by Puck using the powers of Titania's realm.

11 The Bible has various mythic explanations for the first violence by which an original world was wrecked. One of them was the emergence of a race of destructive giants - the progeny of the angels in lust. (A story much elaborated in the *Book of Enoch.*) These destructive beings were the counterparts of the rebellious giants, or Titans, in Greek myth, and of the monstrous Typhon, the giant of storms.

Caliban, the rapist, whose first violence duplicates Prospero's own violence - the storm - is implied to be the offspring of Prospero himself - "…this thing of darkness I acknowledge mine"[12] What we are thus indirectly told is that the 'father' of Caliban was the Duke (alias Prospero). Setebos, the Devil, cited as Caliban's father through Sycorax,[13] was therefore the Duke himself become his own devil of lust and self-fantasy, 'begetting' a monstrousness just as surely as the destructive storm in *Pericles* was 'begotten' from a dark lust - in that case involving self-love imaged as incest.[14]

What it comes down to is that in *The Tempest* the story of a ruler turning into his own monster of vengeance and destruction is given an alternative rendering that is sexually imaged - the ruler siring his own monstrous 'twin' through a feminine enslavement (denoting the pride) in this play represented by Sycorax.

We might see, in passing, why Shakespeare is so obscure in giving us Prospero's story, hiding behind hint and image. It is another case of the 'fallen god' heresy. Prospero is, after all, later in the play so much cast in the role of 'Jehovah' (the storm-god of destiny working the process of life back to a paradise regained) that Shakespeare has no option but to be indirect. Was he blatantly to come out with the idea that God through his own folly in pride and lust created the Satan destructive to the first Paradise?

There are other ways by which Shakespeare indicates retrospectively that the power of Sycorax was at work in the downfall of Milan. First, the many echoes of Troy's story in the play bear the implication that Milan as the first illustrious state is this play's equivalent of golden Troy. This is partly confirmed by the act of treachery by which Milan finally fell, which is like the fate of Troy

---

12 5.1.275

13 Though the name 'Setebos' was taken from a contemporary explorer's account, Shakespeare may have found it useful in its combining the elements *Set* and *bos* ('bull'), and thus linking in idea with the Osiris myth, in which the destructive 'twin' of the true ruler is called Set, whose animal forms included the red-haired bull. (There may be some explanation here of Caliban as the "moon-calf".)

14 Incest involved in the first lust is commonly found in myth. (Two examples may in fact shadow King Lear - the biblical story of Lot and his daughters, and some versions of the 'Cinderella' story in which the father's intent on his daughter is incestuous.)

– "…whereon, a treacherous army levied, one midnight fated to the purpose, did Antonio open the gates of Milan; and i' th' dead of darkness…".[15] The further underlying implication is that if Troy's ruin was caused by a sinister feminine power – Helen – then so also was Milan's. And this indeed must point to Sycorax, who is as strongly linked with Venus as ever Helen was.

Secondly, if we look at Antonio's temptation of Sebastian soon after their arrival on the island, we see not only the continuing presence of Sycorax as the 'spell' to man's ruthless desires, but the further implication of her similar role in Milan. I will explain. The dream-persuasion of Sebastian to murderous usurpation so much resembles Lady Macbeth's upon her husband,[16] that we are almost forced to consider something balefully 'feminine' at work; but then also realise that, as this episode *repeats* the fantasy that befell Antonio himself in Milan earlier, then that 'feminine' influence – the self-dream – must itself have operated there.

Thirdly, there appears the temptation of Ferdinand to a similar rebellion.[17] This also is probably meant, in part, as a repeat showing of the rebellion in Milan, for Ferdinand, whatever his romantic moonshine, is impelled like the earlier rebel (Antonio) by the wishes of the self regardless of obligation to others. And what images this self-ambition? The shimmering beauty of Miranda. And what other figure ever lurks in beauty's power to captivate the mind of man? In short, Ferdinand's drawing his sword upon Prospero re-enacts the first usurpation, and its motive now being imaged in Miranda must be imaged also in Sycorax, for she is Miranda's linked personality.

To sum up on this point. Just as Titania was the central factor invisibly at work in the Court of Athens, which represents in the play the first 'golden' world of humanity, so Sycorax is indicated to have been at work in the original 'Milan'. And in both cases the result is the same. Imaged in both plays variously as rape, rebellion, wrathful vengeance, and a massively destructive upheaval of the

---

15   1.2.127-130   (As a further link between Troy and Prospero's first state it is useful to recall that in one version of Troy's destruction the cause was a vengefully raised sea-tempest.)

16   A resemblance well recognised in commentaries on the play.

17   Act 1, Scene 2

elements, the result is the turning of the masculine character into a force destructive to life. It is a truism of the myths we have considered in this study. They tell the same story about some long-ago disaster that wiped out a primal world. Whether we look at Asgard's fate, or that of Troy or Paradise, or whether we simply look at fairy tales, which often record the same deep wisdom, the same fact emerges as it did in my first concocted Nature myth of Chapter 1. Something banefully turned the lady of life into division, with a force of hate and selfhood thus set against her own nature of love and kindness, as against her own flesh, and then, so powerful upon the masculine mind and action, she turned him into a beast, a violater of that true life, that true bride.

★   ★   ★

The Process of Redemption

I have so far in this chapter, and generally in this study, given much attention to the way the myth shows things going wrong in the first higher state of life, and to the way that 'wrong' persists in this world, pictured in the myth as the world of quest or ordeal. From now on, I shall concentrate more on the happier aspect or purpose to the myth's central ordeal, seeing it as the necessary purging process whereby the cycle of destiny moves into its reformative or redemptive stage upwards to the finally reclaimed higher state of life.

When we look at the start of *The Tempest,* we see a violence - the storm - that, as often in Shakespeare, represents how a wild destructiveness in the male finally wiped away the first state; and when we look further into the play, we see how that villainy persists in the male character. All - with the exception of Gonzalo, the old counsellor - are influenced by the attitudes of the self, which makes them all but different degrees or aspects of Caliban, the destroyer. And this includes even Prospero himself, for, though on one side he is a wise intelligence, he is nonetheless, like many wizards and ogres of romance (and like not a few gods of myth), in the grip of a life-hatred, a spirit of self-righteous vengeance, that renders him also, in part, a 'Caliban'. In this way, in this subjection to the self, all the male personages are in the hold of the one who represents the self - that feminine, quasi-emotional entity who figures often as the Witch, and in this story as Sycorax.

At the same time, there is a glimmer of a lost humanity in all. I have already mentioned the uncanny intelligence of Prospero, which is like the remnant of a lost great mind to a body of life that once existed. In the same way, there is a glimmer of the true 'prince' in the Caliban, figured as Ferdinand, and of the true 'princess' in the Sycorax, figured as Miranda: the lost 'sexual' partnership of a virile life-creativity and of a loving, human kindness. It is Prospero's purpose to bind together these two meanwhile marred and contrary forces in life, so that they mutually strengthen what is human in them, and weaken what is bad, and so finally realise between them a lost unity of harmony as in "paradise" or the "golden age" (using the play's own terms).

In this process of reform, Prospero's grand experiment, we see that even what is base is put to service, working even against its baseness its own refinement. In the following way.

What is wrong with us, at its simplest, is self or pride, that ever makes of the masculine character in us – the mind and creative energies – a fantasist of self-seeking and a destroyer of what is natural and kind. Putting this in equally simple mythical terms, we might say that our distortions of character are, on one side, a 'witch' and, on the other, a 'monster': or, as in Shakespeare's ballad, a "hag" and a "hungry goblin".[18] Now, in pondering on these two sides of our inhumanity, something strikes us. The two sides, though base and inhuman, can serve a humanising purpose. They can to some extent be set to work one against the other, to cancel one another out, so to speak. And this is part of Prospero's method.

Let me give examples. We know, to start with, that something weakening or even breaking to our pride is pain. So amass all the different kinds of pain – all life's hardships, griefs, disappointments, ailments, and so on – and we can see straight away how these, though an evil, have generally the effect of humbling us. We can say therefore that the cruelty factor in life, the destructive spirit – the 'monster' – as well as being hurtful to what is true and kind, can also

---

18 *The Ballad of Loving Mad Tom.* See Appendix A.

be hurtful and ravaging to our pride. So, we might say, using mythic terms, that the 'monster' can serve to break the 'witch'. In biblical terms - using the story of Job as an example - we might say that the 'Satan' of afflictions, the Bible's equivalent of life's 'monster', can likewise serve to a good end - the humbling of Job's pride - and therefore be a means by which the understanding and true vision will be fostered. In all, the 'monster', the dark side of life's masculine energy, is in a way a kind of saviour in frightening disguise, like the Grisly Beard or Beast of fairy tale, a 'ravisher' who actually works the return of the resistant feminine heart to 'fruitfulness'.

We can see this idea in so many stories - in dark Oberon's intent to humble Titania, for example, or in the sorrows of Lear, as his pride suffers the breaking fears and cruelties of life's monstrous forces, the "foul fiend", for his true sight and understanding to be restored. And we can see also why Prospero, as the God-figure behind the same process in *The Tempest,* makes use of the same 'monster' of pains and afflictions against the characters in his power: the two Italian parties, Caliban, Ferdinand, and even Miranda, who is made to suffer in sympathy. It is all to weaken the strength of Sycorax, the pride, within them, for without the breaking of pride there can be no acceptance of truth or true understanding. Where hearts are hard, minds are barren also.

This idea of the 'monster' and his breaking role against pride, the 'witch', introduces another feature of Shakespeare's plays. Once we realize that the destructive is simply another aspect of the productive, as seen in any artistic or innovative process, where the making of the new is ever attended by a 'violence' upon what already is, then we see how the 'monster' and the 'artist' are part of the same masculine character. This is shown in Shakespeare's grasp of the masculine role in life's restorative ordeal. For example, in Hamlet we see that the demon of potential violence is also, once developed, the creative genius of new form, 'violating' now the false forms of art, "habit", "custom", and his mother's proud heart and attitudes, in order to create something new and fine. As this process is run alongside his 'creative' sexual threat on Ophelia, the point is made that this doubleness of the masculine character - part 'violater', part 'creator' - is imaged also in his sexual role in life.

By this, we see that Ferdinand's final consummating act upon Miranda (the marriage rites) stands for the whole process of creativity that Prospero has enjoined him to: converting him from a negative destroyer (a 'Caliban') into a creative power, working upon the feminine form the ultimate 'work of art', the restored Paradise.

A similar idea is used in *The Winter's Tale,* where, alongside the breaking effect of affliction, pain and remorse upon the pride, there is found (briefly) the idea of "art" making the feminine "nature" into its true form.[19] It is also shown in the image of Time as a destinal figure, continually breaking and re-making the forms of life.[20] But it is most clearly brought out in the making of Hermione's statue, shadowing the Pygmalion story, in which the 'violence' of the sculpting masculine artist upon the hard feminine form – the rock – is wedded to the idea of a creative process whereby the true Feminine, like a work of art, is finally produced: the restored kindness and beauty of life.

Thus the masculine as monster and innovator, breaker and maker, is portrayed in life's process. And in all this, we have not travelled far from our original myth of Chapter 1 – the Nature myth – in which the 'wrath' or 'violence' of the winter-king upon the resistant, wintry form of Nature (his 'queen') was both a cruelty and yet a means of softening her to receive at last the idea or seed of a new Spring, which was behind his violence all along. The only real difference between that primitive myth and many of Shakespeare's versions (including *The Tempest*) is that the winter-king, as often in myth and romance, has divided into two figures – the dark director to the process, and the 'energies' (a younger figure) whom he directs in that process. We shall look further at this matter shortly.

Now, to take our bearings, I will remind the reader that the last point began in our recognising that Prospero was using what is debased in the masculine and feminine forces of life – the 'monster' and the 'witch' – for a process in which the two sides might break and refine themselves. Having looked at the way the 'monster' can be used against the 'witch', we can now logically look at the way the

---

19 Part of the idea behind Polixenes' words – 4.4.88-97.

20 The Chorus at the start of Act 4.

'witch' is employed against the 'monster' - likewise to break and refine. We have seen something of this already, in the above argument - the notion of the artistic process, in which the resistance of 'feminine' form helps to convert the urge of violence into the urge to re-make, and to bring out as by a sublimation the creative idea or vision that lurks darkly in the male impulse for destruction.

In the same way, as once widely recognised in mystical thought, all this life of formal limitation and resistance, this material world, is like a woman also, which imprisons, frustrates and disciplines the male spirit, refining him and keenly transmuting his power of mind and impulse. It is a prison that is also a reformatory. The idea is commonly found in older symbolic literature, where we see so often the feminine as the bond upon the man in this life, both inwardly on his desires and aspirations and outwardly as the form of the world in which he seeks and struggles. Whether it is Hamlet, bowing to his mother in obedience at the start of his "prison" reform,[21] or whether it is Chaucer's rapist-knight under the bonds of the hag, or whether it is Leontes of *The Winter's Tale,* bound to the hard lady of discipline (and the statue of rock), the idea is the same. The feminine, though a genius of man's bondage, though a witch of his thraldom, is also the domina in the magic of his refinement. This is a central truth of the myth in so many of its variants.

There is one particular way that the 'witch' can be used to break the 'monster', to change him back into the 'prince'. If we return to the idea of the 'witch' being, in part, the power of man's own ego or pride, we shall see it.

Let us say, to start with, that many of man's endeavours, aspirations and schemes in this life are partly self-centred. He wishes to gain something for himself and achieve the prize, in whatever small or large way. So pride is a major motivation in him, reflected outwardly in all manner of desired goals, glittering objects, and (in romance so often) the ultimate 'goddess' to be gained. And yet in seeking out that prize, that darkly shimmering realisation of his self-dream, he finds he has to make sacrifices, deny himself this or that immediate comfort or satisfaction. Sometimes in a very big way. So

---

21 "I shall in all my best obey you, madam." - 1.2.120

the process of achieving pride's goal, the 'queen' of his hopes, can actually work against his pride and self, and his pursuit of the 'self' paradoxically teach self-sacrifice.

This idea lies behind many romances, especially those that deal with amorous quest or 'Courtly Love', in which so often the point is made. The Queen of Pride turns out to be the Queen of man's discipline and re-nurture, his teacher into true manhood, usually with some final sacrifice on his part for that manhood to be achieved. This process appears clearly, for example, in Chaucer's *Franklin's Tale,* in which Aurelius's ego is martyred in the cause of ego, imaged in the divinely pure and almost unattainable Dorigen. It is clear also in *The Tempest,* where it is used by Prospero on Ferdinand, to turn him from a part-Caliban into a whole Prince. Miranda is used as his pride's goal, or its image, for which he will do anything - even, at length, learn to sacrifice that pride. And with that pride there is also sacrificed of course the monster in man that pride ever creates. Altogether, just as we have earlier seen how the 'monster' can be set to break and refine the 'witch', so we see above a case in which that 'witch' of life can be used, even against herself, to slowly eliminate the 'monster' in man. It is a process in which our myth-writers keenly perceived the strange ambivalence of the feminine character: that what is so strong to debase and bind the male is also right powerful in his re-nurture, his 're-naturing'. 'She' that can turn noble prince into frightful beast, can yet from that beast return the prince. 'She' that brought on the Fall can also bring on the salvation.

By this idea, we look more closely at one of Shakespeare's first portrayals of the feminine role in the destinal myth - Titania. What secret lurks in her fierce hold upon the "boy-child"? As well as being an enslavement of stupidity on the male character, is she not also a refining hold, a refiner of what she has debased? Let us mark, in this, the mysterious promise she makes to be-monstered Bottom: "For I will purge thy mortal grossness so, that thou shalt like an airy spirit go". (3.1.153-54)

It is the same secret that lurks in the stories of the ancient goddesses who shadow Shakespeare's Miranda/Sycorax in *The Tempest*. There is first Demeter (and Isis), who was set to deify the male character (imaged as a boy-child) in her strange transmuting fires;[22] and then Medea, who had a cauldron of a like transforming power on man; and Calypso also, who entrapped the debased and guilty hero (Odysseus) and yet promised him godhead through his bondage.[23] [And Calypso's story, it should be noted, is present not only in the shadows of *The Tempest,* but in Shakespeare's earlier magical play, for Calypso as the daughter of the magical *Titan* (Atlas) is also 'Titania'. By this detail, the two plays are further linked. They are the first and last of the same process of the witch in Shakespeare's work.]

There is something else that might be realised: something that has from time to time already surfaced in this study of the myth. When we reflect, as in this chapter, how the feminine character can first debase, bestialise and make violent the male, and then through a process of bondage upon him bring him into a creative or godlike power, sometimes realised in his final sacrifice, then we see how the whole story is like a sexual act. For there too, man, first egged by the lady to the violent will of lust, is held by her until he is brought to a "sacrifice" in which his base energy is transmuted to a "creative or godlike power". Putting it in religious terms, we might say that 'she' who made the male crazy-violent (the 'Fall') will in process of time – this world – change that violence into life-giving power (as in a final 'crucifixion'), so that she herself will be changed by that power into her lost character of fruitfulness – the return of the summer-queen, the radiant lady of many stories. Prospero's 'experiment', therefore, ending a line of similar versions – perhaps from most ancient times – has at its centre a coital analogy.

This idea will be increasingly explored in the rest of this study. In it, I hope at least to suggest how the idea of an old 'fertility' myth was worked to the finest form of Christian myth – the story of the male spirit, confined to the 'feminine' ordeal of this life, at last being brought to a surge of vision, a force that, like a final virility casting

---

22 In the stories of Demeter's and Isis' wandering search, there is recorded an attempt to immortalise a male child by magical fire.

23 All these goddesses have long been recognised by scholars to shadow Miranda/Sycorax, but for what reason Shakespeare uses them (and others) as such shadows, scholarship alone cannot tell. (See next chapter).

out a cold barrenness, will penetrate like a spiritual fire into the
sorrowful feminine heart, casting out the terrors of sin and death
that so beset it and giving it, as in a quickening, a lost fruitfulness, a
lost paradise of joy.

★   ★   ★

The cyclical stories of Theseus (Oberon) and the Duke of Milan
(Prospero) are two Shakespearean instances of the masculine spirit
turned destructive by a malign alteration in his partnering feminine
personality or nature, and of the ensuing struggle of that spirit to
regain his lost character, status, and the world he once inhabited.
There are many other examples in Shakespeare's work, and in earlier
mythic literature, some of which we have looked at in this study.

Their story-line holds at least two truths that were unpalatable
to patriarchal religious orthodoxy, which I have also touched on in
this study. The first is the implication - very near the surface in some
cases - that the destructive darkening of the masculine character
involved the *whole* of that character, even what the orthodox would
have liked to believe separate and undefiled - the divine element:
their 'God'. The second unpalatable truth focuses when we consider
what was (and still is) the victim of that masculine monstrousness -
the true feminine, the loving nature, the 'body' of life. Putting the
teaching of this preserved primitive myth at its most blatant: 'God'
became his own 'Satan' and ravished, murdered or caused to be lost
his true 'Paradise'. From the early Nature myth, in which the
summer-king became his own demon of wrath, wrecking to his
world's summer love and beauty, through various later versions -
including the fairy tales and myths of the *Snow White* and *Persephone*
type - and into Shakespeare's plays, these combined truths remained,
as witness to the enormity in the male spirit, though disguised to
some extent because of their heretical import.

Two other Shakespearean versions of this idea are worth special
notice in passing. For example, when the King of *Henry IV* (an
example of 'history' adapted to myth) longs to restore the true
feminine, imaged as a reclaimed England, or Jerusalem (or even a
redeemed "Marian" Quickly, restored to her true "Robin"), he knows
he is trying to find again what *he himself* destroyed. Likewise when

Lear strives with equal pain to reclaim his lost state, his 'Grail', his 'Cordelia', he knows that he himself destroyed her. The 'guilty ruler', a variant of the 'sick ruler', is one of a number of destinal directors in medieval and Shakespearean stories in which is hidden the heresy of 'the fallen god'. Prospero is now to be examined as a leading example.

One group of stories that contained the same heresy – and not the least disguised – is that of the Grail romances. I mention these partly because I am sure that in *The Tempest,* among the many myths that Shakespeare hints at by echo and suggestion as parallels with his own final summing-up of *the* myth, the Grail cycle is itself adumbrated. The God who had become his own *Cain* (or Satan) in the biblical cycle is the King who became his own *Balin* in the Arthurian cycle, and both meet in the Duke who became his own *Caliban:* the Arthurian 'sword' of masculine life-vigour (Caliburn)[24] that changed into its own destructive demon and must be re-fashioned to its true character, and thereby restore the Lady of Life it first blighted or destroyed: the Grail itself. This matter will now be examined.

First, let us imagine, like some minds in the ancient world, that the original state of life was a harmonious unity, like a single body, even an androgynous giant-form, a 'god-goddess', as seems to be witnessed by the bisexuality of some early deities. Next let us imagine that the 'ruler' or intellectual part of this unity, its 'king', weakened and darkened in his power for some reason, causing a poisonous change in his feminine life, such as I have tried to convey in the 'Story of Eve' throughout this study. The result of this, as through a poisonous infiltration and frustration, was the turning of the masculine life-energies into a destructive force. Using still the idea of a unified body to this primal life, we might say that the 'phallus' part, as symbolising those energies, turned violently against the rest of the body, wounding or even slaying it. Further, as that life or body was part of the feminine entity in the original unity, then this first 'phallic' violence or rebellion could be imaged as rape. And it is interesting to see how persistent the idea of rape was in mythical stories, to symbolise the first enormity – even remembered as an attempt in *The Tempest.*

---

24 The name of Arthur's sword in Geoffrey of Monmouth's *History of the Kings of Britain.*

It is the 'Persephonal' theme that survived widely, not least in the recurring 'Snow White' motif of fairy tales. It survived in some Grail accounts also, where, as if to confirm our general impression that the wound in the King's body was in fact in his feminine life, we find various figures and symbols that suggest a blighted, barren or disfigured femininity or state of Nature. As further confirmation, we find the story contained in the *Elucidation,* attached to some Grail romances, in which the first crime is shown as the violation of the feminine cup-bearer, who denotes perhaps the Grail-lady or even the Grail itself.[25] Further confirmation might be deduced from the 'Story of Branwen', an account usually seen related to the Grail romances, in which the calamitous slaughter befalling Bran (Bendigeid-Vran) included the smashing of the magical life-cauldron.[26] But perhaps the strongest confirmation of all appears everywhere around us, though some might think it indecorous to mention. It appears in answer to this question - Which of the sexes actually bears a 'wound' in the loins (such as the Grail King is supposed to have had) as if in token of some long-ago violence or separation? And then another question - Is not this woman's 'wound' also one that is 'made whole' (like the Sick King's) when the right 'phallic' vigour again joins with it? Perhaps the symbolism of the Grail stories is less mysterious than some scholars have led us to suppose.

It seems to me that an alteration was made in many versions of this widespread story of a first violence. It was probably through patriarchal influence, or a growing tendency to realism, but whatever the reason, a change of characterisation took place, whereby the body that received the violence, or from which the energies tore away (in Blake's version),[27] became 'masculised'. It was now a king that was murdered, or some elder brother, or some other

---

25 See *From Ritual to Romance* (J. L. Weston) p. 171ff.

26 Branwen's story is found in the *Mabinogion.*

27 See *Jerusalem* (*Blake: Complete Writings* - ed. Geoffrey Keynes) p. 650 & 677. This alternative version of the first rape, which shows rather a violent tearing-away of the masculine energies from the feminine body, seems to be dimly preserved in the story of Balin. He not only beheads the Lady of the Lake (imaging her violation) but also, in the same episode, pulls the sword of destruction from the sheath of the mysterious damsel. (See the opening chapters of Book 2 in Malory's *Morte Darthur*).

male figure of rightful rule. Though the idea of a body being violated remained, the femininity of that body was obscured by its belonging to a ruler or elder male figure, against whom some 'younger' male had rebelliously or murderously acted. For example, the 'Persephonal' idea in the collapse of paradise story - the 'rape' of the first feminine life-form by an angry god - was not only removed by orthodox priestly adaptation, it was further obscured by being attached to another story, that of Cain, in which the first atrocity is shown as a murderous attack on an elder brother. The 'femininity' of the victim has entirely disappeared (though it survived to some extent in the medieval Legend of the Tree, in which it is the tree of life, the feminine life-form, that is stained red by Cain's act).

There are other well-known myths that seem to show the same obscured significance. In the best-known story of Balder, for example, we see the hero (or god) allowing others to hurl dangerous missiles at him, thinking himself invulnerable. The one plant that will penetrate his defence is the mistletoe, and so Loki, drawing blind Hodur to Balder's missile-throwing game, gives him a spear of mistletoe to throw at Balder, who is thereby slain. To my mind, the myth is a distortion of some earlier form, in accord with my argument above. As follows. There was an original unity to life - mind, body, life-energies, and so on, in one being. The 'mind' weakened into folly (still perceptible in Balder's foolish pride) and set in motion events which, in agreement with the pattern, ended in his own 'phallic' life-energies (linked anciently with the mistletoe symbol) turning violently or rebelliously against his 'feminine' body, his true nature, as in a murderous violation.

The same myth, I believe, remains hazily visible in the murders of other gods of the Balder type. Behind the slaying of Adonis and Osiris, for example, I believe there lurks this same idea of the male life-energies turned violent and ravaging to their own 'feminine' body, as in a rape or a tearing-away that leaves a wound in the groin.

In some versions of the myth, the two ideas are found together. That is to say, alongside the first slaying or wounding of an 'elder' ruler there appears the idea, like a memory, of woman-violation. For example, in the Arthurian story of Balin, the first atrocity - the 'Dolorous Stroke' - is duplicated: the attack on the Lord of

Carbonek (one variant of the Grail King) and the murder of a woman. And we might see that Shakespeare himself, by his own insight into the true myth, preserved the idea of woman-violation alongside the first violence upon the male ruler. This is true of *The Tempest,* wherein lurks the suggestion of life-violation (or woman-violation) as a secondary idea to the main theme of elder-murder. It is clearly shown also in Macbeth's crime against Duncan, in which the idea of rape is imaged ("Tarquin's ravishing strides") and the victim is linked with the kindly feminine nature of life.[28]

Indeed, generally speaking, Shakespeare, with what seems to have been a growing sense of the monster in the male character, increasingly made the initial crime of his plays some male outrage upon the natural or the naturally feminine, or else strongly suggested it alongside a crime of rebellion or murder against a male figure.

An example of this will take us back to Arthurian and Grail matters. In the first two Acts of *King Lear,* alongside the subplot's 'rebellion' against an elder figure (Gloucester), Shakespeare strongly depicts a first crime (by Lear) against the feminine nature. It is shown in three ways – the wrath upon Cordelia, the play's 'Persephone', whose supposed marriage to the King of France is quite misleading; the blasting curses on his other daughters in Act 2; and at the end of the same Act a final symbolic tearing asunder of his realm as corrupt and unworthy, a kind of Herculean off-riving of his natural flesh. And, judging by Shakespeare's many reminders of the Arthurian cycle in this play, we might sense that he means all this to parallel events in King Arthur's realm – the wrath upon Guinevere as sinful (and here my earlier link between her and Cordelia should be noted);[29] her own 'Persephonal' abduction by the 'Hadean' Meliagrance (until rescued by Lancelot); and, most strikingly, the final destruction of the first body of life – the golden realm of Albion shattered by civil war.

As the reader will notice in this, Shakespeare seems to be indicating a sequence to events in the Arthurian cycle different from Malory's. Lear's going through the 'waste lands' in search of his lost

---

28 *Macbeth* – 2.2.35-42
29 Chapter 4

true manhood and partnering femininity (Cordelia) only *after* the break-up of the realm (Act 2) suggests that Shakespeare saw the Grail search as the sequel to the stormy collapse of Arthur's realm. This is logical enough, we must agree, for why search for the Grail, the true femininity and beauty of life, before it had been violently lost?

In *The Tempest* Shakespeare returned to the Grail cycle, making the magical island of his play both the goddess-ruled 'Avalon', in which the shattered life might be healed and made afresh, and the setting of the 'Grail' quest – the search for the lost manhood and womanhood that in their union will restore all. By this, we find a focus on Prospero's role and character. There were many previous director-figures in Shakespeare's plays who resembled the controlling, magical Merlin, or even the shadowy Grail King of man's destiny, but Prospero stands clearly in this role. He is like the surviving ghostly 'mind' of a former all-inclusive being, now seeking his re-embodiment as by a resurrection or rebirth. To this end, he is intent to work back from its present debasement the masculine potency of life, turning the 'Caliban' into the 'Prince', so that, as by an insemination, the barren body or feminine nature of his former realm might be made fruitful again, giving birth to all that was lost – the total body, and therefore himself as its crowned head.

In this destinal, re-working process, we see something that, though it may have been derived equally from other myths, reminds us strongly of the Grail accounts and of Chaucer's own brilliant version of the cycle in *The Wife of Bath's Tale*. This 'something' is the coital analogy mentioned earlier in the chapter. The masculine vigour that first fell to violence against life, but then by the remaining holding-power of that life is brought back to a true 'virility' of transforming vision, is like the phallus that after its first intrusive wrong upon the lady's body is then held within her, as to her strenuous discipline and demand, until in a final death to its base energies it releases the spark capable of banishing her barrenness. She is like a fairy ghost working him to a last lightning, reaching her body in the grave and bringing it to life.

And is not this the truly Christian secret in the Grail stories, disguised by Church interference or through fear of its censure?

That the feminine character in this world, though mainly now a witch of spells, is yet both the luring Grail phantasm of man's highest aspiration, and also the means to his release – both into his own true life and hers? The feminine as both the true heaven and highest love he seeks, and the dark means to it? It was part of the essential femininity of Christianity that the spiritual male hierarchy of the established Church could never accept, and made it ever uneasy with these stories wherever it could not bend or tamper with them, as it had done with the Gospels.

It is reading *The Tempest,* I believe, that we most need to have read and understood the Arthurian stories, so that we can bring that understanding as an aid or reinforcement to the meaning of this play, as Shakespeare intended. Most important in this understanding is the meaning that dwells in the name *Caliban.* I indicated at the start of this part of the chapter that it contains, among other things, the names *Cain* and *Balin.* Cain was the biblical figure who – at least by a heretical view – symbolised the masculine energies and desires brought down to destructiveness by the witch-power of the self, but would nonetheless eventually turn up as the sacrificial prince, the Jesus, who on the tree or cross, denoting the feminine hold of discipline and refinement upon the male spirit, would realise the power of true masculinity and thereby transform that feminine power: the tree of sorrows changed at last to the tree of life again, or a wintry land made fruitful. In the same way, in the Arthurian cycle, Balin is the first debasement of the male spirit who will finally turn up as Galahad, with a similar power to restore the feminine nature – in this case, the Grail. And the terms of the story show, though hazily, that he too has gone through the process of feminine purgation and refinement.

To understand this, we need to grasp the significance of the sword, the symbol of the male character, in these stories, for which reason I also earlier indicated that *Caliban* has connection with *Caliburn,* Arthur's sword. The sword turned to murder (or war) is the male character debased and ravaging (Balin), whereas in the hands of Galahad it becomes the life-restoring power again. How had it been changed back? If we discount Malory's illogical sequence once again, and instead logically equate the sword at last drawn by

Galahad from the floating stone with that drawn by Arthur from the
stone or anvil, as a symbol of his true manhood and kingship, then
we shall find the answer.

Arthur's sword of true power is the same as that given him by the
Lady of the Lake, which I believe is the sword re-made or refined
from its fallen character by feminine discipline and nurture, much as
in an alternative story the true hero (Lancelot) is shown being
nurtured by her. In other words, Arthur's gaining the sword, either
from the grinding stone or from the Lady of the Lake, should come
near the end of the cycle, like Galahad's finding of the sword and like
Lancelot's emergence from the grinding wilderness to rescue
Guinevere. All are the same re-fashioned masculinity, the 'phallus'
made life-potent again as if coitally within the 'bond' of a woman.

Remembering Merlin as the magical director in the refining
process of the goddess upon the male (the re-making of the true
'sword') leads us back to *The Tempest,* in which we see another
Merlin likewise using a 'Lady of the Waters' (Miranda/Sycorax) to
refine the male character (Caliban/Ferdinand) as he too makes out
of this fallen masculinity a 'weapon' of creative vision, to shatter at
last this shadow-world and quicken what is dead – the true feminine
nature that within the witch of spells has been working her return.[30]

The coital analogy in this – the lady bringing the man from
crude energy to potency – is only dimly remembered in Malory. In
other Grail accounts it is clearer, and to it we are led by the sexual
symbolism of these stories, prompting many commentators to muse
on their dark origin in 'fertility' ritual or early mystical equivalent.
But let us look for this matter of the coital analogy itself.

I think, to start with, that many will have guessed, as they view
the strange wilderness of these romances, that these dark lands of
male quest and rigour reflect our mortal world in a fantastical way,
and therefore, like Titania's wood of spells or Ariadne's labyrinth or
countless other examples, also represent the dark 'body' of the fallen
life-lady herself, in which the male is trapped and tasked. These
lands are therefore not only the realm of the Grail, but the Grail

---

30 It is of some interest to note in passing that Shakespeare's name for the goddess
    used by Prospero to re-make the lost 'sword' of power recalls another name for
    Arthur's true blade - *Mirandoisa.*

itself, in a darkened and mortal form meanwhile, which prisons like a feminine body the male spirit and energies until they realise again a true 'masculinity', like the phallus brought to a life-restoring godhead, and so restore a 'fertility', a life, a full joy and radiance to that body: the Grail restored to her lost fruitful richness. And if this coital idea in general is not realised, I am sure that at the climax of these quests the analogy will be at least suspected. There is something unmistakably suggestive, for example, in the male spear dripping its vital drops into that vessel (which occurs in a number of versions), or in the fact that the re-entry of the spear into the 'groin-wound' brings relief from woe.[31] And perhaps most telling of all is that episode in which the failed hero is hotly scolded not by the King but by the loathly damsel, the figure of hideous blight and 'wintry' barrenness connected with the Grail itself, who behaves as though the hero has failed to bring the needed 'virility' to her for her own destined rescue, transformation or release into 'Spring'.[32]

To this might be added another fact that comes out more strongly once we realise the coital analogy. The oft-recurring victory over the power of death in these stories, usually fittingly near the end, and the release of lost life from its clutches – isn't this always very close to the idea of a victory over blight and barrenness? Is not the rescue of the maiden from dark death so often a partnering image to her rescue from a sort of sterility? The two ideas have a persistent poetic relationship in myth. Even in the Christ-myth, the harrowing of Hell to raise the dead, for example, is tinged with the idea of the virile energies unleashed into the sterile earth, the 'nether cave' of barrenness, with a quickening power. It survives too even in the relatively late story of Galahad rescuing the prisoners from the enchanted castle. For all the Church influence, likely to have toned down its sexual symbolism, this prison is still called the 'Castle of the *Maidens*'.

★   ★   ★

---

31 This occurs in Wolfram von Eschenbach's *Parzival*.

32 In a number of Grail romances there is found the implication that the *hag* or *loathly damsel* is simply a 'wintry' aspect of the beautiful Grail-bearer (and therefore of the Grail itself?), but the link comes out strongly in *Perlesvaus*. (The lady's scolding of the non-achieving hero appears in Chrétien de Troyes *Perceval*.)

In summary. I have argued in this chapter that *Midsummer Night's Dream* and *The Tempest* are like a clear first and last of Shakespeare's working on a myth of human destiny. In both, though little indication is given as to why a baneful alteration first befell the feminine nature in the human make-up, that baneful change takes place, and drives the masculine character into a darkening of mind and spirit, destructive to life. In the ensuing action – the usual time of quest or ordeal in such stories, mirroring our fallen world – the debased feminine and masculine characters are enjoined to a process whereby, each working on the other, what is base in them is refined, and in their final spiritual coalescence, as in a climax that breaks their lingering debasement, a lost unity and happiness is found. Directing this process is a relic of the old winter-king, who survived in countless romances, and in some patriarchal religions as the father-god: a formidable ghost-intelligence of a lost, tragically violated world of 'summer', now seeking his own return through the death and rebirth of the fallen sexes, as in a child brought forth to which he is the restored mind or head of wisdom.

This symbolic cyclical story survived widely in older times, though often in fantastic, corrupt or bleary form, and even further distorted by the needs of a religious ideology that had no wish to see that the divine might itself have fallen, or that it now yearns, through its fallen elements, to remake itself. Nor did this ideology wish to see that this divine power was part in thrall to its darker feminine being, holding it in life-hatred, monstrous towards its own true bride, and even the spirit of love itself.

Considering this led us to the Grail romances, in which lingered these heretical truths, and also the coital analogy of the divine re-creation or regeneration from the fallen condition, influencing Shakespeare as they did Chaucer before him.

Chapter 9
The Myth of the Sexes and The Tempest

In the first chapter of this study, a simple model of a Nature myth was projected and put forward as the story-basis of many later myths. The model comprised the destiny of essentially two characters or forces in life, male and female, who in harmony formed a 'summer' existence of happiness, but in division brought about a disastrous fall. This fallen state continued until they could mutually reclaim their erstwhile characters and partnership. This was achieved through the cleansing of their deformities in an event that was often imaged in ritual and myth in a mixed sacrificial and sexual way: a climactic burning-out of the base for a restored fineness of humanity, like a rebirth.

This chapter will add to this, following an idea mentioned in the last chapter: that in many cases of the myth's survival it is not only the last climax that shows or implies a sexual, or coital, analogy, but the whole process of ordeal leading up to it.

★   ★   ★

In the last chapter, while considering the nature of Prospero's 'experiment', I took up the idea that pride (the self) and the destructive character in life can sometimes work against one another in a way that mutually breaks down their power. When we consider this further, reflecting that pride is feminine and destructiveness masculine, we see that the 'experiment' in *The Tempest,* yoking together a Sycoraxian Miranda and a Calibanic Ferdinand, is much like a marriage. There also two contrary forces - the sexes - are 'wedlocked' to a process that (ideally, at least) will weaken what is inhuman in each, and bring out what is truly human. But as well as in marriage, the idea can be seen in the sexual act itself, in which two sides mutually burn out and re-make themselves, even as in a child thereby produced, symbolising the lost androgynous harmony reborn. By this view, the whole myth of human ordeal, of which *The Tempest* is just one example, comes down to a sort of lengthy act of coition. Prospero's 'experiment' is very much like that suggested in the ordeal of Mars and Venus, who were likewise bound in their act of love by a vengeful 'magician' (Vulcan) in a way that might likewise denote the sexual principles or characters in this life mutually working towards refinement or salvation.

Strange though the idea will seem at first to some modern minds, the more it is thought on as a way of looking at these myths, the more it takes on relevance. And we might note in such pondering how William Blake, in his own work of creating a single myth of destiny, observed as if for our guidance: "O holy Generation, Image of regeneration".[1] Indeed, the idea of the sexual contraries breaking and re-making one another towards a new humanity and unity is central to his versions of the myth, and inferentially therefore to all the myths he thought contained the same destinal story.[2]

So let us think further on this idea, and, to fix our minds, look first at the 'pride' in the process of life's learning and re-making, relating it to the feminine side of the sexual act.

Let us say first that, among whatever motives there involved, the female wishes to possess the male, to rule this vital power, and even tame it to her will. This is like the pride in its wishes too, and also like the darkened feminine nature that at the Fall (as once thought) sought power over the masculine, even by using her despised true nature, her body, as a victim to his ravage. But what happens in the process, as the dynamics of her action begin to take hold? She finds in time that it is herself that is possessed, and that it is herself that is given to her own crushing and surrender. Something happens that makes this force of pride or self want to yield all, for she has felt a strength that banishes all the fears and shames that made her seek to possess and claim, a strength like a god's that makes her cast aside all the false and hard about herself she has become, and surrender into this new, overwhelming truth and rightness.

In this way, the very will of the feminine pride leads to its own 'death', and to its renewal by a power she then receives, much like a seed that her own true desire, though perhaps unwittingly, has

---

1   *Jerusalem* plate 7, line 65 – p.626 *Blake: Complete Writings* (ed. Geoffrey Keynes).

2   See Appendix D – 'Blake and Shakespeare'.

been urging in the male from the start - perhaps like that 'seed' of truth that we all in our feminine hearts really long for, to banish our poor, resistant and wilful self, and make us spiritually fruitful.

That coital analogy is part of one that has lain behind versions of the myth from its old natural and ritual form right through into the stories of the feminine pride being processed. It explains in part the sense of a sexual idea behind so many of them, especially clearly at the final climax, as in Cleopatra's suicide, for instance. Here we see a death quite unmistakably as 'sexually' depicted, but see also how her bond upon Antony has at last brought upon her a vision of his magnificence - the "dream" of Antony[3] that takes hold of her and makes her former empery a trumpery of no importance to surrender. We see it also in Dorigen's yielding - the quasi-sexual 'Gethsemane' of *The Franklin's Tale,* in which an overwhelming demand of truth, like the masculine force returned, brings her to surrender. We glimpse it imaged also in the final yielding of many another proud princess in fairy tale, when their sufferings under the 'grisly beards' of this life bring them to yield and find again their lost true nature.

It is implied in *The Tempest* also, in which Prospero uses this feminine power even against herself, towards its final yielding in the rocky cave of death. But we might glimpse it there, in addition, in Shakespeare's mystical understanding of the whole world, the whole temporary framework of mortal life, as a feminine fabric of fantasy upon the male, which, having achieved its purpose on him, will surrender to its own dissolution like a "dream".[4] Miranda's island of spells is a later version of Titania's wood, and has theatred the same play.

But this is only half the sexual analogy; this is only half the process that explains why we sense behind such stories, from start to finish, that there is some sort of sexual idea or energy carrying them towards a final climax of dying and rebirth. For the other half, let us look at the coital process from the male point of view.

Whatever other motivations go into his action, I deem there is

---

3   *A&C* 5.2.73-100

4   The famous speech, beginning "Our revels now are ended …" - 4.1.148-58.

in his state of 'lust' both an urge to realise a completion of his ego-dream, to possess the dream-object, and an urge to violate or destroy. This re-enacts the male madness of the Fall, when the feminine became both a goading dream and - in her true nature - a target for punishment. But what happens in the process, as the dynamics for him begin to take hold, as in this fallen world of toil? He is brought to the point where the dream-object fades to little importance, and where a compulsion more mighty than himself drives him to destroy not something else but his own destructive self, in a kind of ecstatic need for his own death, by which he will be changed to godlike power. In this way, what is base is transcended even in the act of hoping to fulfil it, and something of divinity over life is realised even in that death. And thus we see the end of many a romance quest in an extinction of base motive in the man, and see the end of such as Aurelius's labours in *The Franklin's Tale,* by which he self-sacrificially takes on the power of a god, able to loose the feminine nature from her dark bond and raise her again to joyful life. And thus we also see many like a Coriolanus at the climax of his labours, or like a Jesus before the act of his own annihilation, by which divine power-release the joyful life will be restored.

Primed with this, our minds range back over a tradition of stories in which, following the coital analogy, there is found the same idea of man's purgation and refinement through the binding lady-power upon him. So we see, for instance, Odin bound to the lady-tree throughout the ages, till his mind-power sharpens to see the runes of escape and new life; or an Odysseus bound to a tree-mast amid the wailing siren-power, or held by a magical embrace on an island of renewal; or a Satan bound for his wrongs to the same lady-tree of mortal generations, finally to become the lord who dies upon the tree and shatters this fallen life.[5]

In these myths, the tree is a symbol of this mortal life of feminine form and limitation, to which the male is bound for his

---

5   This myth is adumbrated in Chaucer's *Merchant's Tale* and *Wife of Bath's Tale*. In these, the cycle begins with a male wrong and ends (or implies an ending) in the male sacrifice. In both, the bond upon the man is feminine, but also imaged to some extent as a tree. See Longer Notes at the end of this chapter.

refinement back to truth and vision, as if within the body of a woman who awaits this liberating strength like a seed-burst. And what goes for the tree goes also for the wood or forest that appears in some myths as the place of man's bondage, pain, or wearying search. In it, as upon the tree, we find the same toiling hero - a questing knight, for example, a Lysander (*MND*) or an Orlando (*AYLI*) - searching and groaning to the same end of final surrender, as if in sacrifice for his mistress.

The same coital idea lurks in tales of heroes set to impossible tasks, like a Hercules or Culhwch, or ceaselessly in hard servitude like Ferdinand or Little Gwion (*Taliesin*), or else in a prison-mill, grinding their bone-baseness into a gold-seed of life-renewal, or by a seething cauldron or a fire, sweating and burning till made divinely strong. And in some stories we find the seething cauldron now a whole scourging sea about the journeying hero, as he endures the witch's curse through time, longing for that final 'death' by which the lost land will be found.[6]

So widespread was the idea in stories, under various guises, it is no surprise to find its traces even in traditional children's tales, still visible after perhaps hundreds of years. We see, for example, 'Buttons' toiling at the lady's cindery hearth, to win back his true character and hers, or valiant Jack penned in the hot oven of the giant's wife, turning base masculinity to golden strength, and his dominant 'mother' to a queen. The idea survives most strikingly perhaps in *The Sleeping Beauty* in which the male ordeal is one of hard durance in a briary ring, until a point of power is reached at last, by which the true man wakes the maid from 'barren' death, like a Christ that also set his head through a ring of thorns, or like the valiant hero who died through the ring of spiky flames to awake a Brynhild or a Menglad.

Yes, the coital symbolism survived in some surprising places. Take the medieval church building, for instance. It was a 'lady' from the outside, and also a 'lady' within. And so its inner 'cavern' was

---

6   Hence the many instances of the purging sea-quest, including the usually misunderstood Old English *Wanderer* and Shakespeare's mysterious 'Master of the Tiger' (*Macbeth*).

shaped like a grove of the goddess in ancient times, and so too like her dark realm of creation, at the centre of which - aptly enough - a sacrificial image of the male hero, finally bursting in death into a new life-power upon the tree that had held him. And then we see the whole east window at sun-rise, as if in response to his victory, come ablaze with new light and colour, and this lady-church, this 'tree', of sometime darkness and sorrows become radiant and joyful again like a barren form made fruitful.

So that the run of examples does not lead to a confusion by illustration, I might at this point simply say that through a wide variety of symbolism in myth, both secular and religious, there seems to be conveyed a similar story and destiny. There is indicated how the masculine in this life is bound by a feminine control, which might be understood as a sort of inner compulsion on him, but also as an outward containment: a 'feminine' world of finite forms and limitations, that are like a purging and reforming prison to his spirit, even to the point of a final dramatic transcendence of his fallen character. As is suggested by this, and as is actually adumbrated in some of the mythic examples, sometimes clearly, the whole process compares with the sexual act. For just as in that act the male is held within a limiting feminine body and brought from base energy fully into a productive force, so in the containments, frustrations and disciplines of this life the masculine character may be taught and refined to true understanding and manhood, even finally bursting in vision from his crude selfishness and brute desires.

This process, probably in early times depicted fertilistically, as in the 'king' debased to wintry wrath being bound to the dark lady-tree until in a last climax of sacrifice he found the life-energies for his own and her reborn life, passed in various symbolic stories into later times and into the Middle Ages. Here this purgation and process on the male, in a destinal story beginning in some first debased violence and ending in a transcendence through rigour, is commonly found, sometimes in a mixed pagan and Christian colouring of ideas and symbolism.[7] In some of these cases, the analogy with the sexual act is, as if wittingly, indicated, as in

---

7   See Longer Notes at the end of this chapter.

Chaucer's *Wife of Bath's Tale,* in which the cycle begins with a first sexual violence upon woman and ends in a nuptial chamber of male sacrifice and life-renewal, with the whole process contained by a feminine power.

The myth and some of its symbolism passed also into the work of Shakespeare, in which male ordeal in the refining rigours of this feminine world is a key feature, and in which the coital analogy is often adumbrated. So we see Orlando, for instance, being taught by his mistress in her realm of Arden, and brought to a final self-sacrifice, as if to complete her destiny upon him, and that of her magical 'uncle' (foreshadowing *The Tempest*). We also see Lear in the dark ordeal of this world, as within the toils of a witch, first being instructed by his Cordelia-in-disguise (the Fool) and then in the crushing rigours of the law upon him (given feminine connotation) brought to a climax that transmutes mere wrath to power of vision, compelling him to a death in which the grave, as if to represent the place of ordeal all along, is imaged as a woman's genitals (4.6.128-131).

By the central symbolism of *The Winter's Tale* - man bound to a hard feminine statue - we see a similar process of rigour upon the destructive energy, by which it is transmuted to wisdom, and that hard, binding form itself thereby 'fertilised' back into true femininity.[8] The same idea, most clearly, shows in *Measure for Measure.* Beginning with a sexual 'crime' and ending in a consummation, all is set alongside the process of a brothel, wherein man is 'put through it' to his 'dying'. The same is in the play's workings of the law, a feminine power, a hard 'Isabella', to which man is bound, likewise to be 'ground' until crude energies of self turn again to vision, able to loose her hold and in a final death - imaged as of the Cain-like Ragozine - change her to the fruitfulness of mercy - the lost *Torah* in which all are found. The brothel-world likewise symbolises the processing place of Hal (*Henry IV*) towards

---

8   The name of the statue's guardian - Paulina - suggests that some of this symbolism is linked with the 'Pauline' *Epistles,* in which the Law is also imaged as a 'feminine' power in this life, a "bond-woman" that meanwhile has hold upon the man, but only until he rids himself of "the old man" as by a final dying, exchanging this 'body' of bondage for one that is heavenly and free.

a last sacrifice into right kingship and a raising of the true bride from the harlot - England (or Jerusalem).

In looking back on this chapter's argument so far, I realise that it is likely to seem strange to the main modern understanding, which is so bound to the literal or physical perception of sex, that it finds it hard to see in it the mystical metaphor that I am sure some minds of earlier ages were able to see, and to express in their art.

Perhaps we also should try to understand that true masculinity is not simply a physical virility, nor even a strength of courage and manliness, but an ultimate power of vision, a transforming truth, and equally brought about by something 'feminine'. That is to say: in all forms of devotion, frustration, discipline and limitation, by which man finds his true 'power', his true masculinity, whether it be a bodily virility, a strength of courageous character or, further, this 'virility' of imaginative vision, it is 'she' that like a body encloses him and enjoins him to this end, her world of hard bondage and teaching upon him, by which he is worked from the crude monster towards what he truly is.

And in all cases, too, though her darker purpose may be to possess, enslave or crush him, her hidden purpose, like that of a Cinderella within the sister of false beauty, is to bring on a power by which *she herself* shall be realised: a true femininity that is gained through the gaining of a true masculinity. Just as her cursed barrenness and blight of body can be banished for a fruitfulness on a physical level, so a barrenness of fear and shame - that dark fust of sin-awareness within all things feminine - will be banished by a final transforming truth she might raise in him. It is like a voice to her: 'There is no sin, no death; you are everything, and loved, in what you are'. By this, as in the dark heart of all of us, a wonder will be worked, like a conception that brings back the lost 'motherhood', the radiant kindness that has been longing to return, and has lain behind all distorted witcheries of pride and malice, behind all the trapping lures and screens of this material prison.

The ultimate realisation of the myth of sexual destiny, as in the finest of our older art and literature, is therefore 'Christian'. Not the sentimental pieties of self-congratulation, or the moral suppositions of good ('ourselves') and evil (those who are not 'ourselves'), but

Christian in its teaching of our true liberation, a freedom in vision
and love, by which this world is finished in her work, and left behind
like a witch-wood of fantasy, like a dark church of mortal
containment, or like an island of spells set in a sea of time.

★   ★   ★

The artistic method used in *The Tempest* is the presentation of a
simple surface sprinkled with clues, so that the reader, taking those
clues and pointings, will bring to the work its extra colour, mythic
clothing and meaning. We know how in reading *Canterbury Tales* or
Paradise Lost our understanding is the deeper if we follow the
sprinkle of allusions and echoes that their authors lay upon the
textual surface. It is the same in *The Tempest,* where the method is
simplicity in design but complexity by allusion.

One of the things that the allusions lead us to is the symbolic-
sexual process. What are the clues that lead to it? The hint at the
Balin story in the name Caliban, and therefore the process of the
male sword's re-making in the magical lady's watery cave, was
mentioned in the last chapter. To this could be added the play's final
nuptial consummation, as a more obvious clue, but also
Shakespeare's use of the Masque of Demeter (Ceres) in Act 4. This,
in linking with the Mystery rites, links also with sexual symbolism,
and even with the sexual act that in some imaged way (or actual?)
was used in those rites, as in other Mysteries.

In looking more deeply into this, let me first recall, from earlier,
that the feminine nature, as poets have ever owned, has a most
ambivalent power. She can both debase the male and yet at other
times ennoble him. For her, he is capable of the most monstrous
behaviour, and for her also the outstandingly heroic and fine. In the
same way, but more physically, her sexual power turns him into a
grunting beast, but then leads him to be changed into the power of
a god. For what is more godlike than the power to pass on the seed
of a new life, a whole new creation, into her?

This strange ambivalence hangs about the feminine character in
The Tempest in the shadowy figure of the debasing witch, Sycorax,
and the ennobling daughter, Miranda, like twin aspects of the same
power. And Shakespeare adds to the idea of her magical ambivalence

by hints at other mythical figures of the same power in her shadow. Calypso, Medea and Circe, for instance, are well known to the play's commentators, who perhaps recognise also the sexual symbolism in their stories, or the sexual analogy visible in their effect on the male character.

Calypso was earlier mentioned in connection with both Titania and Sycorax, the goddess who enslaves Odysseus and yet promises him godhead. This double power to 'animalise' man, or else bring out his full potential, also appears in the story of Circe; and in the story of Medea it is further shown in the heroine's witch-like power. In this last case, we might particularly note the trace of sexual symbolism given to her power, shown in the episode of Medea's use of her magical cauldron to restore the youth of old Aeson. The analogy between the old man being turned to youthful vitality in her cauldron and the male being brought sexually to a full power of vigour within a woman's body seems to be hinted at.

A cauldron of similar power to change the male is found in the first part of the medieval Welsh *Romance of Taliesin* – a story of marked sexual symbolism. As this romance was put forward by Robert Graves as an influence in *The Tempest*,[9] I shall give it closer attention, starting with an outline of its story: –

The action takes place on a lake-island on which live the witch-goddess Cerridwen and her husband, Tegid Voel, a romance name for Ogyrvran, a magical god of the sea and of the dead. Cerridwen has two children: Creirwy, the most beautiful woman in the world, and Avagddu, the ugliest man. To compensate her son for his extreme ugliness, Cerridwen plans to give him immense wisdom (possibly denoting divinity), and to this end, following the instructions of a magician's book, prepares a magical brew in her cauldron. She is assisted by a servant-boy, little Gwion, who is set to stir the cauldron incessantly, while a blind man (Morda) keeps its fire in fuel.

I think even in this opening situation we already see some parallel with *The Tempest*. There is some resemblance in the chores imposed upon the males, for instance, but also a more important

---

9   See *The White Goddess* p.123

similarity. Cerridwen and Creirwy seem to be joint personages, like Sycorax and Miranda, and moreover, under the guise of adding a compensatory quality to the male character, seem to be similarly working a change in that character. This change is imaged as a turning of his ugliness, denoting crude energy, into a power of wisdom, a power of vision. As this power is the mental or spiritual equivalent of male sexual potency, with a similar ability to transform or recreate things, as I have earlier argued, we realise that the change here promised for Avagddu is very much like that brought about in the male during the sexual act - the gaining of a potent, transforming power. Other symbolic details in this part of the story now fall into place as bearing the same coital connotation, as most noticeably in the males having to toil continuously at the witch's vessel. And this coital analogy stays with the story as it continues:-

One day, by accident, while Gwion is stirring the cauldron, the magical drops that it has made spill out scaldingly onto his hand. He licks his hand in pain, and so absorbs the potion of wisdom. Perceiving by this wisdom that he has accidentally stolen a gift intended for the witch's beloved son, and that he will suffer her wrath, he flees in terror. The cauldron meanwhile, bereft of its precious drops, splits asunder and spills out all the fluid that remains, which is poisonous. Cerridwen in her anger smites Morda with a stick so hard that his eye falls out, and then sets off in enraged pursuit of Gwion. He uses his newly endowed magical powers to shape-shift into various forms to elude her, much like Tam Linn in the Scottish story, but her magic gets the better of him at every stage, for she changes into forms superior to his. At last, Gwion changes into a seed and hides among other seeds on a granary floor, but Cerridwen, changing herself into a sharp-eyed hen, espies him and pecks him up, and swallows him. She becomes pregnant by the seed, and in time gives birth to him again. Still his enemy, but not wishing to destroy her child outright, she puts him in a leather bag and casts it into the sea, from which he is at length washed up onto land as Taliesin, the divine wonder-child of wisdom.

Having earlier noted the sexual symbolism in the physical toil of the male at the hot cauldron, we see in this remainder of the story a continuation of the same idea, especially in Gwion's having to use all his powers (under Cerridwen's pressure) to turn himself into "a seed" that inseminates her. Cerridwen thus, whatever her ostensible anger and earlier disappointment, has in effect achieved her purpose. She has indeed turned male 'ugliness' into a potency equivalent to the transforming power of wisdom, and has also thereby changed herself from the witch of barrenness into the fruitful mother – becoming her own 'Creirwy', as it were. In the same way, we might see that the 'Sycorax' of *The Tempest,* whatever her ostensible purpose upon the male character, is working a similar magic upon him and thus transforming herself fully into the beautiful and fruitful Miranda.

And yet, as a parallel to *The Tempest,* there seem to be some incongruities in the *Taliesin* story. To start with, where is its Prospero figure? The answer is that he is there by implication. First, we notice that Cerridwen works her process by the directions of a magician's book, which suggests that her work and purpose is actually being guided by some shadowy male power. Secondly, we might ponder on a character who, though he does not actually appear in this version of the story, is nonetheless mentioned and could be inferred to be taking some part in Cerridwen's process on the island. This character is Tegid Voel (mentioned as Cerridwen's husband in this romance form) who, as previously pointed out, is a variant of Ogyrvran, a magical god of the dead, who was in turn the shadowy remnant, like a ghost, of a former illustrious ruler. The more we reflect on the mythical connections to this Ogyrvran, the more it appears that his role is that of a shadowy director to Cerridwen's process upon the male hero, Gwion. Let us see.

Ogyrvran is likely once to have been the divine lord Bran (or Vran, as he is sometimes called), whose story in other accounts both reveals a past calamity in which he and his realm violently perished,[10] and also gives us grounds for suspecting that his implied presence in the *Taliesin* romance is that of a sort of remnant, magical 'Prospero', working through events in a succeeding state of existence – the 'island' – so that he and his lost realm will be quasi-

---

10 In the 'Story of Branwen' in the *Mabinogion,* Bran leads a punitive expedition that ends in massive destruction, in which he and the wondrous life-cauldron are lost.

sexually 'reborn'. We might even suspect that there once existed versions of the *Taliesin* story that showed his presence and directing purpose more clearly.

Interestingly, this Bran is often linked in mythic studies with the figure of Arthur, another illustrious ruler who perished violently with his realm and – if we arrange the Arthurian romances into logical order – can also be seen to have been survived by a sort of magical and ghostly intelligence (Merlin), who likewise through events in the succeeding state of existence engineers the return of what was lost. As this ties in with the Grail romances – the quest for the lost world in the wilderness of this – we might glimpse in the 'sick king' of those stories yet another such ghostly survivor of an illustrious past who likewise works the destiny of his own return. Another example is the magical Thoth of the Osiris myth, who is likewise intent on working the return of the true lord Osiris (himself in full form?) and in a process that ties in with both the Taliesin story and *The Tempest*. That is to say, the Osiris myth, in which Thoth is the magical director, centres on the character of the goddess Isis, who holds and preserves within herself (sometimes imaged as a boat or tree) the potential of all that was lost, as within a womb, and awaits the vitalising seed by which it can be quickened and brought back to life as by a birth.

By this example of Isis' role – very relevant in understanding *The Tempest,* as we shall later see – we realise many things. One is that the coital analogy in such stories – the male energies being transmuted by the feminine power into a transforming 'seed' – is but one part of a wider sexual analogy, a wider 'sexual' story. I will explain. When the first higher state of life was destroyed, its potential for forming once again and returning to life was preserved in the feminine character, somewhat like an egg within a womb. To bring it back to life, this feminine force or character must by ordeal convert the male energies that remain in this lower mortal existence into a revitalising spark, much like a woman converting a man coitally, so that this 'egg' of the lost world, containing all its original forms and characters, can be quickened and then re-delivered as by a birth.

So I was wrong if I earlier gave the impression that the *whole* myth is like a sexual act. The 'coitus' is only the central ordeal of the myth which actually begins as the feminine character takes into herself all the collapsing or dying first world, and ends when she re-delivers it.

I will return to this matter later in the chapter. For now, let us look again at the *Taliesin* story, with the above idea in mind, and then a little more at *The Tempest*. The last part of the *Taliesin* story I earlier outlined deals with a sea-journey, beginning with Cerridwen's placing of 'Gwion' in a leather bag and casting it to the waves, and ending when the bag, or the sea itself, delivers him as the divine child, Taliesin. This child, as often in myth, is not simply the hero of labours (the 'Gwion') making a return, but images in the totality of its symbolism the return of the whole state that was originally lost. That is to say, the birth of the divine wonder-child from the sea images the restoration of something that existed before the start of all the pains and labours on Cerridwen's lake-island, which were simply the means to its restoration.

An everyday example will perhaps help clarify this point. When a child is born to us, we might see in it ourselves returned – a living product of those who beforehand laboured and 'died' sweatily for its making – but we might also see in it the return of something much more fundamental: a form of innocent life, like an all-inclusive heaven or paradise, that is now mysteriously brought back, whose loss occurred long before our 'labour' began. We may indeed go even further, and sense of this radiant miracle that it fulfils in living form some divine impulsion, some shadowy urge of destiny that was behind our earlier sweat and strange desire.

In the same way, Taliesin is the product of Gwion's insemination of the witch, and yet also, by the will and arrangement of the shadowy Ogyrvran, the *return* of something – a totality – that existed and perished long before Gwion's labour even began: a totality that includes the original ruling mind, the Lord Bran. In the same way, too, the 'birth' at the end of *The Tempest* is both the product of the labours of Ferdinand and Miranda – summed up in the sexual congress in the cave of consummation – and yet also the image of the whole primal state restored, like the return of *all* from death: including its ruler, who has meanwhile been a ghostly genius arranging its return.

By this view, Miranda, like many a goddess of pagan myth, has borne within her the 'egg' of all the former life, preserved as within a womb or - using some of the symbolism of such stories -as within a fibrous tree, bark or ship of preservation, simply waiting for the right magic from the male to bring on its gestation and rebirth. She is the Mary-ship or Mary-ark, or boat of Isis, holding within her like a potential all the lost realm, including its 'god', until through the coming of the right male seed - the sacrificial prince who will die for her (or into her) - she might bring it back to fully living form.

Pondering this, we see yet another heresy, for these stories tell us not only that what the orthodox call 'God' perished long ago, with all his realm, and is waiting to be born again, but that he is meanwhile simply a ghost arranging the sexual forces in this life, male and female, towards his own rebirth. But the real heresy emerges when we realise the means of this rebirth; for the same stories tell us that Jesus' final dying, like that of many a sacrificial hero, will be the last vital release of energy that, as it were, inseminates the witch of this mortal state, and tell us also that God himself will be the 'child' of the witch resulting. Shall she who brought forth Death bring forth the living God?

It is one of the things of the ancient myth that the Middle Ages inherited: a heresy that appeared shadowily in much of its symbolism - even in that of the Church in some cases. No matter how sanctified or distinct from taint the 'Mary' was made by the purists of the Church, there was ever the shadow to her of the older goddess of destiny, who could play the witch and the final blessed mother equally. So behind Mary's smile flittered ever that of Eve or Magdalen as the same 'Mother of God'. Yet artists and poets of this primitive truth had to be careful to keep it as no more than a 'flitter'. One of these was Shakespeare, who in *The Tempest* therefore only hints that God (the Duke) was to be born of Sycorax, just as Taliesin was born of the goddess-witch Cerridwen. He also hides the essential unity to the characters of Miranda and Sycorax, and - as a further safeguard - pretends that Sycorax died long before the action of the play began.

And yet the truth is obvious. It is verified by simply looking at our own lives. Is the heart, the 'inner lady' of our being, that will one day conceive and bear the form of paradise and even God himself, an entirely holy thing? No, not at all. It is as much a witch of spells as a queen of kindness, as much a trollop as a saint. And that's just as well. Nothing much can be conceived by a virgin.

★   ★   ★

We have not yet looked into all the thickets that lie in the mythic maze we call *The Tempest,* but it is time to pause and take stock of the findings that have made up this chapter.

In one way, these findings are readily summed up, for the whole exploration has taken us round a single idea - the myth's use of an analogy between the course of human destiny in this mortal life and what could be called the sexual process.

The central personage in both, the key factor if you like, is the feminine character, playing two linked roles in the 'drama'. First, just as a woman keeps within her, as within a dark underworld or grave of death, the potential of new life that ever springs from her, so the feminine character or power in the myth is the holder of the potential, the keeper of a ghostly egg in which, though meanwhile in a sort of sleep or death, resides all that was originally lost and will in course of time return. Images of this holding-role in myth are numerous, but in this chapter have appeared mainly as the tree, the boat, the tree-like church, the island - all symbols of the central womb or cauldron, into which all that dies passes and from which all that comes to life shall spring.

The second role of the feminine character follows from the first - the means of bringing this potential, this sleeping form, to its awakening or birth. Just as a woman can by her bodily hold upon the male bring the crude energies orgasmically to a vital charge, for the insemination of her waiting ovum, so in this life the 'feminine character' - a force inwardly on man or outwardly in the formal containments, structures, and bonds of discipline and learning upon his spirit - might bring his desirous energies and intellect to a piercing power of wisdom or vision, by which the sterility in her heart, the psycho-pathetic depths of our being, can be overcome and changed to joyful affirmation. It is the equivalent of a mighty insemination that she has wrought, to cast out a deep negativity and make her the mother of all that was lost.

This negativity was in the time of the myth's last flowering linked in religious ideology with sin-awareness and life-hatred, which in *The Tempest* is shown in the spirit of vengeance and accusation possessing Prospero, a feminine power of darkness that can only be banished by a truth beyond the self it creates, and thus restored to a feminine power of life. What symbolically enters Miranda in her nuptial consummation is therefore what enters the 'Sycorax' in Prospero himself: a force at last realised in the male energies by ordeal.

It does not, however, register as clearly as the symbolic events in the liberating climax of *King Lear* earlier. It seems that in his final summing-up of the myth Shakespeare was more concerned to create an artistic directory to the myth and its variants than try to match his earlier insights.

⋆   ⋆   ⋆

Chapter 9 – Longer Notes

p.173 & p.175   In *The Wife of Bath's Tale,* as the hero is led to his final sacrifice, the loathly lady uses the image of a family-tree while making the point that true virtue is not inherited, but derived from God. Beneath this might lie another meaning - that no true virtue will pass down from our ancestor, because that ancestor is the fallen Adam and the tree is the tree of mortal generations, which will only give virtue through Christ (mentioned here) whose sacrifice, the true virtue, was at last on this 'tree' (the Cross).

We thereby see that the whole process in the tale can be summed up not just as a quest entirely controlled by the feminine character that leads to a final male crisis into restored life, beautiful and abundant, but as a mortal cycle of bondage - with the male bound as if to the 'feminine' tree of this mortal life, from the first rebellion and violence (Satan, who was thereafter bound to the tree in serpent coils) to the finally fulfilled masculinity on the Rood-tree, which also fulfils, as if bringing to Spring-flower again, this 'wintry' tree.

Some of the same symbolism is found surviving in pagan rites, lasting at least into the late Middle Ages, and the same connection made between mortal sacrifice, 'fertility', and the joyful liberation. But to keep this to the main religious form. The pattern of *The Wife of Bath's Tale,* but with clearer symbolism, is found in Chaucer's *The Merchant's Tale,* in which the first violation by the 'serpent' (Damian) is upon the lady and the tree of the garden (Paradise), to which we might picture him thereafter bound until he too symbolically fulfils the destiny as the sacrifice to violence in the same tree.

Now, because the tree, as an image of our mortal limitation from Paradise to Salvation, is feminine, some in the Middle Ages connected it with both Eve and Mary, the 'tragic first' and 'fruitful last' of our controlled destiny. By this, we look with wonder not just at the powerful hag in the Wife's tale but at the Wife herself, for in her Prologue appears a sort of destiny that makes her, so to speak, the Eve (clear enough!) *and* the Mary. It seems strange, but mark the Wife's three journeys to Jerusalem (mentioned in the *General Prologue*). Hardly feasible as fact, but it might remind of the three main journeys of Mary to Jerusalem, as recorded in the Gospels – for the presentation of her new-born child at the Temple; for the Passover Feast, where the boy Jesus was accidentally left behind; and for the Crucifixion. In medieval legend, partly influenced by apocryphal texts such as the Book of James (*Protevangelium*), Mary was also noted for her textile skills (like the Wife), for which she was employed on the Temple Veil, using red and purple strands. She thus perhaps symbolizes the weaving womb of mortal time in which the lost Paradise is preserved, like an egg. It simply awaits the right male energy (divine vision) to be at last 'inseminated', as imaged by such as the entry of Jesus' power into the 'barren' Temple (at the time of his sacrifice) or victoriously into the underworld of death.

The heroine of *The Merchant's Tale* is connected with the tree and its Eve/Mary symbolism by other details. Her craving for the fruit recalls both Eve (her clear role) and Mary, who in pregnancy likewise, according to medieval legend (and *The Cherry-Tree Carol*), craved the fruit of the tree. But it goes further. The controlling axial tree of the biblical destiny was matched then by its pagan equivalent, the May (hawthorn), which is the name of Chaucer's heroine. The hag of *The Wife's Tale* might connect with this tree too, since 'hag', or 'hag-thorn', was one of the old names for hawthorn. Further, this thorn-tree was linked in medieval lore with Jesus' suffering (the crown of thorns) and so the hag bringing the hero to sacrifice takes on more meaning perhaps, as might the tree-image of her lecture to him.

Chapter 10
Other Mythic Wisps and Whispers in The Tempest

Two other sets of myths seem to have a shadowy presence in *The Tempest,* and relate to my argument of a 'sexual' process and renewal in the play. The first is of Germanic or Norse origin, and the second – already touched on in the foregoing chapter – is Egyptian: the Isis/Osiris myth. However, in both cases the influence on Shakespeare is probably unprovable, unless much more time were allowed than I am willing to give, and so I add these to this study speculatively.

$$\star \qquad \star \qquad \star$$

When Sir Israel Gollancz was investigating the Norse background to *Hamlet,*[1] he gave the first eight pages of his book to a curious set of story-fragments. They deal with the primeval giants, and mainly with the "wise giant" Bergelmir, who survived the massive flood of blood in which all the rest of the giant race perished. Details suggest that his survival was by some kind of boat or "ark". There is also a mention of his wife with him, making this a sort of 'Noah' myth. Gollancz's discussion led, by way of the idea that Bergelmir was later "laid under a millstone", to the view of the giant's being ground in the sea-mill, thus linking with the story of Aegir's Ocean Mill of the Nine Maidens, in which another name for the suffering giant is Amlodi (alias Hamlet).

The story seems to connect with a world-wide network of mythology dealing with some past cataclysm, something of which we have seen in this study as the myth's first violence and as the opening disaster in some of Shakespeare's plays. It also seems to connect with the sequel to that disaster, equally widely found in myth and (again) in some of those plays: some kind of purging process by which the masculine character in this succeeding world is refined from the monstrousness he took on in that first calamity.

But apart from this general similarity of idea, has the Bergelmir

---

1 *The Sources of 'Hamlet'.*

story really any relevance in our reading of Shakespeare's work, and specifically in our reading *Hamlet*? In answering this, I must say that many years ago, when pondering this question, I searched about in Norse myth for stories related to that of Bergelmir, to see if I could piece together a fuller account that might in some form have influenced the writing of *Hamlet*. I was partly encouraged by the guess that there was in Shakespeare's text signs of influence from a Germanic or Norse source, either direct or through English folklore (as put forward in an earlier chapter). The upshot of my search and pondering was quite surprising. I came to the realisation that, whether or not a 'Bergelmir' story had influenced *Hamlet,* it probably had influenced *The Tempest*. I will now try to justify this view.

I said earlier that the Bergelmir story was a sort of Norse 'Noah' myth, showing the escape by boat or "ark" from some violently collapsing world, and possibly also implying some idea of preservation in a sea-voyage. We can see, then, that at least generally in its theme it resembles that of *The Tempest,* but must nonetheless admit that this offers no more than the remotest possibility of influence. And yet there are other 'Bergelmir' stories in Norse myth – some now little more than fragments – that, if added to this general theme, makes the possibility stronger.

First, to recall something. I said in an earlier chapter that in some mythic accounts of the first destructive calamity the process by which the masculine character was turned violent – by a change in his feminine nature – is imaged as his falling lustfully for a femme fatale or witch, through whom he then, as it were, sires his own violent double. At the same time, I claimed that the Caliban story provided an example, for there – at least implied by Shakespeare's hints – appears a destructive devil begotten through a witch-like power infatuating the ruler. Now, as it happens, there is an account in Norse myth that likewise variantly suggests that the first violence came about as if by an act of begetting. Moreover, the one thus begotten is a recognisable 'Caliban'. This is Loki, the devil of destruction and mischief, who for his villainies (including the slaying of the god, Balder) had to be later chained in punishment. But Loki's story tells us something else of interest. It tells us that

Loki's father was the same "wise giant" who had escaped by boat from a first collapsing world – Bergelmir.[2] It thus turns out that the Bergelmir story has not one, but two important features to match with that of Prospero: the hero's escape (and possible preservation) by boat, and his fathering of a destructive being.

And it goes further. In *The Tempest,* the "bark" or boat, linked symbolically with Miranda, which preserves the soul of the dead world and its ruler, seems to be connected with another boat – that of Sycorax, which likewise came across the sea, but containing Caliban. The two boats could be seen imaginatively as one and the same, just as their imaging 'owners' – Miranda and Sycorax – could be seen as aspects of the same character. By the same imagination, this 'boat' could be seen to be further represented by the magical island, in which (a) the potential of the lost realm and its ruler is preserved, and (b) the male demonic energies are held in confinement. And something of the same idea seems to be present, though fragmentarily, in the Bergelmir story, in which the boat of the hero seems likewise to be linked with one associated both with Loki's mother and the idea of an island. This might be deduced from the two names of Loki's mother: 'Vessel' (Nal) and 'Leaf-Island' (Laufeia).[3] Was she, like Sycorax, also a witch? We do not know from the Bergelmir story itself, but it is likely she was, because in the possibly related story of Asgard's ruinous downfall the feminine character that breeds the violence is clearly witch-like and so bears as one of her titles 'The Hag of Ironwood'.

Pulling the threads together at this stage, we could surmise that some tale of Norse derivation once existed, incorporating elements of stories that now only appear separately and even fragmentarily – those of Bergelmir, Loki and perhaps also Balder (whose spirit also 'survived' by boat). Such a story, if it existed, would almost certainly have included the following similarities to Shakespeare's play: an escape from a shattering violence, and an ensuing state of life within the sea of time that preserves, as within some kind of feminine embrace or containment, both the potential of the lost world (and

---

2   See on to next footnote.

3   I came across the story of Bergelmir (Farbauti), Loki and Laufeia in H.A. Guerber's *The Norsemen* (p.217).

its ruler) and a character of meanwhile destructive energy.

And wouldn't it be convenient if the Norse accounts also contained (a) a ghostly magician, like a surviving 'mind' of a lost state, working its (and his own) return to life, and (b) some indication of a process by which the destructive energies were being worked back to a vitalising force capable of bringing about that 'resurrection'? To put the wish another way – wouldn't it be convenient if the Norse accounts showed something to match *The Tempest* as closely as did the Welsh *Romance of Taliesin*? Well, perhaps they do.

I said earlier that Sir Israel Gollancz, in his investigation of the Bergelmir story, linked the story of a hero's being ground under a millstone with another Norse story about an Ocean Mill – or 'Island Mill', as it is sometimes called. The presiding god or owner of this sea-mill was Aegir, who, as a magical lord of the dead and sea-god of storms, has some immediate resemblance to Shakespeare's Prospero. In addition, Robert Graves linked this Aegir with Ogyrvran,[4] the spooky background figure of the 'Taliesin' story whom we have already seen to be a Prospero-figure.

Building up the data of resemblances, we might then remember that both Aegir and Ogyrvan owned a magical cauldron. In the 'Taliesin' story it was connected with the witch Cerridwen, who seemed to play a crucial role in the purging and re-making of the true masculine character. It seems possible that Aegir's cauldron played the same role and was similarly 'feminine' in character, and so could be linked with the grinding-mill of his daughters as an alternative symbol of male purgation.

What emerges, in short, is the possibility that on Aegir's island, or in his 'mill', there is taking place a process of masculine transmutation carried out by a feminine power, figured as his daughters or symbolised as a purgative cauldron or a grinding-mill. It is as if the magical Aegir is deliberately using the feminine character as a means of masculine alteration for some reason. This compares with the island-process of *The Tempest* in which the 'wizard' Prospero, a similar master of storms, conducts an ordeal in

4   See the *The White Goddess* p.432 – footnote.

which something feminine – Sycorax/Miranda – is used for a transforming effect on the male character – working a change in its 'virility', in fact.

It is interesting then to find a related Norse story linking the sea–mill, in which the hero is being ground, with one that brings about an enrichment. This is the story of the giant Frothi, who employs two supernatural maidens (Menja and Fenja) to grind out gold and jewels from their mill. This further seems to agree in idea with the process of Prospero's island, which includes not only a purgation but an enrichment of this male character. Indeed, at one point, the idea of enrichment is unmistakably imaged in terms of precious things. This is in Ariel's song about the "drowned father", a former ruling figure who is undergoing a change as if in a bodily transmutation into something precious:– "Full fathom five thy Father lies; *of his bones are coral made. Those are pearls that were his eyes;* nothing …doth fade but suffers a *sea-change into something rich and strange.*"[5]

The same idea is shown in the process that Ferdinand (or Caliban) undergoes. He too is being enriched by a purging of his character that will lead back to the actually stated "*golden age*". And is not the means to this a 'sea-mill' called Miranda, for whom Ferdinand grinds and toils? Is not Sycorax/Miranda and her island used by Prospero as Aegir used his daughters and as Frothi used the supernatural maidens?

Another image proves weighty here. In the story of Ariel, Shakespeare shows a male character imprisoned in a tree by a witch, and about this he uses an image so clumsy he can only be meaning to draw our attention to it – "…where thou didst vent thy groans as fast as *mill-wheels* strike". Does not this image the whole process of the island – the male character in a feminine trap in which he is being painfully ground? I used to think that this image alluded simply to Samson, because he too was in a mill, grinding himself back to a lost gold of regality and power, but with possible Norse shadows in the play, I wonder if the image is another connection with the sea-mill.

---

5   1.2.399.404

What we should not lose sight of in all this is the coital analogy, though I suspect that the reader, prompted by the obvious symbolism of a grinding-mill will have kept full sight of it. Throughout all, the same underlying idea lies – that this purging and processing world of ours, this material limitation and prison of the selfhood, is a 'feminine' bondage and control upon the masculine character, and as such compares with the woman's hold on the man to bring him to his edge. This symbolic sexual connection is sometimes clearly implied as when, in *The Tempest,* the crowning act is made a nuptial consummation or climax. Likewise, earlier in *Measure for Measure,* Shakespeare had run the whole process of man's ordeal – the prison-house of the law – alongside a brothel and its doings. It is not by chance that in both the house of Lady Law and the house of Lady Venus man is equally put through it, and even to the point of dying from the base in realisation of something more vital. I likewise see that the grinding-mill imagery of the Norse myth and *The Tempest* is linked with the feminine character or force in life, through which the debased masculine passes in purgation, even unto 'dying' and a power-release towards a new birth. This power-release' is Prospero's final storm, his last Wild Hunt, or Second Ragnarok.

This 'coital' process is one by which the ghost-character Prospero is hoping to bring himself back from the dead. For this purpose of resurrection, male and female, as separate and debased characters or forces, are as if coitally combined, to work mutually a realisation of a former life-power, and a realisation of a lost unity, even as in an infant offspring, which includes in its radiant totality the former ruling wisdom – the lost 'ruler'. What Ferdinand and Miranda are doing together is in effect re-making the lost 'Milan' and its Duke. The same process is detectable in many destinal, cyclical myths, even beneath the romance surface of the Grail stories, where similarly young heroes are put through ordeal to reclaim as it were a lost 'virility' and so re-charge the feminine 'cauldron', restoring from the dead the 'mind' that has been behind the whole process – the ghostly Sick King. And it is the same process intended, no matter how uncertainly nowadays, by the Church in marriage, for there also a fallen male and female are yoked together so that (hopefully) one day their re-discovered harmony will bring to living strength this ghostly God who enjoins the labours of their tragic-comedy. Marriage stands symbolically for the whole way back to Paradise. Divorce, on the other hand, stands for its smashing – by the same fake-liberal mentality that ever offers us the easy way to some realisation of Utopia, and ever lets us down.

★   ★   ★

Opera-lovers will have noticed a strong likeness between the stories of *The Tempest* and Mozart's *The Magic Flute*. Whether the second was influenced by Shakespeare's play, or whether both were influenced by a story-type that appears also in *Die Schöne Sidea* (sometimes cited as a possible influence on Shakespeare) I do not know. Another thing to be noticed in *The Magic Flute* is that it contains an aria – well known to bass singers – in honour of Isis and Osiris. Emanuel Shikaneder, who devised the plot and libretto for this opera, had seemingly spotted at least a slight analogy between his story-line and that of the Egyptian myth. This prompts another curious glance at *The Tempest*. Did Shakespeare also, in his final, all-comprising master-work, recognise the analogy with the Osiris story?

Not much imagination would have been needed to see a similarity of story-line – an illustrious realm and ruler violently perished, magically preserved, and by a mysterious process finally restored. Particular similarities would have struck him, too, when reading the myth as recorded in Plutarch's *De Iside et Osiride* or some other intermediate source. For example, he would have noticed the resemblance in character between his own Prospero and the Egyptian Thoth – the god of magic who, like a destinal ghost, seems to be working the return of his own former being, the form and majesty of Osiris, who is meanwhile the "drowned one" or "lord of the dead", as recorded in the Pyramid Texts. He would have noted, too, the resememblance between his own Sycorax/Miranda and Isis – the central power over life and death, through which the magic must be worked, the lost elements re-formed and re-made, and all at last re-delivered. Further to this, as partly witnessed by his earlier portrayal of Titania in a play containing Osirian features, and by his portrayal of Cleopatra, he would have noticed the sinister side of the goddess Isis that is visible in details in her story, making her as fitting to the witch-like nature of Sycorax as to that of Miranda: the ambivalent power that can turn a god into a beast, but as readily then turn that beast back again into a divinity of strength and majesty.

Poised now for a full investigation of the Isis/Osiris story in connection with *The Tempest,* I hesitate. This study has been so loaded with mythic parallels, outlined and strenuously explicated. So in this case, I am going to leave most of the chore - and the fascinated delight - to the reader. He will find, if he has not already found, good accounts of the Osiris myth and related ritual in readily accessible places.[6] I feel sure that his own understanding when reading this myth will support my belief in its relevance to *The Tempest.* In it he will find, I believe, not only the destinal cycle, in which the feminine plays her part of womb-like preservation between the first loss and final rebirth, but also - implied in the imagery of some of its episodes - the coital analogy of the male energies being brought, by a death of their own baseness and a transmutation of their power, to a re-vitalising of that stored potential within the feminine 'body' or character. He will recognise, for example, what seems to be the real point to Isis' fire-ordeal upon the boy-child at Byblus, to give him the power of a god, or to her bringing death to the royal youth in the act of kissing and caressing the dead form of Osiris, or even in her 'making' of the vital phallus necessary to the resurrection.

I will finish this chapter, and the book, with a subject that will only touch on the Osiris theme.

★   ★   ★

In my earlier chapters, when marking out the outline form and idea of the myth this study has dealt with, I imagined our distant forefathers' sense of a cyclical destiny, perhaps as partly imaged in the seasonal cycle wheeling about them, which strongly influenced their

---

6   I find one of the best accounts of the Osiris myth and ritual to be in the old favourite - J. G. Frazer's *Golden Bough.* In the abridged edition it is also reasonably compact.

religious rites or dramas and the stories they passed down to later ages. I imagined then also that man has ever been struck in wonder at the mystery of the feminine character or nature – this powerful form that brings forth all living things as from a grave or underworld of secrets. This recognition was not by any means the whole basis of primitive magic, but it certainly played a part in it, and as certainly all early forms and perceptions of the goddess expressing it showed this strange connection between the underworld and the power of fertility, the mysterious link between life and death, affecting religious thinking and symbolism until modern times.

The symbolism for this feminine power was manifold, but it widely showed in the figure of a tree. Probably the primitive sense of wonder imagined in the powers of the tree much the same as in the feminine being – the form that takes the dying summer into itself, and keeps it through darkness and death for a rebirth in the Spring. Another common symbol was that of the boat. Maybe the making of this object from a tree influenced the transference of idea, or maybe there was the notion that this fibrous container, preserving through the storms of the sea, was another symbol of the womb, that preserves life or its promise through the hardships and darkness of existence.

Whatever the reason, two of the main images of preservation and potential rebirth, the containment of promise between the life lost and the life to come, were the tree and the boat (or ark); and so the temporary habitation of many a lost and future king was pictured in accord as the tree or boat: his prison or house of keeping and re-making, as if his own feminine partner in her darkening and hardening had trapped within herself his failing soul.

Both symbols figure strongly in the Osiris myth. His death, for instance, is an encasement in a wooden coffer, which then becomes the seafaring bark, and lastly a tree from which he is magically resurrected as from the womb of Isis who, as that bark or tree, has meanwhile kept and re-made him, like the dark queen that kept the sleeping Arthur. Fittingly, in ritual and icon Osiris was imaged as entombed in a coffer or ark, upon which the goddess was pictured both in the form of winged Isis, the life principle, and of winged

Nephthys, her death-aspect.

It is likely that the same symbolism passed into that of the Jewish Ark, with basically the same idea of a full divinity whose soul, first preserved from the rushing waters of the first disaster (as in *Exodus*), is meanwhile encased in the limited forms of this life and its dark wanderings until some future resurrection - the whole of the first kingship and its realm restored. In this case the winged figures of Isis and Nephthys had become the winged tutelary 'cherubim' that were pictured as arching over the ark like twin mothers. The same idea is vaguely found in the story of Noah's ark - the same preserving of life for a future deliverance as within a womb, with the same protective figures of the twinned female now become the 'dove' - the love and life principle - and the 'raven' as the figure of the death goddess. Yet it holds essentially the same idea - the same goddess of life-in-death, the same feminine nature in whose 'womb' is kept the shattered past like an embryo of the future restoration.

And then we look at *The Tempest* and see how the dying 'Milan', the first world, is imaged as being preserved by a boat, which then becomes an island of magical process within the same threatening sea, and finally gives up, as in a birth from a temporary sleep or death, the whole of the original life. And this means of preservation is linked with the Ark in Jewish symbolism, for Miranda as the tutelary goddess of both the ship of keeping and the island of meanwhile habitation is referred to thus - "O a *cherubim* thou wast that did preserve me". And it is also linked with the Noah myth, for the rainbow of the final Masque (Iris) seems to be meant as a reminder of the rainbow of promise in that story; and the two sides of the goddess in the Noah myth - the raven and the dove - seem to be partly remembered in Sycorax (*corax* means 'raven') and in the loving nature of Miranda, the kinder side of Venus ever emblemed as a dove - the precious love that will finally lead all from the dark seas to the lost land. By Eve we were lost, but by Eve we are restored.

There is something here further to be wondered at. We see how the medieval church resembled from afar a turreted ship afloat on the open landscapes of time, and how inside it was designed arboreally. It was therefore an image of the ancient goddess in her keeping role, but now become Mary, in whose 'womb' all creatures of this mortal life were gathered as in waiting for their birth. And so Mary was also called the 'Ark of the Covenant', that would finally end its wandering and come to the far side of the waters and give birth into the promised land, the paradise regained, like the Ark of Noah that would also bring back all to the land, and like that boat-shaped cradle which would at last shine with a divinity born again, surrounded by the all-life of animal, man and angel, in Bethlehem.

The ancient myth survived in many forms, last flowering in the Middle Ages, to which Shakespeare in his work was increasingly a devotee, against a world that was going to forsake it.

★   ★   ★

Most of *The Tempest* after its stormy start is quiet and dream-like, giving the feeling of the weird and insubstantial, as befits the idea of this life as a dream that will lastly pass away when its purpose is fulfilled. There are exceptions to this mood. One is the more solid description of Antonio and Sebastian as they plot murder and the seizing of power. Other cases are whenever Prospero grows angry – the blasts against Sycorax and Caliban, for instance, or that sudden rasping comment on the Court party – "for some of you are worse than devils".

I think Shakespeare intended these things to stand out. They are linked with a definite message. He is using his last play as a warning, partly implied too in the half-heartedness of the final reconciliation.

It would be a mistake to see Caliban as Shakespeare's idea of the savage and uncivilized, and no more. The so-called civilised may themselves be Calibans, though smartly dressed and differently assuming. This most clearly shows in the self-centred ruthlessness of Antonio, whose plans of murder and ambition are simply a sophisticated version of Caliban's own brutality.

But what, in short, might Shakespeare be aiming censure at? Possibly, at rational humanism, and its tendency, already apparent in his day, to forget our 'fallen' and innate brutality and therefore any need to guard and nurture against the selfhood, but simply assume that freedom and opportunity will make all well. Shakespeare evidently enough, and quite clearly in this play, was of a different tradition – the Judaic-Christian – that was hostile to such ideas of self-development, and rather, by an understanding of the innate monster in us, ever teaches the way of strict re-nurture and re-making, so that we might at length reach something like humanity. Though unpalatable to modern liberal minds, this older view teaches that disciplines, the law, and even sometimes harsh afflictions are part of the way that divine love (as is claimed) chooses for us to learn anything of value, for us to learn the need for self-sacrifice. It is perhaps a point as important as any investigation into myth.

★   ★   ★

A LAST WORD

A wish to keep this study reasonably short has meant that some aspects of the myth it has dealt with have been sketchily handled, or not at all in some cases. Yet, I believe, the two main aims have been reasonably covered.

The first was to show a single story, or 'myth', inherited from an even older world, present in much of our medieval literature. The second aim – and this more important – was to bring out some of the meaning of this myth, something so vital to our older authors, in that it held much of the meaning of life itself, that its recurrence in their work is explained as an insistent testament of belief. It was their powerful alternative gospel of life, and to some extent a secret gospel: the Mother-Story through passionate love of which they continually gave form to new versions of herself.

Yet its importance to them, I suspect, will remain mainly a lost cause today. Its wisdom, even when understood by the modern world, seems likely to be ignored, for the most part, along with much traditional understanding, as the mere stuff of fairy tale and fanciful backwardness. To be ignored also, because, as I have pointed out a moment ago, this wisdom has in it certain things against the grain of modern liberalism, including the teaching that we in this world of present material existence are, whatever the features and possibilities else, in a fallen state of nature, wherein the masculine character needs discipline to rise above the barbarous in intellect and spirit; and the self, given much free allowance and scope nowadays, needs to be re-nurtured, if we are ever to find a true remedy for the fears and shames that the self is a defence and avoidance of.

APPENDIX A:
The Ballad of Loving Mad Tom

Many years ago, in his collection of essays, *A Common Asphodel*, Robert Graves gave what he maintained was a likely original version of this ballad. It was based on one found badly transcribed in a manuscript book of Giles Earle (1615), to which Graves made slight amendments and, to complete the sense, added a stanza from a related ballad, which he claimed had originally belonged to it (stanza 9).

Graves' whole reconstruction is very interesting, but as interesting is what he claimed of this ballad. He believed that it had once belonged to a version of *King Lear*, which does have a bedlamite character called Tom (Edgar in disguise), and he suggested a place in the text where it would have fitted.

If the ballad did belong to the play, then it is of vital importance in our understanding. After all, *King Lear* still holds problems of interpretation. Other cryptic verses and allusions sprinkled in the text seem to hold clues to a kind of inner meaning, so why not the ballad also?

Graves suggested - and rightly, it seems - that the ballad was based on some original bedlamite verses, or song, which had been adapted, and with some additions made to the crude original. Only the stanzas that appear to be adaptations or additions will be looked at in this Appendix, though the other stanzas will be put at the end for the reader's interest. In addition, I have rearranged the sequence of the relevant stanzas, to give what seems to be a more logical order.

Since much has been said already in this study about the 'myth' of *King Lear*, this look at the ballad will be kept to essentials.

Stanza 3
A thought I took for Maudline
    In a cruse of cockle pottage;
With a thing thus tall - sky bless us all! -
    I befell into this dotage.
I've slept not since the Conquest,

Ere then I never wakèd
Till the roguish fay of love where I lay
Me found and stripped me naked ...

Most of the meaning follows from the fact that "cockle" foods were then thought aphrodisiacs. So here we are told of lust entering the world, connected with man's new shamed sense of his 'nakedness'. A link with the Adam myth is made, and more clearly still when we realise that the "roguish fay" (from the underworld) is a folklore version of the *Genesis* serpent. (Snakes were long associated with the underworld.) The "Conquest" (1.5.) probably therefore means the Fall – the 'conquest' of the human by the infernal.

"Maudline" denotes Magdalen, the figure of the harlot in the Gospels. Such a woman satisfies both man's ego-fantasy and his urge to degrade or punish what is natural – the two aspects of Lear's behaviour in the play's opening scene, incited by his flattering daughters (the ego-fantasy) and Cordelia (the natural 'victim'). For closer examination of the link between the Paradise myth and the breakdown of Lear and his kingdom, see Chapter 4.

Stanza 6
I know more than Apollo,
    For oft when he lies sleeping
I see the stars at bloody wars
    And the wounded welkin weeping,
The Moon embrace her Shepherd
    And the Queen of Love her Warrior
When the first doth horn the Star of the Morn
    And the next, the heavenly Farrier ...

The conscious, rational mind (Apollo) is ignorant of deeper truths – among which, all the poetic and inspired imaginings and memories that well up from the 'sleeping mind', the Unconscious. Mad Tom, broken mentally from the rational, has access to this kind of mind. And what does it tell him? About something long ago – an alternative story of the Fall which involved a violent calamity, remembered in many myths as a War in Heaven. What was its cause? According to the last four lines, the cause was a breakdown in the original sexual harmony of life, indicated by two stories of adultery

(Selene with Endymion; Aphrodite with Ares). Similarly, the massive violence in Arthur's story and in the Troy story followed something going wrong in the sexual sphere (the adultery of Guinevere/Lancelot and Helen/Paris). But sexual rebellion is only one aspect of the conflict that must arise once a sense of sin (as indicated in the previous stanza) enters life. Judging by early events in *King Lear,* sin-awareness brings about a consciousness of the self as distinct from and opposed to others. It therefore causes a conflict of self against self, the clashing demands for self-right, found abundantly in *King Lear.* Adultery (imaged later in Edgar's Lancelot-like guilt) is only one example of rebellious self-demand conflicting with the self-demand of order and stability.

Stanza 1

From the hag and hungry goblin
    That into rags would rend ye
The spirits that stand by the naked man
    In the Book of Moons defend ye
That of your five sound senses
    Ye never be forsaken
Nor wander from yourselves with Tom
    Abroad to beg your bacon …

The "hag" and "goblin" are the extremes of the dehumanised sexes in this world. In Shakespeare's work, the first is represented by such as Goneril and Regan ("unnatural hags"), Lady Macbeth, and Sycorax. She is the Pride or Will, the emotional coil of the selfhood, the force of man's binding dream, almost impossible to break free of, which according to this study came into being reactively to a poisonous sense of shame and meaninglessness. The "hungry goblin" is the masculine character she has created in turn: a figure whose imagination is reduced to a glimmer of itself and whose strength is given to destructiveness. He is the monster that fallen man has become, reflected onto gods he wants a reason to serve, and onto others that he wants a reason to destroy. And yet he keeps a little of his original sight, like an instinct by which one day to escape the manic plaything of the witch he has become: a King Hamlet, Lear or Odin, working towards his own destruction and his own release.

Stanza 4

When I short have shorn my sow's face
    And snigged my hairy barrel,
At an oaken inn I pound my skin
    In a suit of gilt apparel.
The moon's my constant mistress,
    And the lovely owl my marrow.
The flaming drake and the night-crow make
    Me music to my sorrow ...

A clue to the first four lines is in the change of clothing, which occurs in *King Lear* after events denoting the breaking of the pride and the monster it has made (Act 4). Lear himself is re-clothed after his healing sleep - taken "out of the grave". As he has by this stage reclaimed his former true majesty or manhood ("Aye, every inch a king!"), we can understand this stanza's "gilt apparel" and also the first two lines' indication that he had cast off the inhuman. Also, as the oak was known as a tree of human sacrifice, the "oaken inn" likewise fits with the climactic acts of self-sacrifice in the play. Perhaps even the shaving as well, for the victim's hair was sometimes shaved before execution.

The last four lines are out of sequence. They should precede the first four lines, since they indicate a process of re-nurture that *leads up* to the final sacrifice. That is to say, the romantic dedication of man to his mistress - the witch employed in a reformative role - is the amorous or 'courtly' equivalent of the process in which he re-learns his humanity and what needs to be sacrificed for its regaining.

This mis-sequence seems to be deliberate, as in stanza 6 (previously) and as in the order of the stanzas itself: a deliberate 'scrambling', as is often found in old cryptic teachings and riddles.

Stanza 8

With a host of furious fancies
    Whereof I am commander,
With a burning spear and a horse of air
    In the wilderness I wander.
By a knight of ghosts and shadows
    I summoned am to tourney
Ten leagues beyond the wide world's end -

> Methinks it is no journey …

This stanza also links with the climactic events of *King Lear* – the hero's defeat of the monster that his own pride or self-righteousness has created in himself – which is correspondingly imaged in Act 4 as a last battle or tourney. Little needs to be added, except to point out in line 3 the Norse details (Odin's spear and horse) which links this final conflict with the last Wild Hunt or Ragnarok – an idea that Shakespeare was to use again in Prospero's final storm in *The Tempest*.

Stories in which heroes are challenged to combat by ghostly warriors are found commonly in our islands, a good few surviving in Arthurian romances, wherein infernal, otherworldly knights are a frequent hazard of the quest. Perhaps all are relics of pagan rites, celebrating the victory of light and life over winter and death, and imaging in later moral allegory man's reclamation of his true manhood – and, of course, the reclamation of true womanhood. The mention of "wilderness" links it fittingly with the Christ myth and the reclamation of the true God through the sacrifice of the selfhood.

Stanza 9

> I'll bark against the Dog Star,
> I'll crow away the morning
> I'll chase the Moon till it be noon
> And make her leave her horning;
> But I'll find Merry Mad Maudline,
> And seek whate'er betides her,
> And I will love beneath or above
> The dirty earth that hides her …

Indeed, the most important stanza of all, but if it needs commentary, then such as Shakespeare wrote in vain, and a host of lesser talent, including somewhere well down the line my eager, explaining self, should have idled and dreamed elsewhere.

––––––––––

The stanzas not considered are as follows:-

2. Of thirty bare years have I
     Twice twenty been enragèd

And of forty been three times fifteen
In durance soundly cagèd,
On the lordly lofts of Bedlam
With stubble soft and dainty
Brave bracelets strong and whips ding-dong
And wholesome hunger plenty ...

5.   The palsy plague my pulses
      If I prig your pigs or pullen,
      Your culvers take, or matchless make
Your Chanty-clear or Solan!
When I want provant, with Humphrey
I sup, and when benighted
I repose in Paul's with walking saules
Yet never am affrighted ...

7.   The gipsies, Snap and Pedro,
      Are none of Tom's comradoes;
      The punk I scorn and the cut-purse sworn
And the roaring boys' bravadoes;
The meek, the white, the gentle,
Me handle, touch and spare not,
But those that cross Tom Rhinoceros
Do what the panther dare not ...

In addition each stanza had this refrain –

While I do sing 'Any food, any feeding,
Feeding, drink or clothing?
Come, dame or maid, be not afraid:
Poor Tom will injure nothing.

APPENDIX B
Hamlet and the Biblical Storm of Destiny

As maintained in this study, realism and myth do not make a happy partnership. Putting them together in a single work asks for contradictions. *Hamlet* is full of them for this reason.

Viewed realistically, its hero and his role come off badly. He appears a self-righteous ego-maniac, forever chuntering and railing against a life not up to his expectations, forever hurting people who get in his way or do not bend to his wishes, and he is even ready to kill them with scarcely a qualm. To make things worse, he then declares that all this comes about because he is appointed by heaven as its "scourge and minister". This is in the Queen's Chamber scene, where his deeds are not only black but absurd. Having angrily murdered an old man behind a curtain, simply for snooping, he turns round to lecture his mother on her misbehaviour - her bad choice of marriage partner.

When we look at the same character and actions from the point of view of myth, however, the picture is quite different. As in a romance or fairy tale, we see the questing knight abroad in a ruined, fantastical kingdom, intent on winning it back for its cheated and banished king and having to contend with a fell enchanter and his accomplice, the original queen now under spell, who seems liefer to ensnare him than be rescued. In such a setting, if evil old men and goblins are detested and slain, the hero who hates and slays them does not make himself a criminal but a grand champion.

I believe an Elizabethan audience was as ready to see *Hamlet* in this second way as in the first. Probably readier, because much of their mental conditioning had been in stories and exempla that called for a mythic rather than a realistic appraisal of things. Part of that conditioning was the largest fabric of myth known in their day - the Bible - further fostering a tendency towards symbolic and spiritual understanding.

In this, it was little different from the influence of romance, allegory and folktale, for its wonders and instruction were very similar in nature. The main cycle of the Old Testament, for example, is very much like the standard romance or fairy tale in pattern. Call the lost and cheated king, Adam (or even God); call the questing knight the prophet; call the fell enchanter the false gods of Canaan; and call the queen under spell the harlot daughter of Zion ... and you have the same story, the same purpose and dynamic, the same end, in a cycle that stretched from the fallen 'once upon a time' to the restored kingdom or marriage, with the conception of the Messiah as its symbol. And that is just the overall cycle. There were many stories placed within this framework like examples-in-little of the same wheeling process of loss, tribulation and final atonement. The stories of Joseph, Ruth, Samson, the Egypt-to-Canaan wandering, Job, and so on, all added with different viewpoint and emphasis to the larger cycle and its meaning.

As part of this upbringing by stories, fostering a readiness to read mythically, there was another idea or understanding - that all the wisest stories somehow belonged together. They were of a piece, repeating and varying on similar patterns, themes and characterisation. This understanding seems to have been part of a tradition shared by readers (or listeners) and writers from earliest times. The Bible itself showed it, and so did Homer in his epics, or Ovid in his *Metamorphoses.* So also did Chaucer in his *Canterbury Tales,* and Shakespeare in his work so often combines - by allusion, echo, shadow, added to the main story - elements of folktale, myth and biblical theme, as if part of a single tapestry. It is not surprising then that *Hamlet,* in addition to mythical and folktale elements, should have in it so many echoes of, and a general correspondence with, the Bible's own overall cycle: the lost marriage of Eden and the quest towards its regaining, centred on the winning back of Eve.

There is a particular sense of correspondence between the action of the play and the Old Testament prophetic books - Jeremiah, Isaiah, Ezekial, and so on - with Hamlet himself shadowing the prophetic role: the agent of truth unleashed upon a world of lies. The rest of this appendix will concentrate on this. The New Testament elements in the play, though important, will for brevity have to be waived.

★   ★   ★

In the Old Testament, the power of moral and spiritual renewal is carried by the prophets, whose fervour beats against the customary spiritual deadness of the people, in order to force them to a higher destiny - to cast out the spirit of untruth in their hearts like a false lover, and take back in what is true and right, like a husband. It compares with the 'energy' character and role of Hamlet, the "prophetic soul", the violence of the word and power of light (indicated by the solar imagery of Act 1, Scene 2), the spark that, like "the dawn in russet mantle clad", threatens the darkness of Claudius's kingdom with a transforming vision, re-awakening the heart. It is possible that one Biblical image for that transformation - a virgin at last conceiving (Isaiah) - is used in the play's sub-plot knowingly for this: Ophelia at length wrested from her father's sterile influence to find the fruitfulness that Hamlet earlier threatened - "Let her not walk i' th' sun: conception is a blessing; but as your daughter may conceive, friend, look to 't" (2.2.180).

The prophets were notorious for a fiery, uncompromising spirit, which made them a thorough nuisance to kings and counsellors - even to the point of drawing persecution on themselves, and death. Serving a higher power, their God (like Hamlet's father) from whom they received their message and mission, they strove against the people's bondage to unworthy practices and false authorities. They were out not only to break customs but to change them, to change the very way people thought and acted, and the law that governed that thought and act. They were out to make a new nature in what they often symbolised as an erring woman or harlot - the stubborn, blind heart of the people. This makes sense of Hamlet's war against custom that numbs, that imprisons to senseless, automatic behaviour, blinding and stifling the instinct of truth and conscience. The re-structuring of Gertrude's behaviour makes first-rate biblical sense:-

> "That monster, custom, who all else doth eat,
>   Of habits devil, is angel yet in this,
> That to the use of actions fair and good
>   He likewise gives a frock or livery
> That aptly is put on ...
>   For use almost can change the stamp of nature

> And exorcise the devil or throw him out
> With wondrous potency ... (3.4.161-170)

The reforming zeal of the Old Testament prophets has further points of correspondence with Hamlet's role. For instance, the prophets' influence led to the Jewish use of the Law and story, precept and example, as a reflection of right behaviour. You might say that 'art' became an instrument of true teaching. In the same way, Hamlet is shown reforming the art of the players, moving drama away from mere entertainment into service of moral truth, like a mirror - "... to hold as 'twere the mirror up to nature; to show virtue her feature, scorn her own image, and the very age and body of the time his form and pressure" (3.2.21-24). It is interesting that in his reform of Gertrude's "heart" later, he uses a similar 'mirror' of instruction - "You go not till I set you up a glass where you may see the inmost part of you" (3.4.18-19). And in the same scene is another instance of art used for reformative purpose - where Hamlet shows Gertrude contrasting pictures of his father and Claudius, "the counterfeit presentment of two brothers", to instruct her. It is worth noting also that just as the prophet Nathan used a story to 'catch the conscience' of King David, whose fault was murder and adultery, so Hamlet uses a play (*The Murder of Gonzago*) to show Claudius his own crimes of murder and adultery. Claudius's prayer soon after this therefore fitly echoes one of David's psalms of remorse - "Wash me, and I shall be *whiter than snow*" (Ps.51:7); "Is there not rain enough in the sweet heavens to wash it (a murderer's hand) *white as snow*?" (3.3.45).[1]

In contrast to Hamlet's use of art is the manipulative "art" of Polonius, mere showmanship for self-promotion or, in the case of his use of Ophelia, for deceit and power. If Shakespeare is reflected in Hamlet, as few can doubt, then we might say that he is fully avowing a use of art as a teacher, a means by which those who see truly may show truly, for the instruction of others. No wonder his last portrayal of the magical artist is also of a "school-master" - Prospero.

The clearest link between the prophets' and Hamlet's mission is

---

1   Pointed out by Thomas Carter (*Shakespeare and Holy Scripture*).

now to be looked at. The prophets' attempts to win back the people, or the heart of the people, is often imaged in the Old Testament as the attempts of the Lord like an estranged husband to win back his erring wife, who meanwhile prefers the flatteries of untruth, which like false lovers (the false gods) are the cause of her "whoredoms".[2] The 'grieving husband' idea is very noticeable in *Hosea,* and it is here, as you might expect, that echoes of Hamlet's dealing with his mother are strong. Notice, for instance, the words of instruction given to the prophet: "Plead with your mother, plead; for she is not my wife, neither am I her husband. Let her therefore put away her whoredoms out of her sight, and her adulteries" (*Hosea* 2.2). In this case, too, part of the reclamation of the feminine heart or character comes through compelled abstinence.

Sometimes a general comparison with Hamlet's mission touches on a similarity of wording. For example, remembering the reformation of Gertrude and the image of the cleft heart - "O throw away the worser part of it, and live the purer with the other half" - we might recall Ezekial's "Cast away from you all your transgressions whereof ye have confessed, and make you a new heart and a new spirit". Likewise in *Jeremiah,* the prophet not only sees the people as a woman gone astray and turned harlot - "the faithless woman, Judah" - he uses images that occur in Hamlet's words. For example, "Behold, I will feed them, even this people, with wormwood" (9.15) compares with Hamlet's wording when he also shows the bitter truth to Claudius and Gertrude in the play-scene (3.2.178). We might note also in *Jeremiah:-*

"... and from the prophet even unto the priest everyone dealeth falsely. They *have healed also the hurt* of the daughter of my people *slightly* (New translation 'but skin-deep only'), saying Peace, peace, when there is no peace. Were they *ashamed* when they had committed abomination? Nay ... neither *could they blush* ..." (13.15).

This compares with Hamlet's "...O shame, where is thy blush'?... Lay not that flattering unction to your soul... It will but

---

2   An image of serving a lie that had some basis in the actual facts of Canaanitish religions, in which ritual prostitution was practised.

skin and film the ulcerous place". Likewise Jeremiah's famous "Can the Ethiopian change his skin or the leopard his spots? Then may ye also do good that are accustomed to evil" (13.23) seems to be remembered in Gertrude's "...my very soul (where) I see such black and grainèd spots as will not leave their tinct". This is especially likely since it is followed by Hamlet's making the same point as Jeremiah: that customs as well as working for the bad can be used to work for good also ("This monster, custom..." etc).

One of the most powerful comparisons between the unworthy people and the woman erring in her pride and beauty is found in *Ezekial* 16 (7-39), which I am sure would put the reader in mind, as it did me, not only of the situation in *Hamlet* generally but of that first soliloquy of deep regret over the fickleness of the wife ("Frailty thy name is woman"). The end of the passage in *Ezekial* is interesting also, in that the false woman, like the prostitute, is humbled by stripping. The same image is used elsewhere in the prophetic books to denote the humiliation of the proud people, delivered over by God's wish to their enemies and conquerors. Once we remember how the term 'habits' can mean both automatic behaviour and clothing, the point of Hamlet's humiliatingly tearing away Gertrude's old habits is realised. His 're-clothing' her with fresh 'habits' is also found in the prophets. Isaiah, for example, as well as matching with the other prophets' view of the people as a harlot ("How is the faithful city [Jerusalem] become a harlot!") and in imaging the final humiliation as a stripping of her clothes and finery, then goes further. When the wrath is spent, the Lord will take the woman again and give her new clothes or 'habits' - "for he hath clothed me in the garments of salvation, he hath covered me with the robe of righteousness, as a bridegroom decketh himself with ornaments and a bride adorneth herself with her jewels" (61:10).

The idea of a second marriage, indicated here, is also important. As the right relationship of the 'sexes' was imaged at first as a marriage (Adam and Eve), so at the end of the 'sexual' war, when the wrath of the cheated and resisted 'Adam' is spent and the proud feminine brought low, so a re-marriage or re-harmony can take place. *Isaiah* is full of this spirit of reconciliation - the Lord angry no more but as a lover to his bride, as if it were only the proud resistance that made him a monster. The same is true of Shakespeare's work, wherein, the world of proud error having been overcome, there is often a marriage (or re-marriage), most clearly shown in the story of Prospero who so much in mood resembles the successful Lord in *Isaiah* - "Yet with my nobler reason 'gainst my fury do I take part; the rarer action is in virtue than in vengeance; they being penitent, the sole drift of my purpose doth extend not a frown further" (*Tempest* 5.1.26-29).

There is a brief moment of reconciliation between Hamlet and Gertrude, slightly comparable with the mood in *Isaiah,* when the long-resisted Lord or 'husband' returns, as it were, to the humbled 'wife'. For instance, the expression of the ghost is such that Hamlet feels it will "convert my stern effects: then what I have to do will want true colour; tears perchance for blood", and the ghost also bids Hamlet comfort Gertrude. Likewise a meeker, more thoughtful Hamlet says to her "…and when you are desirous to be blest, I'll blessing beg of you". But it is a brief and shallow reconciliation compared with its equivalent point in the Bible.

Is the failure in *Hamlet* Shakespeare's own reflection on the actual failure of the prophetic spirit and of the Christian religion that followed it? Hamlet stays self-righteous after all, and his 'reforms' seem dangerously like a cult of superior virtue so likely to foster pride, involving all the old hatreds and cruelties. So maybe the play's failure is a reflection of Shakespeare's own view of failure in the Judaeo-Christian quest, and a failure therefore of the cycle of destiny. Perhaps all is doomed to plunge down again to darkness and the iron hand of tyranny.

APPENDIX C:
Other Eves – Other Stories

Through a study of myth, I have shown in this book that its key to our fallen situation, or – if you prefer modern terms – the key to our underlying psychosis, is that our feminine nature bears a deep-set awareness of shame and emptiness: in the words of the Paradise story, an awareness of "sin" and "death". It is something lodged deep in our emotional or psycho-pathetic being like a self-hatred. From this, I have shown – at least have tried to show – the ills of life arise, and among these an alteration in what is masculine in us into something life-hating and destructive, in love with the fantasy that hides the dreaded sense of shame and emptiness.

So important do I believe this fact to be, that I would ask all who search into myth, as well as into the human condition, to hold it like a key, perhaps worded in the way of fairy tales: 'The lady with the Witch is twinned, and so the Wise King twins with Beast'. They will find the idea also in the wisest of myths, which show or imply a first poisoning, a first alteration in the kindly lady, from which a mad woe arises. Among such wise stories I would include certainly the Paradise myth, but would prefer to that the medieval romance of *Sir Orfeo,* because that story more clearly shows an important truth. It shows that our lady-self had no choice, any more than we as children have choice in the feelings of emptiness, fear and self-hatred that sooner or later beset us, from which we escape into the protective fantasies we call 'growing up', or any more than the trees and flowers in Autumn have choice in the blight that comes upon them and causes them to wither into the dusky raiment of the Winter Queen.

Unfortunately many distortions crept into other versions of the myth. Some I think came about through an increased literal-mindedness, mentally converting female figures in the myth into actual women; but also, I feel surer, occurred a weakening of insight into the feminine nature and, with that, into her essential blamelessness in what she did. Patriarchal societies did not like (do not like) woman. It's as simple – and as complex – as that. This had its effect in altering the story. The woman was seen with fault, even full responsibility; and so the myth took on a range of Pandoras and Zuleikas. Even the Paradise myth, for all its wisdom, was listing that way, towards a blame on Eve, for betraying the man. It had almost forgotten that it was a masculine weakness to start with, that allowed the lady partner to be beset by dark thoughts and misgivings, just as the weakening sun and life-force in Autumn allows to creep in a darkness and a canker to the fields and woods.

Some versions of the myth carried this misogyny further. If we look at typical *Delilah* versions, for instance, woman is a bad lot from the start. Indeed, in some cases no better side to her is mentioned. In the Blodwed story, for example, the only excuse she might have – and that faint – is that she was alone and separate from her husband at the time of temptation towards a lover. Clytemnestra comes off hardly better, though somebody thought fit to give her a grievance. Likewise the lady Freyja in the Brisingamen story seems to choose voluntarily her path of betrayal and damnation, as do Shakespeare's Lady Macbeth and Lear's "hag" daughters later.

Typical of this misogynistic version is a very old story that might stand for a whole type. In it I think the reader will see how the true story may have been altered – perhaps unwittingly indeed, but nonetheless surely – so that now the feminine urge to power has no terrible and irresistible cause, but comes about simply by whim to rise 'above her station'. The first poisoning in this version is not what afflicted her but what she uses on the man:-

Isis, weary of her place in a world of mortals, desired to be divine. To this end, she decided to get for herself the power of Ra, by having him tell her his secret name. He was old, and sometimes the saliva from his mouth dribbled to the earth, and Isis, secretly mixing this earth and saliva, made a serpent, placing it on the path she knew that Ra must, as sun-god, daily travel. When Ra therefore in the majesty of his rays passed by, the serpent bit him. He fell ill with a shaking fever, and none of the gods knew how to help him. Isis asked him about his illness, and offered to cure him in return for his secret name. At first he put her by with unclear answers, because he knew that his main power was held within his name; but with his illness worsening, and she persisting, he finally told her. And so the power passed from within his breast, and into hers. Isis became a goddess.

There is another story about Ra that seems very much like a sequel - perhaps it once was - because the behaviour of the male agrees with the normal pattern in such stories: he grows destructive against the natural feminine as sinful, it goes as follows:-

Nut, the wife of Ra, was in love with another - the god Geb. Ra, discovering her infidelity, was enraged, cursing his wife with childlessness, and declaring that the fruit of her womb would never be delivered. There is of course a happy ending, because the magical Thoth, who also loves her, finds a way round the curse, and Nut finally gives birth to offspring.

★   ★   ★

But the details of particular myths may be less important than the appearance of the Eve theme in so many of them, and sometimes with so much insight into her first fundamental alteration of character as to leave her exonerated. Our older poets, much taken up with man's sexual situation, even what we might call man's sexual destiny, inevitably touched on different versions of Eve's story. With different degrees of fairness and insight. Spenser and Milton, for instance, seem usually unwilling to stray far from suspicion and denunciation, and only able to accept some ideal fabrication of womanhood. Chaucer, on the other hand, showed such sympathy and understanding as made him the wisest of our poets and a true spokesman, with Malory, for the age of chivalry: the lady, whatever, is not to blame. Shakespeare is more variable, sometimes a poet of Venus and sometimes of Jehovah. If *The Tempest* could be taken as a final witness, then he was more of the latter. But he is puzzling. Judging by his portrayal of Ophelia, for instance, we see that he seems to have been well aware of feminine blamelessness, which then at other times he preferred to ignore. Perhaps he wanted a reason to be fascinated by the witch and her world, or a reason to storm at her, and so suppressed the insight that would have robbed him of this reason.

APPENDIX D:
Blake and Shakespeare

William Blake in his *prophetic works* was intent to write his own versions of a myth, the same cycle of destiny that this study has dealt with. The major scheme was to survey the whole of man's spiritual history from the disastrous Fall, whose causes he shows, through the process of tribulation and clarification of error, up to the final breakthrough and man's salvation.

These works were his own versions of the Bible, so to speak, or of Milton's major epics. But his intention was very ambitious, because into these works he incorporated, sometimes simply by allusion or 'echo' and sometimes more substantially, ideas and forms from all the writers he knew that he suspected to be dealing with the same myth. The *prophetic works* are therefore a stupendous compilation or poly-amalgam, brilliant but, it has to be admitted, incredibly obscure and sometimes quite maddening to read. The reader, if interested, would be well advised to approach these works by way of very able scholars who have managed to work out an overall pattern and distinct exegesis. Among these, on the matter of Blake's restoration of a mythic tradition, is the masterly study by Northrop Frye - *Fearful Symmetry*. It is a book that any interested in the mythic tradition of literature might read in entirety (along with 'The Archetypes of Literature', in his *Fables of Identity*). The argument throughout is that Blake's purpose was to re-create a myth or form of lost vision, in which the work of some earlier artists was to be used and adapted so as to show them in relation to this overall "archetype" or pattern.

But what has this to do with Shakespeare? In answering this, I hope the reader will allow a spell of autobiography. In the late 60's, favoured by fortune to be teaching on the major works of English literature, I had formed the notion that there was in the work of our older writers a sort of mythic tradition, to some extent wittingly engaged in. In whatever older text I happened to handle, despite its surface differences or the differences of apparent subject, I had often the quite uncanny sense that I was dealing with the same underlying story.

Probably, in the normal way of things, this notion would have led nowhere, but by chance in these same years I took up a part-time study of Blake. In reading his *prophetic works* I kept noticing how there occurred occasional echoes of Shakespeare's plays. I was for a long time too preoccupied with other aspects of Blake's work to give these much attention, even though I knew that similar (though more obvious) connections with Milton in his pages had led Blake scholars to important insights. Eventually I began, however, to take the Shakespearean adumbrations more seriously, and then saw their possibly major import.

As Blake was writing Myths of Destiny, and as he was well known as an amalgamator of many kinds of old, even ancient, mythic and religious material that he believed aspects of this supreme myth, then by such echoes and allusions he might be indicating that some of Shakespeare's plays could be seen as variants of the same myth. Even at this early stage I saw real possibilities in this, for some of Shakespeare's plays did indeed seem to deal with a cycle very much like Blake's, starting with a catastrophic fall from a higher state, and moving through earthly tribulations to a point where wisdom either succeeds in regaining the first state of happiness, or else fails, and allows another plunge into darkness and woe.

Eventually the lures of possibility grew too strong to resist, and so, pushing aside the piles of notes amassed on my earlier subject, I set to work to write on Blake's use of Shakespeare. Alas for the hopes of youth, even when we are not so young! It was sometimes a fairly easy matter to pick out from Blake's pages echoes of Shakespearean ideas and sometimes actual wording. For example, there is a strong shadow of Oberon and Titania, mixed in with reminders of *The Tempest,* in the quarrel of Los and Enitharmon in the early Books ('Nights') of *Four Zoas.* It proved, however, extremely hard to use the notoriously obscure *prophetic works* to support lucidly a then unusual reading of Shakespeare. I ended up with a manuscript that though interesting to me was likely to interest nobody else – except perhaps a student of that serious academic disease, *explicia gravis.* Apart from anything else, I was a nobody with an unusual subject – not the sort that publishers or professors were likely to embrace like a returning prodigal. Instead of pushing faint hopes, therefore, I simply set to work once again to write a study of Shakespeare's plays as myth, using some of the ideas and insights that my earlier labours had led to.

Feeling then very tired – for these endeavours had been followed up on top of a very taxing full-time job for almost eight years – and having grown very diffident in my isolation about the whole business, I set the whole thing aside, making only one half-hearted attempt to canvass my findings and ideas. It was not until, many years later, I caught by chance a broadcast interview with Ted Hughes about his newly published book on Shakespeare as myth,[1] that my interest revived and, with it, the first glimmerings of assurance that perhaps there was something in the work after all. I wrote to Ted Hughes with an outline of my earlier work, and he generously offered to read it, giving me much encouragement in reply.

It was that encouragement that led to the writing of this present study. I hope that those interested in Blake's work, either for itself or in connection with Shakespeare, will find this study helpful, for, even after so many years, I have largely followed what I believe is a Blake-ian approach.

---

1   *Shakespeare and the Goddess of Complete Being*

APPENDIX E
Further Notes on *King Lear*

There are three further points I would like to make about *King Lear*. These are here tacked on as appendices because I could not work them easily into the main discussion in Chapter 4.

    1.   Lear's original kingdom, Arthur's realm, and paradise are all linked in Shakespeare's *King Lear* as the first higher state of life that suffered woeful decline and finally violent collapse. We have seen that this collapse is due to a combination of sin-awareness, like a spiritual poison, and its frustrating effect on the masculine life-energy, causing a dangerous darkening in it, which finally breaks out violently against the life it should sustain. It is as if Osiris, another figure of this first divine energy, had not only been trapped in a box,[1] but was also poisoned; or as if Samson had not only been bound by his own feminine 'flesh' but by a 'flesh' with a poison running in its veins.

This 'as if' does not need to be applied to the similar fate of Hercules, because the combination of the two factors is clearly indicated in the story of the 'Nessus robe' - the gift of a jealous wife - which not only bound the hero but held a poison. Its effect is interesting. He went mad, and tore from him this feminine form, his own flesh, which is equally shown in the other story of his madness, in which he murdered his wife and children. The 'lion' Hercules, for this, did penance by command of Delphi. Another 'Leo' did likewise in a Shakespeare play - Leontes in *The Winter's Tale*. But Hercules' fate is as clearly shown in Lear's mania, when, in a poisonous sense of the sinfulness of life, and in a similar maddening sense of bondage, he likewise is imaged as tearing off his garments (and his whole nature?) - "Off, off, you lendings"[2] - underlining the meaning of his action at this point in the play: the violent renunciation of all life as corrupt.

---

1   In one version of his downfall, Osiris is lured by Set (his usurper) into an ornate coffer, which is then murderously sealed.

2   3.4.110

Maybe all these cases – and many more – are linked, like a mythic memory recorded in many variants of some long-ago violent catastrophe. Maybe they record what the 'scientists' only came upon much later – some long-ago *Big Bang* that shattered and scattered the original state of life. And maybe they are warnings of what might befall again, for this same denial of true masculinity and this same moral poison still operates.

2.   That last 'maybe' in fact brings us to something in *King Lear* that has often puzzled its readers – that in Act 5 all plunges *again* into violence and darkness. Why? It seems to go against the main drift of the play, in which so much has been endured and so much learned. And it goes against the 'happy ending' which the source-story actually included, and which all mythic sense demands. The man "all tattered and torn" should find again "the maiden all forlorn", and live with her happily, as the wise children's verse has it. And yet it doesn't happen.

The reason may lie in what I said above, at the end of Note 1 – "… this same moral poison still operates". Shakespeare may have looked at the early stages of what is for us the modern world, and not felt hopeful. The overall historical cycle of destiny for man, of which *King Lear* was a mythic reflection, may have seemed to him unlikely to have a happy ending, whatever individuals like Lear might learn through the process of affliction. The underlying capacity for malice, for violence, remained unchecked, as did man's lack of wisdom towards his suppositions of good and right – his own self-righteousness. So the conditions that had brought the first major calamity were still there, ever able to precipitate a repeat disaster. Indeed, new humanistic attitudes, freed of the deep suspicion about human nature such as had prevailed in the Middle Ages, made this basic foolishness in man more likely to take hold. Men were free to become enslaved to the intoxications of their own goodness and right, whatever the cost.

In fact Shakespeare had shown his pessimism as clearly – and the reasons for it more clearly – in *Hamlet,* a few years before *King Lear,* centred on the attitudes and behaviour of Laertes. He is the product of an upbringing that has concentrated on image as all-important, that has lacked the restraints and disciplines of Church and chivalry, by which self might have been checked and a wisdom to the truly monstrous potential of that self perceived. In such a one, self-interest as a ruling principle soon turns to self-righteousness as a ruling passion, convinced of the goodness of its suppositions. He is easy prey for the manipulator (Claudius), who plays on the stupidity that sees no right other than self-right, and is ready to destroy whatever opposes the rabble-banners of its cause.

Blake and Dostoievsky were two others that reflected darkly on the modern world's liberated capacity to believe in its own goodness and on its failure to face what is rootedly at fault in our nature. The first had the French Revolution to warn him of the falsehood of the liberal enlightened dream. The second realised by intuition the hollowness of our rational liberation, and would not have been surprised by either the horrors of the Russian Revolution or those of the First World War soon after his death. Shakespeare likewise may simply have looked at the New Thinking, man's assured self-celebration in rational development, as at the words and smiles of a well-disguised Caliban.

It is odd that we are so eager to include Shakespeare in our modern industry of educant, or enshrine him our mock-marble foyer of Kulturama International. He stands for a world whose wisdom and disciplines were even in his own day being dismissed by some as archaic, fanciful and rather foolish. Those some were the modern men, whose world we now live in.

3.   When reflecting on Lear's wandering in the wilderness in search of the lost happiness, truth, or completeness, we might think not only of the Arthurian parallel - the Grail Quest - but of something biblical. The wandering in the wilderness is a reminder of the story of Moses, found in the Old Testament books, *Exodus* to *Deuteronomy.*

In this semi-mythical account, the first state is represented as Egypt, as it was also in Hermetic symbolism. What happened to this 'Egypt' that led to calamity? There was an attempt to emasculate the people of the true Lord,[3] perhaps symbolising an attempt to deny

---

3   Recorded as an attempt to reduce the Israelite numbers by killing their male offspring.

the true masculinity in life. This compares with what I have said about the fate of Lear and his party in Act 2, as the new regime sets about to deny or frustrate them. And the result in both cases is the same. First, the restrictive regime is smitten by curses inflicted by the Lord in retaliation - the plagues brought upon Egypt; Lear's angry curses upon Goneril and Regan.[4] Secondly, there is brought upon Egypt an overwhelming deluge,[5] which links in with the final stormy deluge of rage that ends Act 2 and images the wipe-out of the original kingdom. Moreover both calamities are preceded by another similarity. Lear's angry "Go, go, my people!" seems to be a direct reminder of Moses' (or the Lord's) "Let my people go!"

This wipe-out of the first state by deluge or flood is a commonly found variant of what may be a mythic memory of a long-ago calamity. The *Exodus* drowning of the Egyptians itself links with the more famous story of Noah's Flood, as might be judged by Jewish texts,[6] and we might further link it with disasters like that of Atlantis, or Deucalion - and even of Troy, for one version of its downfall is imaged not in war but by vengeful sea-flood. More interesting for us, perhaps, is that the medieval world tended to see all these primal disasters as the same, and linked with the main story of the paradisal collapse.[7] This is important to know while reading Shakespeare, for otherwise we might miss the point of some of his descriptions. In the account of the elemental chaos in Act 2 of *Midsummer Night's Dream,* for instance, Shakespeare by imagery links the paradisal disaster, caused by 'sexual' disharmony, with Ovid's description of the Deucalion flood, a Greek counterpart to that of the biblical Noah. (MND: 2.1 .87-117)

More important to this present topic is the likeness between what happens in the Moses story after the 'deluge' and what happens in *King Lear* after the equivalent upheaval of the elements. The

---

4   1.4.284-97; 2.4.163-9 & 280-4.

5   Recorded as the drowning of the Egyptian army in the sea.

6   In *Isaiah,* for instance (51:9-10), two stories are combined as if as one - the Lord's fight to quell the chaos-dragon of the waters (connected with the Flood) and the Israelites' passing through the sea (Exodus).

7   To some extent still true of modern biblical scholarship. See, for example, S.H. Hooke's *Middle Eastern Mythology* (particularly p.105-8; 139-43).

wandering in the wilderness. In the Moses story we see that the refugees from this first disaster, led by Moses, attempt to formulate some basis of moral control and understanding again, picking up the pieces and forming an idea of law and truth (including the famous Ten Commandments). This is also true of *King Lear,* for in Act 3 the hero is clearly engaged on a quest to re-formulate truth and understanding out of madness. There is even included in this a garbled allusion to the Ten Commandments.[8]

But there is another parallel of even greater importance. At the end of the wandering in the Moses story, just before the crossing into the Promised Land, Moses died. This was taken symbolically in Christian thinking, because, as Moses was linked with the making of the Law, then his death at this point indicated how the Law, though of great service in refining the spirit and clarifying the intellect to truth, had to 'die' before we could pass over into the regained Paradise - our spiritual 'promised land'. This was because at the heart of the Law, for all its merits and benefit, was a spirit of vengeance or negative accusation of life - the law of sin - from which we should need to be freed for the final salvation. It involves a complex network of ideas in Christian thought, but - narrowing the matter to the literary, and to Shakespeare - we should by this idea have a better understanding of certain events in Shakespeare's plays. For instance: why Isabella in *Measure for Measure,* who images the stern Law, should finally have to yield herself; why the hard statue of life's control in *The Winter's Tale* should finally have to melt from hardness into the kindness of flesh; or why the interim patroness of that statue, Paulina, should be linked in name and symbolism with *Pauline* - that is, 'of Saint Paul' - whose work in the Epistles had been much given to discussion of the Law as a teacher of man which yet needed a final surrender; or why Prospero, the Lord of Vengeance, should have a "book" of life's control that he must finally destroy, just as Jankin (the scholarly accuser of *The Wife's Tale*) must finally burn his. But, for the present topic, we should chiefly now see why at the climax of *King Lear,* before the play's equivalent of finding again the Promised Land (the lost Nature - Cordelia), there is a final breaking

8   3.4.80-82

of the power of the Law and all it represents in pride and accusation in the human spirit.

The Moses story (*Exodus* to *Deuteronomy*) is another example of the cyclical myth - the collapse of a higher world that climaxes in a violent event, followed by a period of ordeal in which errors are clarified and the spirit refined, followed then by a final crisis (Moses' death) that ends the time of ordeal and restores the lost happiness. It thus serves to reinforce the cyclical process of *King Lear,* along with another parallel indicated by Shakespeare's allusions and 'echoes' in the text - the Arthurian cycle, which, if rightly ordered, also starts with a collapsing golden age, is followed by a questing ordeal, and ends in a restoration - the achievement of the Grail.

★   ★   ★

Appendix F
The 'Male Rivals' in the Myth

As I said in *A Last Word* at the end of Chapter 10, my wish to keep reasonably short a wide and complex study of myth in our older literature led inevitably to some aspects of the subject being skimped or missed out altogether.

One omission – the most serious, to some – is the subject or theme usually referred to as the *male rivals*. I had hoped that in my survey of the main myth (the 'myth of sexual destiny') the connection with this other subject would be readily inferred by the reader and therefore need no separate treatment. In case this is not so, and some readers are uncertain, I will add here some explanation.

The subject or theme of the *male rivals* occurs in a wide range of mythical stories, usually involving a good deal more than simply male 'rivalry': indeed, very often villainy, dark deeds and bloodshed. Sometimes the story features brothers or lovers in competition for the same object of fulfilment; sometimes a husband and a rival lover; at other times it features a father and son, or an 'elder' in authority and a 'younger' in challenge; and sometimes, as an extension of this 'elder/younger' idea, there is involved the wider subject of tyranny and rebellion (not least in Shakespeare's plays).

The variations are almost endless, and so for brevity let it simply be said that from the relatively early myths of Cain-and-Abel and of Prometheus-and-Zeus (perhaps themselves derived from even earlier myths of rival male forces in the natural cycle) right through at least as far as Shakespeare's *The Tempest,* we find many myths containing one or more of the *male-rivals* elements.

But what has this type of story to do with the main 'sexual' myth? A clue that there is a connection, somewhere, is found in the frequency in which the two types of story are found alongside or interwoven. Notice, for example, how the Jewish writers of *Genesis* attached to the main Paradise myth the story of Cain and Abel, as if recognising (no matter how dimly or clearly) that some sort of idea-connection existed. Notice, too, how often Shakespeare shows the same recognition, in weaving his main myth with features of male hostility, particularly clearly in joining the main plot of *King Lear* with the sub-plot of the Gloucester family.

But the main clue to a connection is found in realising – as I am sure my readers already have – that not only is the main myth of sexual destiny centred on a feminine character (or presence) of control/motivation upon man, but so too is the male rivals story. Sometimes it is made quite clear by the object of male fulfilment (and contention) being figured as a woman, but as often perceptible by the slightest hint to the weakest imagination. I mean, this 'identity' that men strive over, this fulfilment to be gained or guarded against other claimants – isn't it ever *feminine* in some sense? Garb or dress it as you will – a title, a position, an honour or whatever – it is the same hoped-for addition or affirmation of a ghostly queen within them, a queen that the sharpest versions related to the self or pride that dominates man's mind and action.

And this ghost-queen of self-ambition (or 'ghost-mother', to Freudians) is quite the same as operates in the main myth. In *The Tempest,* for example, the force that incites the mania of male conflict, usurpation, and rivalry, is the same Sycorax, the same witch, that binds the spirit of Prospero in the main story, and from which he struggles to be free. In the same way, Titania in the earlier *Midsummer Night's Dream* operates as the same 'Queen of the Night' to two separate yet intertwined stories: Oberon's destiny and that of the lunatic lovers.

However, I suspect that this link between two kinds of myth is one of those ideas that is either grasped fairly quickly or else never, whatever the argument. And so I will simply add a brief generalised guide, and leave it at that. As follows: the main myth – e.g. *The Wife of Bath's Tale* – shows the male character turned to fantasy and monstrousness. *Fantasy* in that his identity, his fulfilment, his meaning, is a dream fabricated for a darkness in his heart – the sinister feelings, the dark lady or nature, closely akin to ego and pride – and *monstrous* in that his striving, first to gain this identity and then maintain it, is attended by contempts and hurts inflicted on life or the true nature, his real feminine partner or fulfilment. Until the end, that is, for there he reaches a wisdom to dissolve and loosen the dark feminine hold upon him, and therefore dissolve also the monster ever created by such a prisoning, as he discovers in the abused nature his long-ago lost 'bride'.

If we look now at Chaucer's *The Knight's Tale,* an example of the 'male rivals' myth, we see that more or less the same story is being told - and the same destiny depicted - but with the hero having now become two (Palamon and Arcite) and the monstrousness therefore 'twinned' or inter-reflected. The same pursued fantasy-identity is shown - the 'dream' Emily - and the same victim: the kindly order and the flesh of life, that must suffer their blows.

And the same climactic resolution follows, with one side of the duo - Arcite - as is often the case in such stories, representing more the monster to be cast off in the gaining of the true nature.

In much the same way that we match two Chaucerian stories to see the same in different terms, so we might pick up a number of Shakespeare's plays and see a match or overlap already carried out for us, as two myths run in parallel. For example, in the *Henry IV* cycle, the main 'myth' shows Bolingbroke,[1] much like the later King Hamlet, Lear, Leontes and Prospero, as a figure of bemonstered manhood striving to be free from the dark hold of the self, with its attendant hatreds, guilts and violences, so that he might realise, though by a death to this old distortion of being, his true nature - his "Jerusalem". At the same time, as if Bolingbroke has been split up into particulars or aspects of the one character, we see in the rest of the play's action a world of mad male rivals - hostile sons and fathers, youth and youth divided, aspirant and tyrant etc - all acting out the same nightmare shadow-life like drunkards in a tavern, under the watchful harlot-eye of pride. Acted out, that is, until the same resolution is reached: the death of pride or self, the controlling harlot, and the lunatic monster she creates, so that the true 'bride' might then return - the raised realm of England, matching Bolingbroke's "Jerusalem".

In all, the 'male rivals' myth is hardly more than the main myth with one adaptation: the hero has been divided, and so acts out his destiny in duality or multiple.

---

1   The two Henry IV plays are a good example of Shakespeare adapting historical material to the pattern of myth, most markedly in his unhistorical 'rival-youths' portrayal of Hal and Hotspur.

Appendix G   Two Medieval Stories

The Wife of Bath's Tale

The happiness of King Arthur's realm is riven through by an act of violence: a young knight rapes a maiden. The knight is sentenced to death for this but then, by the mercy of the Queen, he is given a year to save his life by finding out the answer to a question – What do women really and chiefly desire?

He collects many answers from many women but despairs of having found the right one until he meets an old, coarse and hideously ugly woman who, in return for his promise to publicly marry her, tells him that woman wants her own way and 'mastery' (maistry) in all.

The knight goes through the humiliating wedding ceremony, and then in the nuptial chamber his old wife begins to address him on the subject of true virtue and nobility as against his own inherited social superiority. She then gives him a choice – to have her very beautiful but utterly false to him, or ugly still but true in all. Unable to decide, he yields his choice to her, and she magically straight off becomes both very beautiful and true, for it is claimed that his surrender has given her 'maistry' after all and thus broken some former curse on her.

And yet it seems, as in other tales, the given 'moral' is misleading. Once we look at the three parts of the story's climax – the humiliating wedding, the lecture and the final choice – we realize we are in the commonly found medieval subject of fallen man's condition of pride, linked with vain desires and a nature ever liable to violence, and all centred on the real curse that causes it: the sense of shame and emptiness deep in the feelings, the stricken 'feminine' heart, that gives rise reactively to self and pride.

Sir Gawain and the Green Knight

King Arthur's joyful Yuletide feast is disrupted by the entry of a fearsome green giant who challenges any of the knights to strike off his head, on condition the roles are reversed in a year's time. Gawain takes the challenge and beheads the giant, who then simply picks up his head and, after a reminder of the condition to Gawain, departs.

Gawain sets off almost a year later to seek the place of peril. At length he comes upon a mysterious castle, where he is entertained by a knight (the giant in another guise, it seems) and by the giant's wife. He undergoes sexual temptations from the wife and almost fully withstands them. (This kind of test, like the 'beheading game' itself, is commonly found in anciently derived medieval romance.)

He next faces his own execution in a wild mysterious place, but instead of death receives only a token blow, as a reward for having passed both the test of his sexual virtue and of his courage. In addition, not only he, but the giant also, thus achieves (or re-achieves) true nobility, lifting a bemonstering curse cast long erewhile by a witch.

I think there will be no prizes for realizing that the two stories are much the same thing in different terms, or for further suspecting that they are also both 'Grail' quests in miniature.